Melinda G. Kramer

Krannert Graduate School of Management
Purdue University

John W. Presley / Donald C. Rigg

Augusta College　　　　　*Broward Community College*

W9-CDD-766

PRENTICE-HALL
WORKBOOK
FOR WRITERS
ALTERNATE EDITION

PRENTICE-HALL, INC., ENGLEWOOD CLIFFS, NEW JERSEY 07632

Printed in the United States of America

10   9   8   7   6   5   4   3   2   1

ISBN 0-13-696591-1

PRENTICE-HALL INTERNATIONAL, INC., *London*
PRENTICE-HALL OF AUSTRALIA PTY. LIMITED, *Sydney*
EDITORA PRENTICE-HALL DO BRASIL, LTDA., *Rio de Janeiro*
PRENTICE-HALL CANADA INC., *Toronto*
PRENTICE-HALL OF INDIA PRIVATE LIMITED, *New Delhi*
PRENTICE-HALL OF JAPAN, INC., *Tokyo*
PRENTICE-HALL OF SOUTHEAST ASIA PTE. LTD., *Singapore*
WHITEHALL BOOKS LIMITED, *Wellington, New Zealand*

CONTENTS

LARGER COMPOSITION ELEMENTS

EFFECTIVE SENTENCES

WORDS

PREFACE

The Alternate Edition of the *Prentice-Hall Workbook for Writers* was conceived to give instructors and their students a choice. If students need more exercises than are supplied by the third edition alone, or if they have already used the third edition of the *Workbook,* the Alternate Edition will fill their needs. Not only does the Alternate Edition offer a fresh batch of exercises, it also contains even more entirely new ones than were presented in the third edition. Of particular interest is the new section (64) on business correspondence that introduces students to some of the stylistic and formatting requirements of business letters and memos.

We have also chosen a new theme for the Alternate Edition. Because college students are preparing themselves to enter the job market, the examples and exercises in this edition of the *Workbook* focus on careers and career preparation. They scan a variety of career opportunities, discuss some of the tasks these careers involve, examine the kinds of educational background students need, and often present people and events associated with certain career fields.

The Alternate Edition also maintains features developed for the third edition of the *Workbook.* It uses a functional format, separating instructional material from exercise pages, and provides an expanded number of new "practices" at the ends of many of the instructional sections. These practices, for which answers are given, enable students to check their understanding of the subject matter and to receive immediate feedback. Used in class, the practices enable instructors to identify and address problems that need special attention—before students work the exercises rather than after the fact.

The *Workbook* has always had a dual purpose. It was conceived as a companion to the *Prentice-Hall Handbook for Writers,* providing explanations and exercises to complement those in the *Handbook.* But it has also been effectively used alone in composition courses and is written as a totally self-sufficient text. The Alternate Edition continues to fulfill those two aims.

Teachers using the Alternate Edition of the *Workbook* with the eighth edition of the *Handbook* will find that both texts follow the same order of presentation. Referring students to the *Workbook* for supplementary exercises is a simple matter; the sections are appropriately sequenced and matched. References to corresponding *Handbook* sections are given in parentheses in the *Workbook's* section headings and in the table of contents.

Classes using the *Prentice-Hall Diagnostic Test for Writers* will also find the *Workbook* to be a valuable aid. Its explanatory sections and exercises can give students additional instruction and practice in problem areas. The Alternate Edition also contains review sections intended to familiarize students with the kinds of material in, and the format of, the *Diagnostic Test.*

Because we recognize that there are nearly as many methods for teaching writing as there are writing teachers, we have used a variety of approaches in the Alternate Edition's exercises while striving to keep the majority of them key-gradable. We advocate no one theory but acknowledge the best of our profession's pedagogy. We understand the concerns of traditionalists and at the same time value the innovations derived from recent research.

Our aim throughout the Alternate Edition has been to present what colleagues and students tell us is sensible—and what works.

The support and assistance we received from Prentice-Hall has once again been outstanding. We thank Phil Miller, our acquisitions editor, who encouraged us to develop an alternate edition; Joyce Perkins, our manuscript and production editor, who saw to it that we did the job right; and our principal reviewers, whose suggestions were both valuable and timely—Stanley J. Kozikowski of Bryant College, June M. England of Brevard Community College, and Judith Comnes of Hillsborough Community College.

To our students we owe the biggest debt of all. The writing classes at Purdue University, Augusta College, and Broward Community College are our perpetual sounding board, our finest test market, and our most precious resource.

MELINDA G. KRAMER
JOHN W. PRESLEY
DONALD C. RIGG

GETTING DOWN TO BUSINESS

This book is about language, particularly written English, and specifically *standard* written English. Few of us always speak standard English; we frequently use slang, jargon, or dialects easily recognized by our family, friends, and coworkers. But when we pick up a popular magazine or newspaper, open a textbook, or look at a notice on a bulletin board, what we see—and *expect* to see—is standard English.

Because they are widely accepted and generally followed, the rules and conventions governing standard English ensure that the greatest number of people will understand a written message. We use standard English not necessarily because it is "good" or "right," but because it is the accepted norm; in fact, *standard* means "the norm." Of course that's the purpose of communication—to get the message across, to be easily understood by as many of our readers as possible.

Having a standard language is important to the development of a society. Amid the variety of our ethnic origins, personal goals, and individual experience, it allows us collectively to get down to business.

This book, concerned with our common language, is also about getting down to business. Specifically, most of its examples and exercises focus on careers or career preparation. Our overview of the world of work is by no means exhaustive; indeed, at times it is downright whimsical. Nevertheless, we find the topic particularly appropriate to our audience—you, who are establishing your career goals; and to our purpose—that most fundamental career preparation, writing well.

A WORKING VOCABULARY

One way people analyze a subject to find out how it works is to break that subject into categories, into its various parts, so they can more easily examine how the individual parts work together as a whole. They may also develop a special vocabulary or set of terms for naming the parts and their functions.

You have performed this kind of analysis and naming many times during your life. In order to know how to improve your car's performance, you must learn how the engine works. To do that, you have to learn the names for the parts: the carburetor, the pistons, the distributor. In order to understand the way the human body functions, you learn about its various systems—the cardiovascular system, the nervous system, the digestive system—and their parts, such as the heart, the brain, the stomach.

Learning about language is no different. It too is a system with parts and functions described by a vocabulary of terms. Just as you breathe without analyzing how to do it, so you write and speak without worrying much about the system or the terms for explaining how language is used. But in order to talk *about* language, about writing, important first steps are understanding the system and knowing the vocabulary.

The following paragraphs introduce some of the basic vocabulary used to describe how written language works, how individual words come together in larger groups that convey meaning. **Part** and **function** are key terms describing how English works. Both words and sentences can be classified by part (what they are called) and function (what they do).

We can categorize words by the parts of speech to which they belong—such as nouns or verbs. We can also categorize sentences by their parts—such as subjects, predicates, or objects. Word functions are naming, predicating, modifying, or connecting. Sentence functions are asserting (stating), interrogating (questioning), or exclaiming. For now we'll concern ourselves just with the categories for words.

TYPICAL WORD FUNCTIONS	PARTS OF SPEECH	EXAMPLES
naming	nouns, pronouns	Shakespeare, he, that, money, means, content, friends
predicating (stating, asserting)	verbs	wrote, wants, is
modifying	adjectives, adverbs	three, good
connecting	prepositions, conjunctions	without and

That parts of speech can change their functions from sentence to sentence can sometimes be confusing. For example, a noun is always a noun, but it can modify as well as name.

NAMING NOUN	*Shakespeare* wrote, "He that wants money, means, and content is without three good friends."
MODIFYING NOUN	*Shakespeare's* play says people need money.

In the first sentence, *Shakespeare* is a straightforward noun telling us who wrote about money, means, and content. In the second sentence, however, *Shakespeare's* takes the possessive form and tells us whose play says people need money. In the second case, we say *Shakespeare's* is a noun functioning as a modifier. In fact, we can say the noun functions as an adjective, describing or qualifying *play,* another noun.

Now you know why the list used the heading *Typical Word Functions*. First you learn how a part of speech usually functions. In time, as you become familiar with the way language works, you will learn to recognize and be able to explain the variations.

1

NOUNS AND PRONOUNS   (1a)

NOUNS

A **noun** names a person, place, or thing. A **concrete noun** names something that can be seen, heard, touched, smelled, or tasted, something that can be perceived by the senses; an **abstract noun** names an idea, quality, or concept, not a substance. A **proper noun** names a particular person, place, or thing and should be capitalized; a **common noun** is the general name of a person, place, or thing and is not capitalized. A **collective noun** uses the singular form to name a group of individuals in a unit.

CONCRETE NOUN	Most *people* work for two main reasons: *money* and satisfaction
ABSTRACT NOUN	Money is a *necessity*, but *satisfaction* is very important, too.
PROPER NOUN	*Sally*, my best friend, got a summer job at *Disney World*.
COMMON NOUN	She needed the *money* to pay her college expenses, but she also thought the *experience* would be good.
COLLECTIVE NOUN	Today's student *population* wants jobs that are meaningful as well as lucrative.

Practice A: Identifying nouns   Underline all the words functioning as nouns in the following sentences. The answers are listed at the end of this section.

[1] Each summer, thousands of college students compete for positions working in theme parks and resort areas. [2] Though the entertainers may have the most prestigious and most visible jobs, for each of these glamorous positions there are dozens more positions available as sales or desk clerks, lifeguards, cashiers, maids, waiters, ride operators, or attendants. [3] Surprisingly, the pay is about the same for all jobs, and all the jobs offer a chance to enjoy oneself, to enjoy meeting people, and to work in very pleasant surroundings.

PRONOUNS

A **pronoun** is a word used in place of a noun. Pronouns (and other words that substitute for nouns) are sometimes called **substantives**. There are several types of pronouns.

PERSONAL	I, we, you, he, she, it, they, me, us, him, her, them, mine, our(s), your(s), his, hers, their(s)
RELATIVE	who, which, that
INTERROGATIVE	who, which, what
DEMONSTRATIVE	this, that, these, those
INDEFINITE	one, any, each, anyone, somebody, all, *etc.*
RECIPROCAL	each other, one another
INTENSIVE	myself, yourself, himself, *etc.*
REFLEXIVE	myself, yourself, herself, *etc.*

	Relative		**Reciprocal**
Students	*who*	seek summer jobs tell	*one another*

Personal		**Indefinite**	
they	want	*something*	useful for readying

Reflexive
themselves   for permanent employment in the profession they

Intensive		**Interrogative**	
themselves	have chosen;	*who*	has not hoped for

Demonstrative
that   kind of summer opportunity?

Practice B: Identifying pronouns   Underline all the pronouns in the following sentences. The answers are listed at the end of this section.

[1] You might prefer that your summer job be overseas. [2] Many a student has claimed that his or her travel in Europe was the highlight of his education; and if you can't pay for a long vacation abroad yourself, you might combine work and travel for a summer. [3] Students who have successfully done this say they started out by contacting their college's placement office or its international study office. [4] Be warned, though, that most of these are unskilled jobs. [5] You may pick grapes, pitch hay, or wait tables—but it'll be in France, Germany, or Austria. [6] Who would be unhappy about that?

Answers to Practice A   [1] summer, thousands, students, positions, parks, areas [2] entertainers, jobs, positions, dozens, positions, clerks, lifeguards, cashiers, maids, waiters, operators, attendants   [3] pay, jobs, jobs, chance, people, surroundings

Answers to Practice B   [1] you, that, your   [2] Many, that, his, her, his, you, yourself, you   [3] who, this, they, their, its   [4] that, most, these [5] You, it   [6] Who, that

EXERCISE 1, NOUNS AND PRONOUNS   (1a)

In the blanks, copy all the nouns and pronouns in the following sentences. If a noun or pronoun is repeated in a sentence, write it out each time it appears.

Example   Many college students work at temporary jobs in the summer.

students   jobs   summer

1. Most summer jobs taken by college students are temporary or seasonal.

_____

2. They often work in factories, at construction sites, in hotels or stores, or with seasonal-harvesting companies on farms.

_____

3. These kinds of jobs require little experience, and the pay is often quite good.

_____

4. But these traditional jobs are often unrelated to a student's education.

_____

5. You might prefer work that relates to your college major.

_____

6. Some colleges offer cooperative-education programs.

_____

7. A co-op student alternates between campus and a job in his or her major area at local businesses.

_____

8. An accounting major, for example, might work several months in the accounting department of a local bank.

_____

9. You can test your choice of a career this way.

_____

10. You can also graduate with job experience already behind you.

_____

11. Internships also give students work experience related to their educations.

_____

12. Large firms often hire summer interns to work on special short projects that require specialized knowledge.

_____

13. A chemistry student might work as an intern in a research lab, for instance.

_____

14. You should apply for internships directly to the company whose work interests you.

_____

15. These interns are also sometimes recruited at campus placement centers.

_____

16. Government jobs are also recommended by students who have worked in them.

_____

17. In January and February, the Summer Employment Test is taken by those interested in clerical jobs with the federal government.

_____

18. Apply for other federal jobs by contacting agencies directly.

_____

19. Professional and "subprofessional" jobs do not require a test.

_____

20. If one is interested in only summer work, one can find almost every federal agency listing summer openings.

_____

21. State and local governments often have summer hiring programs for students.

_____

22. Some of the jobs available are for recreation specialists, park rangers, road workers, typists, and clerks.

_____

23. To apply for these jobs, contact your state employment service.

_____

24. If you can afford a summer without pay, the last resort might be volunteer work in your career area.

_____

25. A month's work as a veterinarian's aide, for example, might be of more use than a job taken just for its salary.

_____

2

VERBS AND VERBALS   (1a-b)

A **verb** provides the energy in a sentence. It usually expresses action, occurrence, or condition and indicates time relationships by its tense. For example, "I *worked* in a restaurant during summer vacation" expresses the action of working and places the action in the past. "My summer employment *ended* on Labor Day" expresses an occurrence that happened in the past. "Waiting on tables all day *was* tiring" expresses a condition that existed in the past: being tired.

Verbs may appear as single words or in groups called **verb phrases**. Verb phrases are composed of **main verbs** and **auxiliaries**; auxiliaries are also known as **helping verbs**. The most common helping verbs are *have, had, is (am, are), was (were), does (do), did, will, would, can, could, shall, should, may, might,* and *must*.

We will look at verbs in more detail in Sections 11–14.

	Auxiliary	Main Verb		Verb	
Because I	*could*	*earn*	wages and good tips, I	*decided*	the restaurant

└─**Verb Phrase**─┘

	Verb	
job	*was*	best for the summer.

Practice: Identifying verbs   Underline all the verbs and verb phrases in the following sentences. The answers are listed at the end of this section.

[1] If you have ambition, determination, and a good idea, you might start your own summer business. [2] One group of college students bought a small van. [3] They advertised their services as household movers and quickly gathered a large percentage of the business in San Francisco, where a smaller truck has been more useful for the narrow driveways. [4] Two brothers in Alabama invested their summer time and energy in a watermelon crop they planted on land they had borrowed. [5] A big success, the crop has paid all the brothers' college expenses.

Verbals is the term used for verb forms that are not functioning as **predicators**. In other words, verbals do not assert, ask a question, or otherwise work like verbs. Instead, they name or modify. Verbals act as noun substitutes, adjectives, or adverbs. The forms of the three types of verbals can help you distinguish them from verbs functioning as predicates.

TYPE OF VERBAL	FORM OF VERB	FUNCTION OF VERBAL
Infinitive	*to* + verb	Naming or modifying: noun substitute, adjective, adverb
		To start your own business is not easy. [Used as noun.]

TYPE OF VERBAL	FORM OF VERB	FUNCTION OF VERBAL
Participle		
Present form	verb + *-ing*	Modifying: adjective only Many *planning* sessions should come first. [The participle *planning* modifies *sessions.*]
Past form	verb + *-ed* or *-en* or internal vowel change *squandered, stolen, shrunk*	*Squandered, stolen,* or *shrunk* by inflation, your profits can disappear overnight. [The participles modify *profits.*]
Gerund	verb + *-ing* *planning, investing, starting*	Naming: noun substitute only Careful *planning,* sensible *investing,* and a bit of luck are essential to *starting* your own business. [*Planning, investing,* and *starting* function as nouns.]

Some predicating verb phrases are composed of participles and helping verbs (as in *Max was running*). To further add to the confusion, of the three types of verbals, both participles and gerunds can have the *-ing* form. You have to check the function of an *-ing* word to know which it is. Participles used alone (without helping verbs) function only as adjectives. Gerunds serve only as nouns. All verbals, however, are modified by adverbs, as are true verbs. For more practice with verbals, see Section 6, Phrases.

Answers to the Practice   [1] have, might start   [2] bought   [3] advertised, gathered, has been   [4] invested, planted, had borrowed   [5] has paid

EXERCISE 2, VERBS (1a)

In the blanks, copy all the verbs and verb phrases in the following sentences. Circle the main verb in each verb phrase you write.

Example   Your search for a summer job should follow a systematic process.

should (*follow*) _____

1.   Last year, two and a half million students entered the summer labor market.

   _____

2.   But this year over a million summer jobs will be available.

   _____

3.   You can improve your chances of success with a good plan.

   _____

4.   A smart candidate will start preparing for summer as early as January.

   _____

5.   First you should have a Social Security card.

   _____

6.   If you're interested in federal clerical jobs, the SET is given in January and February.

   _____

7.   The Postal Service says 10,000 summer workers will be hired this year.

   _____

8.   Apply at the largest post office in your area.

   _____

9.   Group IV jobs, which require no training or experience, have an April 15 deadline.

   _____

10.   Group II jobs have always been popular.

   _____

11.   These pay well and require college study.

   _____

12. College graduates must apply for Group III jobs before March 15.

   _____

13. Temporary employment agencies are located in most large cities.

   _____

14. A serious job hunter should be registered with one of these firms.

   _____

15. If resorts or theme parks are your interest, you can write to them directly.

   _____

16. Restaurants and food service outlets provide thousands of summer jobs.

   _____

17. People often overlook some very profitable jobs.

   _____

18. Good Humor, for example, has hired nearly 2,000 summer truck drivers every year.

   _____

19. According to the company, many drivers have earned the next year's tuition.

   _____

20. Summer camp counselors are often paid low salaries.

   _____

21. These positions do provide room and board, however.

   _____

22. Counselors with art or dramatic talent may earn high salaries.

   _____

23. The camp cook is the person who really rakes it in, though.

   _____

24. A good cook will often earn more than the camp director does.

   _____

25. Don't you wish you'd learned how to cook?

   _____

3

ADJECTIVE AND ADVERB FUNCTIONS   (1b)

ADJECTIVES

An **adjective** modifies a noun or pronoun. It describes, limits, or qualifies the meaning of the word it modifies, often telling *what kind, how many,* or *which one.* An adjective cannot modify an adverb or another adjective. There are several types of adjectives:

DESCRIPTIVE	It is a *good* idea to practice for your first job interview.
POSSESSIVE	*Your* first few minutes with the interviewer can be crucial.
DEMONSTRATIVE	Experts say the interviewer forms his or her main impression of you during *those* minutes.
INTERROGATIVE	*What* difference can practicing the interview make?
NUMERICAL	For *one* thing, it can help you rehearse answers to questions you may be asked.
ARTICLES	If you have considered *the* possible questions and thought through *an* answer or two, you will have *a* less nervous interview.

Several words above also appeared in the previous list of pronouns. *Those* is listed both as a demonstrative pronoun and as a demonstrative adjective. *What* shows up twice, once as an interrogative pronoun and once as an interrogative adjective. Remember that classifying a word by its part of speech sometimes depends on its function in a sentence. The appearance of *those* and *what* in two categories illustrates this point very well. In the examples here, *those* and *what* could be described as pronouns functioning as modifiers, pronouns performing the function of adjectives.

Practice A: Identifying adjectives   *Underline all the words (including the articles) that function as adjectives in the following sentences. The answers are listed at the end of this section.*

[1] The best way to avoid seeming nervous in a job interview is to prepare ahead of time. [2] It is amazing that people enter some of the most crucial few minutes of their lives with only a vague idea of what they intend to do and say. [3] Use standard reference books to learn basic facts about the company which is about to interview you. [4] How old is the company? [5] Who owns it? [6] What are its future plans? [7] Make yourself a list of a few questions you want to ask the interviewer. [8] Don't be passive. [9] A successful job interview may determine much of your life for the next thirty years.

ADVERBS

An **adverb** modifies, describes, limits, or qualifies the meaning of a verb, an adjective, or another adverb. Besides modifying single words, adverbs can also modify whole sentences or parts of sentences. Adverbs frequently indicate time, place, manner, or degree, telling *when, where,* or *how.* Negatives such as *no, never,* and *not* may be used as adverbs. Some adverbs have a distinctive *-ly* ending, making them easy to spot in sentences. The following examples show the use of adverbs.

TIME	Arriving *late* for your job interview gives the impression that you are unreliable. [*Late* modifies the verbal *arriving*, telling when.]
PLACE	When you arrive, be sure to tell the receptionist you are *there*. [*There* modifies the verb *are*, telling where.]
MANNER	Sometimes the interviewers themselves fall *slightly* behind schedule. [*Slightly* modifies the verb *fall*, telling in what way.]
DEGREE	At busy college placement offices, you may have a *fairly* long wait. [*Fairly* modifies the adjective *long*, telling how long.]
NUMBER	After you have interviewed for jobs *once* or *twice*, you will have learned the routine. [*Once* and *twice* modify the verb *interviewed*, telling how many times.]

Practice B: Identifying adverbs   *Underline all the words functioning as adverbs in the following sentences. The answers are listed at the end of this section.*

[1] The worst possible impression you can make during an interview is to seem confused about your major or career. [2] While it may undeniably be true that some people chose their college majors because the lines at registration for everything else were too long, that's probably not the answer to give a prospective employer. [3] Always be prepared to summarize the connection between your career goals and your major precisely. [4] Quickly pointing out the relevance of your education and experience to the employer's needs creates a very positive impression. [5] Routinely, many interviewers first ask the candidate for a summary statement. [6] A well-prepared candidate knows that answering this question truthfully, candidly, and specifically is crucially important.

Answers to Practice A   [1] The, best, nervous, a, job   [2] amazing, the, crucial, few, their, vague   [3] standard, reference, basic, the   [4] old, the   [6] its, future   [7] a, a, few, the   [8] passive   [9] A, successful, job, your, the, next, thirty

Answers to Practice B   [1] worst   [2] undeniably, too, probably, not   [3] Always, precisely   [4] Quickly, out, very   [5] Routinely, first   [6] well, truthfully, candidly, specifically, crucially

EXERCISE 3, ADJECTIVE AND ADVERB FUNCTIONS   (1b)

Each of the following sentences contains at least one adjective or adverb. Some sentences contain both. In the blanks, copy the adjectives and adverbs, labeling them *adj.* or *adv.* Write the words they modify in parentheses. Do not copy or label the articles *a, an,* or *the.*

Example   The most important step in any job search is the interview.

adv.   *adj.*   *adj.*   *adj.*
most   important (step)   any job (search)

1. A good interview may land you either a temporary or permanent job.

   _____

2. Interviews are often held at placement offices.

   _____

3. They are sometimes held at a firm's central office.

   _____

4. Try to arrive early for the interview.

   _____

5. Reliability and promptness are critical traits the employer observes.

   _____

6. You also need to carefully allow a few minutes for relaxation.

   _____

7. Realizing that most people are nervous is helpful.

   _____

8. Carry any necessary papers in a neat briefcase or folder.

   _____

9. You should previously have prepared any application forms.

   _____

10. Questions asked in the interview are really chances to "sell" yourself.

    _____

11. Be ready with prepared answers for standard questions.

    _____

12. Experienced friends or placement counselors can help you anticipate questions.

   _____

13. Finally, you should summarize your main credentials and thank the interviewer.

   _____

14. Always be positive about your experience and your future.

   _____

15. Never criticize a previous employer or professor.

   _____

16. Some interviewers are quite cordial.

   _____

17. This cordiality is an invitation to talk too frankly.

   _____

18. Most interviewers look first for a professional appearance.

   _____

19. Next they note the interviewee's communications skills.

   _____

20. Personality, however, is most seriously considered.

   _____

21. A successful interviewee should seem confident, poised, and enthusiastic.

   _____

22. Self-confidence is a trait of prime importance.

   _____

23. A good sense of humor may also help create a favorable impression.

   _____

24. Do not relax enough to look passive or indifferent.

   _____

25. The positive characteristics that are developed in college will also help you land a job.

   _____

4

PREPOSITIONS AND CONJUNCTIONS   (1b)

PREPOSITIONS

A **preposition** is a connecting word that typically indicates time, place, or movement. Some common prepositions are *about, above, across, after, around, at, before, behind, between, by, during, for, from, in, into, of, off, on, out, over, since, through, to, under, up, with.*

A preposition connects its object (a noun, pronoun, or noun substitute) with some other word in a sentence. Together the preposition, its object, and any words modifying the object form a prepositional phrase—for example, *at business schools*—that modifies the word to which it is connected.

	Preposition		Object of Preposition		
Enrollments	at	business	schools		have jumped recently.

└Prepositional Phrase Modifying Noun ┘

Prepositions and prepositional phrases can modify nouns, verbs, adjectives, or adverbs, supplying additional information about the words they modify.

USED AS ADJECTIVE	The number *of business school applicants* has doubled in a decade. [The prepositional phrase modifies the noun *number*, telling what/whom.]
USED AS ADVERB	Thus, admissions requirements have become tougher *at many business schools.* [The prepositional phrase modifies the adjective *tougher*, telling where.]
USED AS ADVERB	Graduates count *on their business degree* to help land a good job. [The prepositional phrase modifies the verb *count*, telling what.]
USED AS ADVERB	Once *upon a time*, an M.B.A. was a rarity; now it is almost commonplace. [The prepositional phrase modifies the adverb *once*, telling when.]

Practice A: Identifying prepositions   *Underline all the prepositions in the following sentences. The answers are listed at the end of this section.*

[1] A group of students at Yale is attempting to raise money from alumni for investing in the stock market. [2] With their goal set at $100,000, the students hope to learn investment management by actually doing it. [3] Profits gathered from their experiment will be reinvested in the fund. [4] After learning of the group's aims, several alumni have donated money to the new investment club, claiming that they wished they had been exposed to the stock market when they were "at that age."

CONJUNCTIONS

A **conjunction** connects words, phrases, or clauses, creating a relationship between sentence elements. Conjunctions can establish the following relationships between words or word groups.

Coordinating conjunctions show equal rank or importance. The coordinating conjunctions are *and, but, for, nor, or, so, yet.*

A master's degree in business can open the door to high-paying jobs, *but* some employers think M.B.A. graduates are overpriced and overconfident. [The first half of the sentence states a fact. The second half, expressing a contrasting opinion about the value of an M.B.A., is given equal grammatical emphasis by *but. And* connects *overpriced* and *overconfident,* establishing their equal status as modifiers.]

Subordinating conjunctions create unequal rank or dependence. They join words, phrases, or clauses that depend on other parts of the sentence to complete their meanings. The subordinating conjunctions are *after, although, as, because, if, since, that, unless, until, when, where, whether, while, why.*

Although experience is a good teacher, today's young business man or woman increasingly needs an M.B.A. for career success. [The *although* clause depends upon, or is subordinated to, the second clause, since without the second clause the meaning of the first clause is incomplete.]

Practice B: Identifying conjunctions   *Underline all the conjunctions in the following sentences. The answers are listed at the end of this section.*

[1] Although traditionally considered liberal arts schools, many Ivy League colleges find students more interested in business and finance. [2] The colleges expected the renewed interest, but applications outnumbered available seats by four to one. [3] Corporate finance and capital are popular, but investment theory and real estate are equally in demand. [4] School officials aren't sure whether to be happy or not; they worry that students may ignore more traditional study, yet many students still keep in touch with both liberal arts and business. [5] Since one history-business major just went to work for Merrill Lynch, combination majors still seem attractive.

Answers to Practice A   [1] of, at, from, for, in   [2] With, at, by
[3] from, in   [4] After, of, to, to, at

Answers to Practice B   [1] Although, and   [2] but   [3] and, but, and
[4] whether, or, that, yet, and   [5] Since

EXERCISE 4, PREPOSITIONS AND CONJUNCTIONS   (1b)

Prepositional phrases function as modifiers, adding information to sentences. Expand each of the following sentences by supplying prepositional phrases that add modifying information.

Example   Professor Smith is an expert.

Professor Smith is an expert in his fields of counseling and placement.

1. A counselor can help you.

_____

2. I want a degree.

_____

3. I am interested.

_____

4. I want to work.

_____

5. You can find the counseling center.

_____

Conjunctions connect sentence elements, allowing us to combine information and ideas. Combine the sentences in each pair below, using coordinating conjunctions, subordinating conjunctions, or both.

Example   You should find the placement center. You should make an appointment.

You should find the placement center and make an appointment.

6. Your first job may not be important. It may not even pay well.

_____

7. Placement counselors do not need licenses. They do not need certificates.

_____

8. They only need experience. Many have backgrounds in business. Many have backgrounds in industry.

_____

9.   A college degree does not guarantee a job. A degree doesn't limit you to one field.

_____

10. Most people have more than one career in a lifetime. Your choice may not be final.

_____

For each of the following sets of sentences, use prepositional phrases, conjunctions, or both to compose one sentence including all the information given. You may have to rearrange or omit words to create a smooth sentence.

Example   There are over forty thousand possible careers. You may choose one. You may choose two.

You may choose one or two from over forty thousand possible careers.

11. Adults return to school. They want new knowledge. They want new careers.

_____

12. An industry may change. External pressures may be responsible. Internal changes may be responsible.

_____

13. A person returns to school. A job has changed. A job has disappeared.

_____

14. Adult students want new skills. Their job has changed. It may have become more difficult.

_____

15. A chosen career may make you miserable. A few years have passed. You have not assessed your skills.

_____

18

5

SUBJECTS, PREDICATES, AND SENTENCE PATTERNS   (1a)

All complete sentences have a **subject** and a **predicate**. The **subject** of a sentence is most often a noun, pronoun, or noun substitute that names someone or something. A subject with all its modifiers is called a **complete subject**. A subject without any modifiers is called a **simple subject**. The sentences below show various types of subjects. Each complete subject appears in italics, and each simple subject is in boldface italics.

> *Business schools* train students for management careers. [Noun as subject]
> *They* offer courses in finance, operations, marketing, and so on. [Pronoun as subject]
> *Learning to use a computer* has become essential. [Verbal phrase as subject]
> *Computer programs and models* help managers solve business problems. [Two nouns as subject, called *compound subject*]

The **predicate** of a sentence gives information about the subject, making an assertion or asking a question. The most important part of the predicate is the **verb** or **verb phrase** that makes up the **simple predicate**. The simple predicate expresses action, occurrence, or condition (state of being). Other words in a **complete predicate** either are modifiers or receive the action of the predicate's verb. In the following sentences, the complete predicate is italicized and the simple predicate is in boldface italics.

> Employment recruiters *look for graduates with strong quantitative skills.* [Action]
> These skills *will be tested by on-the-job situations.* [Occurrence]
> Good communications skills *are also important for business managers.* [Condition; state of being]

Practice: Identifying subjects and predicates   Underline the simple subject and simple predicate in the following sentences. Be sure not to overlook possible compound subjects or verbs. The answers are listed at the end of this section.

[1] The ultimate degree for students wanting business careers remains the master's in business administration. [2] During the 1960's and 1970's M.B.A.'s received more job offers and garnered higher starting salaries than almost any other degree-holders. [3] Obviously, this made the degree popular, and students flocked to enroll in M.B.A. programs.

SENTENCE PATTERNS

Pattern 1   The simplest sentences contain only a subject and a verb, as in *Japan leads.* We can add information to these simple, or **core**, sentences by supplying modifiers—adjectives, adverbs, prepositional phrases.

	Subject	**Verb**	
Today	Japan	leads	the world in high-technology manufacturing.

Besides the pattern shown in a core sentence, English sentences can follow four other patterns that provide additional information in the predicate. The pattern variations all occur in the predicate—in the verb and what follows it.

Pattern 2   The predicate may contain a **direct object**, a noun, pronoun, or noun substitute that receives the action of the verb and answers "what" or "whom."

Subject	Verb		Direct Object
Japanese products	have captured	the world	market.

Pattern 3   The predicate may contain a direct object followed by an **object complement**, a noun or modifier that renames or describes the direct object.

Subject	Verb	Direct Object		Object Complement (Noun)	
Critics	call	Japan	an	imitator	of American know-how.

Subject	Verb		Direct Object	Object Complement (Adj.)
But high quality	has made	Japanese	products	popular.

Pattern 4   The predicate may contain a direct object preceded by an **indirect object**, a noun or pronoun that identifies the receiver of whatever is named in the direct object.

Subject	Verb	Indirect Object	Direct Object	
Someone	loaned	me	a book	on Japanese management.

Indirect objects function rather like prepositional phrases with the *to* or *for* left out: *Someone loaned* [*to*] *me a book.*

Pattern 5   The predicate may contain a linking verb followed by a **complement**—either a **predicate noun** or a **predicate adjective**. Linking verbs are discussed in Section 12. Some common linking verbs are *is, are, was, were, has been, might be, see, appear, become;* sometimes *feel, act, look, taste, smell,* and *sound* function as linking verbs. You will be able to spot predicate nouns if you remember that they rename the subject of the sentence. Predicate adjectives modify the subject.

SUBJECT	VERB	COMPLEMENT PRED. NOUN	PRED. ADJ.
Robotics	is	an industrial technique.	
The Japanese	are	robotics leaders.	
Robotic assembly	appears		very cost effective.
Some assembly-line jobs	may become		obsolete.

These patterns are the basis for all English sentences. All of their elements can be compounded without changing the sentence pattern. That is, a sentence may have two or more subjects, verbs, indirect objects, direct objects, and/or complements. *Someone loaned my classmate and me a book on Japanese management* has a compound indirect object (*classmate, me*), but the basic sentence pattern remains unchanged.

Other sentence variations are created by rearranging or recombining the elements in these patterns. One variation is worth special notice because it can be confusing. Certain sentences use *there* or *it* plus a verb as something called an **expletive**. Such words are never the subject of a sentence. For instance, in *There are many routine tasks, there* is an expletive. The verb makes a statement about *tasks*, not about *there. Tasks* is the subject. The sense of the sentence is "Many tasks are routine."

Answers to the Practice   [1] degree, remains   [2] M.B.A.'s, received [and] garnered   [3] this, made; students, flocked

EXERCISE 5, SUBJECTS AND PREDICATES   (1a)

Underline and label the subjects (*s*), verbs (*v*), direct objects (*do*), indirect objects (*io*), and complements (*c*) in the following sentences.

Example   An M.B.A. studies a specialized field for a year or two after the bachelor's degree

1. These extra years give the student concentrated knowledge in a particular area of business.

2. Accounting, finance, marketing, and personnel are some of the more common specializations.

3. Many of the best schools use the case method of instruction.

4. The case method gives students the chance to see case histories of actual companies and their problems.

5. Employers feel this is almost as valuable as experience on the job.

6. Professors in business schools include as much detail as possible in each case studied.

7. This gives M.B.A. students the chance to solve real problems with real solutions.

8. A typical case might include, for example, a union election and the accompanying personnel issues.

9. Or a student might learn the ways to raise money for a publicly held company.

10. Beginning salaries for M.B.A.'s range from $21,000 to $29,000 a year.

11. A slowed economy often causes a drop in the demand for M.B.A.'s and a drop in the demand for business graduates altogether.

12. However, some fields are still in demand.

13. Students with work experience and technical training are needed by more employers.

14. Officials estimate higher demand in the accounting, banking, management consulting, and electronics fields.

15. Opportunities for M.B.A.'s seem excellent.

16. (Write your own sentence with a direct object.)

_____

17. (Write your own sentence with an indirect object preceding a direct object.)

_____

18. (Write your own sentence with an object complement following the direct object.)

_____

19. (Write your own sentence with a linking verb followed by a predicate adjective.)

_____

20. (Write your own sentence with a linking verb followed by a predicate noun.)

_____

Revise the following sentences according to the instructions given.

21. After decades of world leadership, U.S. factories are experiencing falling productivity. [*Make the subject compound.*]

_____

22. The productivity problem perplexes corporate managers. [*Make the verb compound.*]

_____

23. Consequently, many companies are hiring people who have specialized in production at business school. [*Make the direct object compound.*]

_____

24. Robotics will be useful for increasing productivity. [*Make the predicate adjective compound.*]

_____

25. Believing people will lose their jobs to robots, some labor unions oppose robotics. [*Add another verb and another direct object, making the predicate compound.*]

_____

22

6

PHRASES (1c)

If you have read the sections in this book on verbs and prepositions, you already have a working knowledge of phrases. A **phrase** is a group of related words that differs from a clause in that a phrase lacks either a subject or a verb. A phrase may contain a subject or a verb but never both. For example, the following sentence is constructed of a **noun phrase** containing a subject and a **verb phrase** composed of a finite verb and its auxiliary.

The engineering student   has finished.

The sentence *The engineering student has finished her degree requirements* contains two noun phrases (*the engineering student* and *her degree requirements*), each having its own subject (*student* and *requirements*); and a verb phrase (*has finished*).

Keep in mind that while a phrase may contain its own subject or verb, these do not necessarily function as the subject or predicate of the entire sentence. For example, while *requirements* is the subject of its noun phrase in the sentence above, it is also the direct object of the verb and is thus a part of the predicate in the sentence as a whole.

Other types of phrases usually consist of a **preposition** and its object or a **verbal** and its object.

PREPOSITIONAL PHRASES	*out of sight, before this century*
PARTICIPIAL PHRASE	A person *designing a bridge* is an engineer.
GERUND PHRASE	*Civil engineering* is an old profession.
INFINITIVE PHRASE	It took engineering *to build the Pyramids*.

You also know, if you have read about verbals (Section 2) and prepositions (Section 4), that phrases frequently function as modifiers. They act as adjectives when they modify nouns or noun substitutes. They act as adverbs when they modify verbs, adjectives, or other adverbs. Some verbal phrases and, occasionally, prepositional phrases can also function as nouns. The following examples show how phrases (in this case, prepositional phrases) can function as adjectives, adverbs, and nouns.

ADJECTIVE MODIFYING NOUN	Originally there were only two kinds *of engineers*. [Modifies *kinds*.]
ADVERB MODIFYING VERB	Civil engineering existed *before the Industrial Revolution*. [Modifies *existed*.]
ADVERB MODIFYING ADJECTIVE	Military engineering is apparent *throughout history*. [Modifies *apparent*.]
ADVERB MODIFYING ADVERB	Other engineering disciplines developed quickly *in some cases*. [Modifies *quickly*.]
NOUN SUBSTITUTE	*"In step with scientific discovery"* is the rule governing engineering. [Acts as subject of sentence. Note that the object of a preposition, by itself, can never be the subject of a sentence.]

Phrases are among a writer's most versatile tools. They enable you to elaborate, to amplify, and to qualify the core of a sentence—its subject and its verb. With a few well-chosen phrases, you can give your readers a wealth of information, adding substantially to their understanding of a sentence's meaning.

For example, suppose you have read the simple sentence *The profession grew rapidly.* Naturally you are wondering "Which profession? Grew how much—as compared to what?" The writer has left too much "detail work" up to your imagination. In fact, the writer has exerted almost no control over the reader-writer relationship because the sentence is so bare. Chances are, the writer had a full mental image of a particular profession's development; but unfortunately the sentence conveyed none of that information to you. Phrases used to expand a core sentence are the means for providing a reader with a more complete understanding of just what the writer means.

```
 ┌──── Participial Phrase ─────────┐ ┌─Prepositional Phrase─┐ ┌─Prepositional
Beginning in the early nineteenth century with the development of mechanical
       └────Prepositional Phrase ────┘
```

```
                                                              ┌─Prepositional─┐
 Phrase ──┐ ┌──────── Participial Phrase ────────────┐ ┌  Phrase   ┐
engineering, adding mining, metallurgical, and chemical engineering toward the end
```

```
 ┌─Prepositional─┐
   Phrase      ┌──────── Core ────────┐ ┌──── Prepositional Phrase ────┐
of the 1800's, the profession grew rapidly during the twentieth century,
```

```
                           ┌─Infinitive─┐
                           ┌  Phrase  ┐
when technological innovations really began to explode.
```

Two participial phrases, an infinitive phrase, and six prepositional phrases have expanded the four-word core sentence, *the profession grew rapidly,* into a well-developed, information-filled explanation. Of course, you will not always need so much information in the sentences you write, but phrases give you the tools for building detail and adding information when you want it.

Practice: Expanding a sentence with phrases Write a brief core sentence; then expand your sentence with details, using at least one participial or gerund phrase, at lease one infinitive phrase, and at least two prepositional phrases. Be sure that the resulting sentence is grammatically correct and that it makes sense.

EXERCISE 6, PHRASES   (1c)

Write sentences with prepositional phrases using the given prepositions.

Example   with _*I should be happy with that kind of job.*_

1. in _____

2. of _____

3. behind _____

4. for _____

5. by _____

6. between _____

7. on _____

8. under _____

9. above _____

10. with _____

11. through _____

12. before _____

13. upon _____

14. across _____

15. during _____

Form participles, gerunds, and infinitives from the following verbs; and write
sentences using them as participial, gerund, and infinitive phrases. Review the end of
Section 2 on verbals if you need a refresher.

Example   *lament*

(participial phrase) _*Lamenting my luck, I left the office.*_

(gerund phrase) _*Lamenting my misfortunes is not my style.*_

(infinitive phrase) _*I don't want to lament my luck; I want to change it.*_

16. *run*

(participial phrase) _____

(gerund phrase) _____

(infinitive phrase) _____

17. *write*

(participial phrase) _____

(gerund phrase) _____

(infinitive phrase) _____

18. *beat*

(participial phrase) _____

(gerund phrase) _____

(infinitive phrase) _____

For each of the following sentences, indicate whether the italicized phrase functions as a noun (*n*), an adjective (*adj*), or an adverb (*adv*) by writing the appropriate abbreviation above it.

Example   *n*
If you want *to major* in engineering, check recent demand for engineers.

19. Engineers have seen their field go through abrupt shifts *in popularity.*

20. *Slowing the pace* of space exploration caused a drop in demand.

21. When fewer engineers are graduated *from engineering schools,* salaries go up.

22. *Attracted by the higher salaries,* more people will pursue engineering degrees.

23. But the oversupply *of engineers* will cause starting salaries to drop again.

24. *Meeting the country's needs* in energy will require more engineers, though.

25. Demand seems strong, particularly *for petroleum and geothermal engineers.*

7

CLAUSES (1d)

Clauses can be divided into two categories: (1) independent or main clauses and (2) dependent or subordinate clauses. Both types of clauses have subjects and verbs, but only independent clauses can stand alone as sentences.

MAIN CLAUSES

An **independent clause**, often called a **main clause**, has both a subject and a verb. It makes a complete, independent statement, and it is not introduced by a subordinating word.

A sentence may have one main clause, or it may have several. When two or more main clauses are present in a sentence, they are usually joined by **coordinating conjunctions**. The most common coordinating conjunctions are *and, but, or, nor, for,* and sometimes *so* and *yet.* Ordinarily, a comma is used before a coordinating conjunction that joins independent clauses.

> Leonardo da Vinci is best known for his paintings, *but* he was also an accomplished engineer.
> Da Vinci was born in Italy in 1452, *and* he died in France in 1519.

Conjunctive adverbs are another group of words used to connect independent clauses. When a conjunctive adverb is used between independent clauses, it is preceded by a semicolon and followed by a comma. The principal conjunctive adverbs are these:

accordingly	consequently	hence	moreover	then
also	else	however	nevertheless	therefore
besides	furthermore	likewise	otherwise	thus

The following sentences use conjunctive adverbs between independent clauses.

> People know da Vinci's works of art; *however,* they are unaware of his remarkable engineering feats.
> He designed a forerunner of the military tank; *moreover,* his drawings include plans for a triple-tier machine gun.

SUBORDINATE CLAUSES

A **subordinate** or **dependent clause**, like an independent clause, has both a subject and a verb. However, it functions as an adjective, adverb, or noun and thus cannot stand alone as a complete sentence. Some subordinate clauses are a necessary part of their sentence's structure, the so-called restrictive modifiers. Other subordinate clauses offer only tangential information, the so-called nonrestrictive or nonessential modifiers. (See Section 31 for further discussion of restrictive and nonrestrictive clauses.) This is the most important fact to remember now: whenever a group of words contains a subordinate clause, the group must also contain an independent clause before it can qualify as a sentence.

> Although da Vinci was a Renaissance man [Subordinate clause is not a sentence; the meaning is incomplete.]

27

Although da Vinci was a Renaissance man, his engineering concepts were far ahead of their time. [Subordinate clause is joined to an independent clause that completes its meaning; the construction is a sentence.]

A subordinate clause is always preceded by a **subordinating conjunction** or a **relative pronoun**. Some of the most widely used subordinating conjunctions follow:

after	how	though	when
although	if	unless	where
as	since	until	whether
because	then	whatever	why

Relative pronouns often introduce subordinate clauses. When used in this way, a relative pronoun may also be referred to as a conjunctive pronoun. Common relative pronouns are the following:

that	which	who	whom	whose

A subordinate clause can function as an adjective, an adverb, or a noun. An **adjective clause** modifies either a noun or a noun substitute.

Anyone who sees da Vinci's drawings never fails to be impressed. [Subordinate clause *who sees da Vinci's drawings* modifies the pronoun *anyone.*]

The **adverb clause** modifies either a verb, an adjective, or an adverb.

If the technology had existed, his "modern" ideas might have been implemented. [Subordinate clause *if the technology had existed* modifies the verb phrase *might have been implemented.*]

His drawings of flying machines are amazing because they resemble today's helicopters. [Subordinate clause *because they resemble today's helicopters* modifies the adjective *amazing.*]

Since they were so advanced, some of his ideas were not taken seriously. [Subordinate clause *since they were so advanced* modifies the adverb *seriously.*]

The **noun clause** may serve as either a subject, a complement renaming the subject, an indirect object, a direct object of a verb, or an object of a preposition.

Whatever da Vinci examined was studied thoroughly. [Subordinate clause *whatever da Vinci examined* serves as the subject.]

His drawings' meticulous detail is what is striking. [Subordinate clause *what is striking* serves as the complement, the predicate noun of the sentence.]

Scholars speculate that some of his ideas were heretical. [Subordinate clause *that some of his ideas were heretical* serves as the direct object of the verb *speculate.*]

Scholars have also been puzzled about why he wrote his notes in code. [Subordinate clause *why he wrote his notes in code* serves as the object of the preposition *about.*]

USING CLAUSES TO COMBINE IDEAS

Clauses enable a writer to combine several related ideas into a single sentence, instead of having to use a separate sentence for each thought. In elementary school you may have learned this definition of a sentence: a sentence is a complete statement expressing a single thought. While that definition is true in a very general way, sentences containing several clauses allow for the expression of complex or multifaceted thoughts.

Consider, for example, the following sentences:

Leonardo da Vinci was a scientist and an engineer. He was also an artist. He combined these three fields. The Renaissance emphasized realistic imitation of nature in art. Da Vinci believed an artist must know mathematics. He must also know the laws of nature. Da Vinci believed the eye was the perfect instrument for gaining this knowledge. He made many detailed technical and anatomical drawings, His drawings show his practice of this belief. He is cited as the creator of modern scientific illustration.

Notice how short and choppy many of these sentences sound. As you read them, you probably began combining some of the related thoughts in your mind to smooth out the bumps. The practice with phrases in Section 6 gave you some tools for expanding sentences with details. By using clauses to form additional relationships, you can also coordinate and subordinate ideas:

Independent Clause
Subordinate Clause
Leonardo da Vinci, who was a scientist and engineer as well as an artist,

Subordinate Clause
combined these three fields. If art was to imitate nature realistically,

Independent Clause
Subordinate Clause
da Vinci believed that the artist must know mathematics and the laws of nature;

Independent Clause
Subordinate Clause
moreover, he believed that the eye was the perfect instrument for gaining this

Subordinate Clause
knowledge. Because of da Vinci's many detailed technical and anatomical drawings,

Subordinate Clause
which show his practice of this belief,

Independent Clause
he is cited as the creator of modern scientific illustration.

In place of the choppy statements, we now have three sentences that combine ideas from the original ten. Besides being smoother, these three sentences establish relationships between ideas by means of their interlocking clauses.

Practice: Using clauses to combine ideas   *Revise the following sentences, using* **subordinate** *clauses to combine the original nine sentences into no more than five sentences containing the same ideas. One possible answer is listed at the end of this section.*

[1] Ergonomics is the study of working conditions. [2] It takes into account human capabilities, skills, and talents. [3] Ergonomics can be applied to office furnishings. [4] It

29

involves such things as how well your desk chair helps you do your job. [5] Office ergonomics is a special form of engineering. [6] It uses basic equipment design and construction principles. [7] Well-engineered desk chairs enable people to work more productively. [8] They do their jobs better. [9] They are more comfortable.

CONFUSING PHRASE AND CLAUSE CONNECTIVES

Certain words that can be either prepositions or conjunctions sometimes cause students to confuse phrases with clauses. This confusion can occur if you try to identify a word group on the basis of the connective alone instead of examining the entire word group. For example, the following sentences use the same connective; but in the first sentence the connective introduces a phrase, and in the second it introduces a clause.

Da Vinci left Italy sometime *after* 1515.
After he settled in France, he worked on at least one engineering project—a canal.

Rather than rely on the connective alone, examine the entire word group it introduces. Remember that a preposition introduces a phrase—the noun, pronoun, or substantive that is the object of the preposition, and any words that modify that object. A conjunction, on the other hand, introduces a clause—a group of words containing a subject and a verb. A phrase never contains both a subject and a verb.

Some of the words that may be either prepositions or conjunctions are *after, before, for, until,* and *since.*

Answer to the Practice   Many answers are possible; the following revision shows
one representative type.

Ergonomics is the study of working conditions that takes into account human capabilities, skills, and talents. When it is applied to office furnishings, ergonomics involves such things as how well your desk chair helps you do your job. Office ergonomics is a special form of engineering that uses basic equipment design and construction principles. Well-engineered desk chairs enable people to work more productively. They do their jobs better because they are more comfortable.

EXERCISE 7-1, INDEPENDENT AND SUBORDINATE CLAUSES (1d)

Write sentences with two independent clauses joined by the listed coordinating conjunctions and conjunctive adverbs. Be sure to punctuate your sentences correctly.

Example   nor   _He never was absent, nor was he ever late for interviews._

meanwhile   _I studied engineering; meanwhile, she studied math._

1. *accordingly* _____

2. *thus* _____

3. *so* _____

4. *also* _____

5. *besides* _____

6. *nevertheless* _____

7. *however* _____

8. *therefore* _____

9. *else* _____

10. *furthermore* _____

11. *hence* _____

12. *or* _____

13. *moreover* _____

14. *otherwise* _____

15. *for* _____

16. *likewise* _____

17. *and* _____

18. *consequently* _____

19. *but* _____

20. *then* _____

Write sentences, each with an independent clause and a subordinate clause. Begin the subordinate clause with the given subordinating conjunction or relative pronoun.

Example   *until* _I was happy until I saw my grade._

              that _I wished that I could take the course again._

21. *although* _____

22. *as* _____

23. *after* _____

24. *because* _____

25. *how* _____

26. *if* _____

27. *though* _____

28. *which* _____

29. *unless* _____

30. *who* _____

31. *until* _____

32. *when* _____

33. *where* _____

34. *whose* _____

35. *whether* _____

36. *whoever* _____

37. *why* _____

38. *whatever* _____

39. *then* _____

40. *since* _____

EXERCISE 7-2, FUNCTIONS OF SUBORDINATE CLAUSES   (1d)

In the following sentences, underline main clauses once and subordinate clauses twice. Indicate whether a subordinate clause functions as an adjective (*adj*), adverb (*adv*), or noun (*n*) by writing the appropriate abbreviation above the clause.

Example

adv.
If a student is strong in math and science courses,

she might be interested in an engineering career.

1. Most of what we consider modern inventions are actually the work of engineers.

2. Engineers are the people who are responsible for the extension of technology into almost every area of modern life.

3. When a new product is developed, an engineer probably developed it.

4. Because invention is almost a requirement of most engineers' jobs, they must have a strong practical streak.

5. They must be able to visualize how a nonexistent tool or machine must look.

Underline twice the subordinate clause in each of the following sentences. Indicate whether it functions as an adjective clause, an adverb clause, or a noun clause by writing *adj*, *adv*, or *n*, above it. Then underline once the word that the clause modifies or complements.

Example

adj.
Any company that invests in research and development hires engineers.

6. Much of the work that is done by industrial engineers helps the country's productivity.

7. An engineer studies basic science and mathematics and specializes in a field that interests her.

8. Whether you're interested in medicine or geology, an engineering field is suitable for you.

9. Biomedical engineering and petroleum engineering are two fields which might interest you.

10. Though metallurgy, chemical, and electrical engineering are popular, newer fields are also interesting students.

Write sentences containing subordinate clauses that perform the stated functions.

Example (adverb clause modifying verb)

I'll be ready after I've taken a month-long internship.

11. (subordinate adjective clause modifying noun)

_____

12. (subordinate adjective clause modifying pronoun)

_____

13. (subordinate adverb clause modifying verb)

_____

14. (subordinate adverb clause modifying adjective)

_____

15. (subordinate adverb clause modifying adverb)

_____

16. (subordinate noun clause, subject)

_____

17. (subordinate noun clause, complement)

_____

18. (subordinate noun clause, direct object)

_____

19. (subordinate noun clause, object of verb)

_____

20. (subordinate noun clause, object of preposition)

_____

EXERCISE 7-3, CONFUSING PHRASE AND CLAUSE CONNECTIVES   (1d)

A few connectives may be either prepositions or conjunctions and can thus introduce both phrases and clauses. These connectives are *after, before, for, until,* and *since.* In the following sentences, carefully examine the word groups introduced by the italicized connectives. Then write *P* above the connective if it is a preposition (introducing a phrase) or *C* if it is a conjunction (introducing a clause).

Example   *P*
After graduation, on-the-job training can make you a petroleum engineer.

1. Opportunities *for* engineers are plentiful in machine design.

2. *Since* the invention of computer graphics, techniques of design have utterly changed.

3. *Until* recently the design of any new machine component took months.

4. The time was necessary *since* any new component had to be field tested.

5. Field testing is thorough, *for* no one can afford to lose production time.

6. An entire factory or process might be shut down *until* one new machine component is

    repaired.

7. *Until* computer graphics became cheaper, only huge industries could afford it.

8. *After* the price of the systems dropped to the $20,000 range, their popularity

    increased.

9. *Before* a machine component is actually made, a computer graphics system can create

    an image of it and test its operation.

10. A process that involved hundreds of worker hours *before* the invention of computer

    graphics now may take less than a day's time.

In each of the following sentences, word groups are italicized. Write *P* above it if the italicized word group is a phrase or *C* if it is a clause.

Example   *P*
Demand is heavy *for engineers* with computer-graphics experience.

11. Schools have quickly added computer graphics to their curricula, *for its applications*

    are amazing.

12. *Since the 1970's,* dozens of schools have made computer work required.

13. *Since dozens of consoles are required,* using computers can be very expensive.

14. *After seeing the benefits,* most faculty are eager to change.

15. An entire electronics design can be tested *before one wire is run.*

16. A rear-axle design can be refined *before its introduction to the assembly line.*

17. An entire airplane can be tested *for efficiency* before a mock-up is even built.

18. A nuclear reactor design can be subjected to hypothetical disaster situations *until all its flaws are known.*

19. Design may be better now, *for computer graphics allows a designer to pursue every possible refinement or change.*

20. Computerized production of computer-graphics designs, *until recently impossible,* can speed up production still further.

Write sentences using the listed connectives to head a phrase or clause, as indicated.

21. (*before,* phrase) _____

22. (*before,* clause) _____

23. (*until,* phrase) _____

24. (*until,* clause) _____

25. (*after,* phrase) _____

26. (*after,* clause) _____

27. (*since,* phrase) _____

28. (*since,* clause) _____

8

SENTENCE TYPES   (1d)

Since you began studying the parts of speech in the first section of this book, you have been increasing your knowledge of the way words function individually and in groups. You have been learning to analyze sentences and to describe the way their components work together. Beginning with words and progressing through phrases to clauses, the relationships of the components have grown more and more complex.

Being able to analyze the components in a sentence is likely to make you a better writer. When you understand how sentences work, you have better control over the ones you write. When things go wrong, you can figure out why. When you want to achieve a certain effect, you can take sentence structures apart and put them back together in new, planned ways.

For example, if a paragraph you have written sounds monotonous because all the sentences seem the same, probably you have used only one or two sentence patterns. Your knowledge of sentence patterns, clauses, and phrases will enable you to vary those sentences, creating a much more pleasing paragraph.

Now we are ready to examine the broadest category in our analysis of word groups: sentence types. There are four. A **simple sentence** is composed of a single independent clause. A **compound sentence** is composed of two or more independent clauses. A **complex sentence** has an independent clause and one or more subordinate clauses. A **compound-complex sentence** contains two or more independent clauses and one or more subordinate clauses. Examples of each type of sentence follow:

SIMPLE SENTENCE   ⌐——— Independent Clause ———⌐
Advertising has existed for centuries.

COMPOUND SENTENCE   ⌐——————— Independent Clause ———————
The 1000-year-old frescoes at Pompeii may seem only

⌐——————⌐ ⌐——— Independent Clause ———
decorative, but some of these paintings are actually

⌐——————⌐
advertisements.

COMPLEX SENTENCE   ⌐— Independent Clause —⌐ ⌐Subordinate Clause ———
One fresco shows wine jars because it once adorned a

⌐——————————⌐
wine merchant's shop.

COMPOUND-COMPLEX
SENTENCE

Subordinate Clause
Throughout human history if someone had wares to sell

Independent Clause
or trade, some form of advertising was used, and some

Independent Clause
consumer responded to it.

Practice: Identifying sentence types   *Examine the following sentences and decide whether each is a simple, compound, complex, or compound-complex sentence. The answers are listed at the end of this section.*

[1] Advertising is the nation's largest service business. [2] It is a service business because advertisers help other businesspeople in selling their products. [3] There are over 200,000 people employed in advertising, and their work involves everything from skywriting to television ads. [4] Over half these people work in New York or Chicago, with the rest working in smaller agencies throughout the country. [5] However, two-thirds of the entire number do not work directly at ad agencies, since much advertising work is performed at television studios, radio stations, newspapers, magazines, printers' offices, and so on. [6] Because ads must constantly change, the industry always looks for new people and ideas, and the rewards for articulate and creative people are high. [7] The risks, though, are also high, and the pressure can be intense. [8] Whole teams of advertisers may be fired when an account is lost to another agency. [9] The challenge, the reward, the stimulating work, and the chance to work with stimulating people keep people knocking on the doors of ad agencies every year.

Answers to the Practice   [1] simple   [2] complex   [3] compound
[4] complex   [5] complex   [6] compound-complex   [7] compound
[8] complex   [9] simple

EXERCISE 8, SENTENCE TYPES (1d)

Using subordinate and independent clauses, expand the following simple sentences into the sentence types indicated in parentheses.

Example   Advertisements are always around you.

(compound) *Advertisements are always around you, and you are always aware of them.*

(complex) *Advertisements are always around you whether you are aware of them or not.*

(compound-complex) *Advertisements are always around you, and you are always aware of them, although your awareness may be sub-conscious.*

1. There are thousands of advertisements on television every day.

    (compound) _____

    (complex) _____

    (compound-complex) _____

2. I have a list of my favorite television ads.

    (compound) _____

    (complex) _____

    (compound-complex) _____

3. Most television ads ask you to buy some product.

    (compound) _____

    (complex) _____

    (compound-complex) _____

4. There are other places we see advertisements every day.

    (compound) _____

    (complex) _____

    (compound-complex) _____

5. Billboards are one common advertising medium.

    (compound) _____

    (complex) _____

    (compound-complex) _____

6. Music on the radio is interrupted by ads.

    (compound) _____

    (complex) _____

    (compound-complex) _____

7. Even the sign at a business is an ad.

    (compound) _____

    (complex) _____

    (compound-complex) _____

8. And don't forget newspapers.

    (compound) _____

    (complex) _____

    (compound-complex) _____

9. Nowadays, many ads are delivered in the mail.

    (compound) _____

    (complex) _____

    (compound-complex) _____

10. Some people think we're subjected to too many advertisements.

    (compound) _____

    (complex) _____

    (compound-complex) _____

9

CASE (2)

The function of nouns and pronouns within clauses and sentences is indicated by their **case**. There are three cases in English: the **subjective case**, used for the subject of a verb or for a pronoun serving as a predicate complement; the **possessive case**, used to show ownership; and the **objective case**, used for the object of a verb, verbal, or preposition.

Nouns and pronouns change form to show their case. Nouns have a **common form**, such as *consumer;* and a **possessive form**, such as *consumer's*. Personal pronouns and relative or interrogative pronouns are **inflected**; that is, they have different forms for the subjective, possessive, and objective cases. The table shows these various pronoun forms.

	PERSONAL PRONOUNS			RELATIVE PRONOUNS		
	Subjective	*Possessive*	*Objective*	*Subjective*	*Possessive*	*Objective*
		Singular			**Singular**	
First Person	I	my, mine	me	who	whose	whom
Second Person	you	your, yours	you			
Third Person	he, she, it	his, her, hers, its	him, her, it			
		Plural			**Plural**	
First Person	we	our, ours	us	who	whose	whom
Second Person	you	your, yours	you			
Third Person	they	their, theirs	them			

Using the correct case and form to indicate a particular function requires a little care.

SUBJECTIVE AND OBJECTIVE CASES

All parts of a compound subject should be in the subjective case. All parts of a compound object should be in the objective case.

SUBJECT	My *husband Gary* and *I* were looking through old magazines.
OBJECT	His mother had asked *him* and *me* to remove them from her attic.

After the conjunctions *as* and *than,* use the subjective case if a pronoun is the subject of an understood verb. Use the objective case if it is the object of an understood verb.

SUBJECT	Gary was taking even more time than *I* (was taking).
OBJECT	The magazine advertisements fascinated my husband as much as (they fascinated) *me.*

A pronoun in an appositive describing a subject or complement should be in the subjective case. A pronoun in an appositive describing an object should be in the objective case. An **appositive** is a word or phrase following a noun or pronoun that identifies or explains the noun or pronoun by renaming it.

SUBJECT	*We*—my husband and *I*—noted that ads hadn't changed much in 70 years.
OBJECT	An old automobile ad showed a charming couple—*us*, of course!

Relative pronouns should be in the subjective case when they function as subjects: *who, whoever*. They should be in the objective case when they function as objects: *whom, whomever*. Remember that the case of the relative pronoun depends upon its function within the clause and not upon the function of the whole clause within the sentence.

SUBJECT	The charming couples *who* pose for today's auto ads make the same consumer pitch. [*Who* is the subject of the subordinate clause modifying *couples*.]
OBJECT	From the Model–T to the Mustang, *whom* the advertisers appeal to has not changed. [*Whom* is the object of the preposition *to* and requires the objective case, even though the whole clause *whom . . . appeal* functions as the subject of the sentence.]

Pronouns following forms of the verb *be* (*is, are, was, were*, etc.) should be written in the subjective case because they function as complements renaming the subject.

It is *we* who imagine ourselves behind the wheel.

POSSESSIVE CASE

Be careful when forming the possessive case of personal pronouns. For most nouns, the *'s*-possessive shows ownership. But personal pronouns show possession through inflection: *my, your, his, hers, its, theirs*, etc. No apostrophe is used. Be particularly careful with the possessive form of *it*. The possessive is *its*, not *it's*. *It's* is the contraction for *it is*.

It's [*It is*] often status or sex appeal with which an ad sells *its* product.

The *'s*-possessive is generally used for nouns naming living things. Conventionally, the *of*-phrase is preferred for inanimate things.

ANIMATE	an advertiser's product, a consumer's money
INANIMATE	the wheel of the car, the pride of possession

There are many exceptions, though, including a number of familiar expressions: *a dollar's worth; for pity's sake; yesterday's news; heart's desire; last year's fashions.*

Nouns and pronouns preceding gerunds should be in the possessive case.

I told my mother-in-law that the reason for *our* failing to finish cleaning the attic was her *son's* reading old magazine ads.

EXERCISE 9, CASE (2)

In the following sentences, decide which of the pronouns in parentheses is correct, and cross out the incorrect choice.

Example   (We / ~~Us~~) marketing students toured an advertising agency.

1.   (They / Them) were proud to show (us / we) around.

2.   They try to give a company an image to use in selling (its / it's) products.

3.   A copywriter has to be someone (who / whom) can relate to an audience.

4.   Words are a copywriter's tools, and he or she uses (them / they) to persuade.

5.   Women are often excellent at copywriting, and many of (them / they) have become famous.

6.   Some advertisers say women are good copywriters because of (they / them / their) familiarity with shopping routines and consumer goods.

7.   You must look for an original approach to persuade (your / you / yours) reader.

8.   To persuade a reader, a copywriter has to imagine (him or her / he or she) seeing the ad and reacting to it.

9.   A copywriter (who / whom) neglects researching the product may not write successful ads.

10. Mark and I decided copywriting was not for (him and me / he and I / he and me).

In the following sentences, cross out any incorrect uses of case and write the correction above the error. Write *Correct* after correct sentences.

Example   We looked at the art department carefully, Mark and ~~me.~~ I

11.   Ad art has to hold the viewer's attention while the message is given to he.

12.   An artist whom cannot work together with a writer is useless.

13.   An art director isn't just someone who can draw but someone who can contribute ideas to a team effort.

14.   This made more sense to Mark than me.

15.   Whomever studies art can design, but an advertising artist is part of a team.

16.   One media buyer told Mark and I that buying was an interesting job.

17. Buyers are not as highly paid as artists and writers, but it is they who transform ideas into reality.

18. They study a client's sales and distribution and decide which media will reach his or her market most efficiently.

19. Us knowing the number of media in the country pleased Janine, a media buyer.

20. Hers is not a simple task.

21. Perry, another media buyer, must decide that the audience of a program or publication is the people who he wants to reach.

22. He has to decide whom reads and whom listens to the agencies' ads.

23. Since ads are so expensive, a buyer can't waste money on a program who's listeners won't or can't buy the client's product.

24. Much research is produced in agencies to convince a client of the success of an ad campaign or to suggest ways it's emphasis should be changed.

25. Consumers are interviewed and their opinions tabulated.

26. It made sense to all the students and I that market research firms are often independent companies.

27. People who's backgrounds are in business or statistics often work in this allied field.

28. Print production teams and broadcast production teams are the people who actually produce the commercials.

29. An account executive, who coordinates all this work, is the agency's representative to the client.

30. Students whom have backgrounds in business, marketing, advertising, art, journalism, English, sociology, or statistics might consider advertising an interesting and rewarding career.

10

ADJECTIVE AND ADVERB FORMS   (3)

In Section 3 we examined adjectives and adverbs as parts of speech with a particular function—modifying. **Adjectives** modify nouns, pronouns, or other noun substitutes. **Adverbs** modify verbs, adjectives, or other adverbs, and occasionally whole sentences. Both adjectives and adverbs limit or qualify the meaning of the words they modify.

Now that you are familiar with sentence patterns and types (Section 5 and 8), as well as with all the parts of speech, we can examine some other characteristics of adjectives and adverbs.

Some words, such as *fast, much, late,* and *well,* can function as **either adjectives or adverbs**.

ADJECTIVE	She is a *fast* runner. [*Fast* modifies the noun, *runner.*]
ADVERB	She ran *fast.* [*Fast* modifies the verb *ran,* telling how she ran.]

Linking verbs such as forms of the verb *be* (*is, are, was, were, become,* etc.) and verbs such as *seem, remain, prove,* and *stand,* as well as such verbs relating to the senses as *feel, look, smell, taste,* and *sound,* are followed by **predicate adjectives** that describe the subject of the sentence or clause.

You must be careful when you use such verbs, since they may or may not be linking. *That meat tasted good* uses a linking verb and hence requires an adjective after the verb. However, in *I tasted the meat,* the verb *tasted* takes an object and hence is not a linking verb. In *She looked tired, looked* is a linking verb followed by the adjective *tired.* In *She looked away tiredly, looked* is not a linking verb. The modifiers *away* and *tiredly* do not describe the subject, *she,* but rather provide information about the verb and thus are adverbs.

Most adverbs are distinguished from their corresponding adjectives by the *-ly* ending: *grateful, gratefully; free, freely; pleasing, pleasingly.* However, an *-ly* ending does not automatically mean a word is an adverb. Some adjectives, such as *friendly, slovenly, cowardly,* also end in *-ly.* Furthermore, some adverbs have two forms, one with *-ly* and one without: *quick, quickly; slow, slowly.* The key, as always, is to see what part of speech a word modifies or what role it plays in a sentence pattern when deciding whether it is an adverb or an adjective.

Adjectives and adverbs show degrees of quality or quantity by means of their **comparative** and **superlative forms**.

For the **comparative** form, which permits a comparison of two, *-er* is added to the adjective, or the adverb *more* is placed before it (*pretty, prettier; rapid, more rapid*). For the **superlative** form, which involves a comparison among three or more, *-est* is added to the adjective, or *most* is placed before it (*pretty, prettiest; rapid, most rapid*).

Most adjectives and a few adverbs of one syllable form the comparative and superlative with *-er* and *-est.* Adjectives of two syllables often offer a choice (*lovelier, loveliest* and *more lovely, most lovely*). Adjectives of three or more syllables and most adverbs usually use *more* and *most* in making their comparisons (*more industrious,* not *industriouser; more sadly,* not *sadlier.*)

The comparative and superlative forms of the adjectives *good* and *bad* are irregular:

good	bad
better	worse
best	worst

Some adjectives and adverbs are absolute in their meaning and thus cannot logically be compared. Examples of such words include the following:

complete	final
dead	perfect
empty	unique

Practice: Identifying adjectives and adverbs   *Underline once all the words that function as adjectives in the following sentences. (Do not underline the articles.) Underline twice all the words that function as adverbs. The answers are listed at the end of this section.*

[1] Many of today's children are very comfortable with computers. [2] They play with computers more easily than previous generations played with dolls and electric trains. [3] Formerly, computers were commonly found only in business offices, universities, or scientific laboratories. [4] Now minicomputers are fairly common in elementary schools, where they are used for computer-assisted instruction. [5] More and more homes also have "personal" computers. [6] These machines most often help with managing the family's finances or are used for computer games that young and old can enjoy together. [7] Computers have fast become child's play.

Answers to the Practice   *Adjectives:* [1] today's, comfortable   [2] previous, electric   [3] business, scientific   [4] common, elementary, computer-assisted   [5] more (and) more, personal   [6] These, family's, computer   [7] child's   *Adverbs:* [1] very   [2] more, easily   [3] Formerly, commonly, only   [4] Now, fairly   [5] also   [6] most, often, together   [7] fast

EXERCISE 10-1, ADJECTIVE AND ADVERB FORMS   (3)

In the blanks, indicate with the appropriate abbreviation whether the adjectival (*adj*) or the adverbial (*adv*) form of the given word should be used.

Example   *slow*   In the '60's people said, "Don't walk __adv__ through the computer room."

probable   "You'll __adv__ be hired."

1. *virtual*   The computer is used in _____ all fields of work now.

2. *total*   Before the '50's, information was processed _____ by hand.

3. *slow*   One census official grew frustrated with this _____ process.

4. *eventual*   He invented what _____ became the first computer.

5. *usual*   His company, International Business Machines, is _____ referred to by its initials.

6. *sure*   This one man _____ transformed the American workplace.

7. *real*   Data processing is a _____ volatile field.

8. *continual*   Machines, jobs, and software are all _____ developed.

9. *basic*   There are _____ three kinds of jobs in data processing.

10. *logical*   Making, selling, or running the machines are all, _____ enough, called hardware jobs.

11. *ordinary*   Software jobs _____ concern writing programs or instructions for the machines.

12. *original*   Keypunch or entry operators put the _____ data into forms the machine can read.

13. *typical*   Computers _____ perform bookkeeping, scheduling, and analysis.

14. *frequent*   For scientists, computers are _____ used to solve equations too long for a human to solve easily.

15. *excellent*   Computer work seemed an _____ way for young people to move into administrative or managerial work.

16. *late*   Only _____ has education become a requirement for the field.

17. *relative*   As a _____ new field, computer operating requires experience of its new employees.

18. *primary*   Employers now hire _____ graduates in math, computer science, systems analysis, or electronics.

19. *heavy*   Any company or government agency with _____ paperwork uses computers now.

20. *fair*   A _____ new development is the minicomputer.

In each of the following sentences, cross out the incorrect choice in the parentheses.

    Example   Some computer jobs seem (simple / ~~simply~~).

21. The ability to think (logical / logically) is necessary.
22. You must also be (imaginative / imaginatively) to solve some problems.
23. You must also remain (patient / patiently) for long jobs.
24. A computer operator must be able to organize tasks (logical / logically).
25. Data processors absolutely must work (accurate / accurately).
26. Skill with numbers is (firm / firmly) required to enjoy this work.
27. You must also work (easy / easily) with details of all kinds.
28. The future demand for computer operators seems (good / well).
29. The use of computers is (current / currently) being introduced to many fields.
30. Doctors may receive (instant / instantly) diagnosis from a computer.
31. And computers can maintain patient files (thorough / thoroughly).
32. Communications systems are beginning to rely (heavy / heavily) on computers.
33. Banks are (eager / eagerly) to use computers to provide better service.
34. Such expansion (general / generally) means good job opportunities.
35. The field seems (inviting / invitingly) for women and for minorities.
36. The field is so (new / newly) that few ideas or positions are entrenched.
37. Hardware and software develop so (quick / quickly) that constant training is needed.
38. Flexibility has proved (important / importantly).
39. (Traditional / Traditionally) two lines of advancement are open for programmers.
40. They move (eventually / eventual) into senior programming or managerial jobs.

EXERCISE 10-2, COMPARATIVE AND SUPERLATIVE FORMS   (3)

In each blank, write the appropriate comparative or superlative form of the modifier given in italics to complete the sentence correctly.

Example   *fast*   Data processing is developing *faster* _____ than people expected.

profitable   It may be the *most profitable* business existing today.

1. *low*   Keypunch or computer operators hold the _____ level jobs.

2. *less*   These jobs are also, of course, the _____ paying jobs.

3. *less*   Operators' positions require _____ education than others.

4. *important*   But they may be the _____ jobs for an employer.

5. *responsible*   Operators are _____ for the accuracy of data processing.

6. *technical*   Programmers' jobs are _____ positions.

7. *logical*   Programmers have to think the _____ of all people.

8. *accurate*   Solving problems _____ than others makes a programmer better.

9. *experienced*   The _____ programmer in a firm may become a senior program or systems analyst.

10. *familiar*   Since analysts plan the uses for the computer,

      they must be _____ with the whole business than must programmers.

11. *accountable*   Analysts are, therefore, _____ than programmers.

12. *bad*   This would be the _____ job for someone who hates pressure.

13. *well*   The analyst may be the _____ known data processor in the company.

14. *quickly*   Analysts plan computer use to solve other executives' problems

      _____ than the executives could solve them alone.

15. *skillfully*   The analyst must juggle capabilities, scheduling, and

expenses _____ than any other executive.

16. *unique*   The analyst's job is _____ in the data processing field.

17. *perfect*   That would be the _____ job for me.

18. *happy*   That job would make me _____ than any other.

19. *frequent*   Data processing jobs require overtime _____ than other jobs.

20. *serious*   I am _____ about this field than any other.

Write sentences using the form called for—comparative or superlative—of the listed modifiers.

21. (*smart,* superlative)

_____

22. (*good,* superlative)

_____

23. (*high,* superlative)

_____

24. (*badly,* superlative)

_____

25. (*obnoxious,* comparative)

_____

26. (*speedy,* comparative)

_____

27. (*hateful,* comparative)

_____

28. (*soft,* comparative)

_____

29. (*joyous,* superlative)

_____

30. (*truthful,* comparative)

_____

11

VERB FORMS   (4-5)

Section 2 sketches the general role verbs play, but it only begins to suggest the amount of information a verb actually conveys. The single word comprising a verb (or the few words of a verb phrase) tells us not only the exact nature of an action or condition but also—

1. the time when it occurs and whether the action is completed or continuing (**tense**);

2. whether or not the verb passes its action to an object (is **transitive, intransitive,** or **linking**),

3. whether the subject is performing or receiving the action (**voice**); and

4. the attitude of the speaker or writer (**mood**).

TENSES

Verbs show present, past, and future time by means of their three tenses. Each of these tenses is further subdivided into categories, according to whether the action or condition is continuing (in progress) or completed at the time indicated. The following table lists, explains, and gives examples of the categories of tense. Notice which helping verbs are used to form each of the tenses.

TENSE	TIME	EXAMPLE
Present	Present or habitual action	I *call* my parents.
Present perfect	Action completed at an indefinite time in the past or extending up to the present time	I *have called* my parents every Sunday.
Present progressive	Present action continuing or in progress	I *am calling* my parents now.
Present perfect progressive	Continuing action occurring up to but not including the present	I *have been calling* my parents.
Past	Past action	I *called* my parents.
Past perfect	Past action completed before another past action	I *had called* my parents before lunch.
Past progressive	Continuing action that occurred in the past	I *was calling* my parents.
Past perfect progressive	Continuing past action that occurred before another past action	I *had been calling* my parents when you arrived.
Future	Future action	I *shall/will call* them later.
Future perfect	Future action that will be completed before another future action	I *will have called* them before I see you again.

TENSE	TIME	EXAMPLE
Future progressive	Continuing action that will occur in the future	I *will be calling* them again next Sunday.
Future perfect progressive	Continuing action that leads up to a point in the future	If I arrive late, the reason is I *will have been calling* my parents.

REGULAR AND IRREGULAR VERBS

The verb previously used to illustrate tenses, *call,* is a **regular verb**. Most verbs are regular; that is, the past tense and past participle (the combining form used with many helping verbs) are formed by adding *-ed* to the present tense form: for example, *help + ed* and *show + ed* yield *helped* and *showed*. If the present tense form of a regular verb ends in *e*, the past tense and past participle are formed by simply adding *d: hoped, filed.*

Irregular verbs, as the term suggests, follow another pattern. Of the more than 200 irregular English verbs, about 20 have the same form for the present tense, past tense, and past participle: *cut, cut, cut.* Many change an internal vowel for the past tense and past participle: *spin, spun, spun.* Some irregular verbs have three distinct forms, a different one for each of the present tense, past tense, and past participle: *forgive, forgave, forgiven; do, did, done.* The following list shows the three forms for the most commonly used irregular verbs.

PRESENT INFINITIVE	PAST	PAST PARTICIPLE
awake	awoke, awaked	awaked
arise	arose	arisen
bear (carry)	bore	borne
bear (give birth to)	bore	borne, born
beat	beat	beaten
become	became	become
begin	began	begun
bet	bet	bet
bid	bade, bid	bidden, bid
bite	bit	bitten
blow	blew	blown
break	broke	broken
bring	brought	brought
burst	burst	burst
buy	bought	bought
catch	caught	caught
choose	chose	chosen
come	came	come
cut	cut	cut
dig	dug	dug
dive	dived, dove	dived
do	did	done
draw	drew	drawn
drink	drank	drunk
drive	drove	driven
eat	ate	eaten
fall	fell	fallen
feel	felt	felt
find	found	found
fly	flew	flown
forget	forgot	forgotten, forgot
forgive	forgave	forgiven
freeze	froze	frozen

PRESENT INFINITIVE	PAST	PAST PARTICIPLE
get	got	got, gotten
give	gave	given
go	went	gone
grow	grew	grown
hang (suspend)	hung	hung
hang	hanged	hung
hid	hid	hidden
hit	hit	hit
hurt	hurt	hurt
keep	kept	kept
know	knew	known
lay (place)	laid	laid
lead	led	led
leave	left	left
let	let	let
lie (recline)	lay	lain
lose	lost	lost
make	made	made
mean	meant	meant
pay	paid	paid
read	read	read
ride	rode	ridden
ring	rang	rung
rise	rose	risen
run	ran	run
see	saw	seen
set	set	set
shake	shook	shaken
shine	shone	shone
shrink	shrank, shrunk	shrunk
sink	sank, sunk	sunk
speak	spoke	spoken
spin	spun	spun
spring	sprang, sprung	sprung
stand	stood	stood
steal	stole	stolen
stink	stank	stunk
strike	struck	struck
swear	swore	sworn
swim	swam	swum
swing	swung	swung
take	took	taken
teach	taught	taught
tear	tore	torn
tell	told	told
think	thought	thought
throw	threw	thrown
wake	woke, waked	woken, waked
wear	wore	worn
weave	wove, weaved	woven, weaved
weep	wept	wept
win	won	won
wind	wound	wound
wring	wrung	wrung
write	wrote	written

The verb *be* is also an irregular verb. It appears often in many forms, and it is used frequently with the combining forms of other verbs. Study it carefully.

SINGULAR	PLURAL	SINGULAR	PLURAL
Present Tense		**Present Perfect Tense**	
I am	we are	I have been	we have been
you are	you are	you have been	you have been
he, she, it is	they are	he, she, it has been	they have been
Past Tense		**Past Perfect Tense**	
I was	we were	I had been	we had been
you were	you were	you had been	you had been
he, she, it was	they were	he, she, it had been	they had been
Future Tense		**Future Perfect Tense**	
I will be	we will be	I will have been	we will have been
you will be	you will be	you will have been	you will have been
he, she, it will be	they will be	he, she, it will have been	they will have been

Practice: Identifying verb tenses   *Name the tenses of the verbs in the following sentences. The answers are listed at the end of this section.*

[1] Most of the time, when people think of careers in the media, they think only of actors. [2] But actors certainly aren't the only workers in the media. [3] For almost any show you watch, dozens, perhaps hundreds, of people have performed their jobs before you see the actors. [4] For a television show, for example, a script writer will have written the script up to a year before. [5] Designers have been working for months to prepare the sets and the costumes. [6] Lighting designers will have established new ways to use lights. [7] Then, perhaps months later, lighting technicians will carry out the designers' instructions. [8] Stage carpenters and painters build the sets, while sound technicians set up the sound system, electricians wire the set, and property masters obtain or make all the props needed. [9] All these people have been working all along, as the cast and director have been rehearsing the script. [10] A stage manager will coordinate all these people, together with an orchestra, if needed. [11] If, in fact, it is a television show, all the engineers, cameramen, and technicians necessary to put the show on the air will be working on the final production itself. [12] And I have produced only a partial list of the people involved. [13] Next time you are watching some actor or actress work, think of all the people who are working "behind the scenes."

SPECIAL PROBLEMS WITH VERB TENSES

Problems writers face in using verbs correctly sometimes arise from difficulties with tense forms. Several of the most common problems are discussed below.

Writers sometimes omit necessary verb endings, especially if they do not audibly pronounce these endings when speaking. The two most frequently omitted endings are -*s* and -*ed*. The -*s* form is required for present tense verbs used with singular nouns, third person singular pronouns (*he, she, it*), and indefinite pronouns such as *each, someone,* and *everybody*.

She *loves* the smell of the grease paint she *wears* for performances.

For the present tense verbs ending in *o,* the form is *-es: goes.* For the verbs *be* and *have,* the *-s* forms are *is* and *has.*

The smell *is* sweeter than perfume to her because it *goes* with the theater, which *is* in her blood: she *is* an actress.

The *-ed* form is required for the past tense and past participle of all regular verbs. When the next word following the verb in a sentence begins with a similar sound, the *-ed* can be hard to hear and may be difficult to remember when you write. Be particularly careful to include it when you write the past tense for constructions such as *used to* and *supposed to.*

I *used* to get stage fright. [*Not* I *use* to get stage fright.]

Writers sometimes use nonstandard forms of irregular verbs. Remember that although most English verbs are regular, a great many are irregular. *See* is an irregular verb, so you should not write *I seed him yesterday* instead of *I saw him yesterday.*

Also, the principal parts of an irregular verb are not interchangeable; that is, you need to select the correct tense for the time you wish to indicate. *I done my homework* is incorrect because *done* is the past participle form (*do, did, done*); it requires a helping verb and cannot be used for the past tense. *I did my homework* is correct.

Writers sometimes have trouble choosing the appropriate tense sequence for verbs in main and subordinate clauses in complex sentences. When the verb in the main clause is in any tense except the past or past perfect tense, the verb in the subordinate clause will be in whatever tense the meaning requires.

Because I *used* to get stage fright, I now *meditate* before performances. [The meditation occurs in the present even though it is the result of past events.]
I *know* meditation *will help* me *avoid* the jitters later. [The knowledge exists in the present but refers to a future condition.]

When the verb in the main clause is in the past or past perfect tense, the verb in the subordinate clause will usually be in the past or past perfect tense, too—unless the subordinate clause states a general truth.

I *had thought* that stage fright *was* my fate. [The main clause uses the past perfect verb to express an action completed; the subordinate clause uses the simple past tense to express a condition occurring in the past.]

BUT

I eventually *found,* though, that mind over matter *works.* [Here the subordinate clause is offered as a general truth and so is in the present tense.]

Answers to the Practice   [1] present, present   [2] present   [3] present, present perfect, present   [4] future perfect   [5] present perfect progressive   [6] future perfect   [7] future   [8] present, present, present, present, present   [9] present perfect progressive, present perfect progressive   [10] future   [11] present, future progressive   [12] present perfect   [13] present progressive, present, present, present progressive

EXERCISE 11-1, VERB TENSES   (4-5)

Change the present tense verbs in each of the following sentences to past tense, rewriting the sentence with past tense verbs in the blank provided. Be sure to choose the correct form for irregular verbs.

Example   The director of the program works with everyone else involved in its production.

The director of the program worked with everyone else involved in its production.

1.   The director consults with the writer, helping shape the final script.

_____

2.   He or she checks to make sure set designs, costume designs, and lighting designs present a single idea.

_____

3.   The director isn't a tyrant.

_____

4.   A good director requests rather than commands.

_____

5.   But directors have to have the final word.

_____

6.   Final responsibility for the quality of a movie or play is the director's.

_____

7.   The director casts the movie or film.

_____

8.   He or she reads and understands the script completely.

_____

9.   A plan forms in the director's mind.

_____

10.   He or she directs the performance of every line and every move.

_____

11.   The director possesses all the skills of a good actor.

_____

12. In addition, the director organizes work into manageable units and plans a schedule, sometimes a year in advance.

_____

13. Our director has worked at almost every job in the theater: actor, stagehand, cameraman, writer, film editor.

_____

14. All this work becomes necessary when she decides to direct.

_____

15. All designers know the effects of stage lighting.

_____

16. Costume designers familiarize themselves with all materials and methods of designing clothes and makeup.

_____

17. A set designer matches his or her materials to the ideas and actions in the script.

_____

18. Experience helps the designer's range of possibilities to expand.

_____

19. Director and designer meet for the important first reading of the script, where basic ideas take form.

_____

20. Designers sketch, draw floor plans, and build models to test and to illustrate their ideas.

_____

21. A designer also supervises the construction of the scenery and the buying of props.

_____

22. They read the script over and over.

_____

23. Lighting and sound designers weave their designs too, but know electricity and electronics.

_____

24. Each designer "comes in" on budget.

_____

25. He or she lists and records the cost of each component of the design.

_____

EXERCISE 11-2, SPECIAL PROBLEMS WITH VERB TENSES (4–5)

In the blank in each sentence, write the correct form of the listed verb in the tense indicated

Example   (*go,* present)   Rehearsals sometimes _____ on well into the night.

1. (*believe,* past)   I _____ I wanted backstage work.

2. (*do,* present perfect)   The stage manager _____ every kind of theatrical work.

3. (*suppose,* past)   We _____ she ran everything smoothly.

4. (*want,* present)   A drama student _____ experience above all.

5. (*build,* past perfect)   I _____ dozens of community theater sets.

6. (*ask,* present)   An actor usually _____ for work since want ads for creative people are rare.

7. (*do,* present)   That _____ put a premium on aggressiveness.

8. (*use,* present perfect)   He _____ all the tricks to find an acting job.

9. (*have,* present)   As an actor or director, you _____ to create the demand for your services with your work.

10. (*prepare,* present perfect)   A wise actor or director _____ for a second career or job.

11. (*see,* past)   I _____ the contradiction of work in the media.

12. (*burst,* past)   No career ever _____ forth without years of work.

13. (*begin,* past)   Almost all successful careers _____ with part-time work.

14. (*lead,* present perfect)   Many people _____ interesting lives with this kind of work.

15. (*take,* present)   It _____ real dedication to be an actor or director.

For each of the following sentences, select the appropriate verb for the tense sequence from the choices in parentheses, and cross out the incorrect choice.

16. It is not clear whether college or practical experience (is / was) the best preparation.

17. Many of these jobs were unionized, which (makes / made) a college degree necessary.

18. I know I (have / had) to get technical training for a media production job.

19. You will be ready for a job in electronic production once you (received / have received) some very specific training.

20. Technical directors, who coordinate camera shots, sound, lighting, and other aspects of the electronic production, (deserve / deserved) respect.

21. I'm not sure if you (knew / know) how difficult a cameraman's job really is.

22. A film or tape editor created the film you see, since the director (has shot / shot) the scenes out of sequence.

23. If you see a man fly or a world explode, a special-effects director and crew (created / had created) the illusion for you.

24. What if none of these careers interests you and you still (want / wanted) to work in the theater and media?

25. Don't (forget / have forgotten) that sales, administrative, and managerial jobs are available, since the media are businesses, too.

12

TRANSITIVE, INTRANSITIVE, AND LINKING VERBS   (4)

A transitive verb transmits or passes action from a subject to an object.

She *bought* a ticket.

An **intransitive verb** does not transmit action and has no object or complement.

The train *arrived* on time.

Some verbs can be either transitive or intransitive. For example, in the sentence *She watched the train,* the verb *watched* is transitive; it is followed by the direct object *train.* However, if the sentence is changed to *She watched carefully,* the verb becomes intransitive; it has no object.

Two pairs of verbs that are often confusing and used incorrectly as a consequence are *lie, lay* and *sit, set.* If you remember that *lie* and *sit* are intransitive but *lay* and *set* are transitive, it will be easier to use them correctly. To help you distinguish their uses, the principle parts of the four verbs are illustrated below.

	PRESENT	PAST	PAST PARTICIPLE
INTRANSITIVE	I *lie* down	I *lay* down.	I have *lain* down.
TRANSITIVE	I *lay* the book down.	I *laid* the book down.	I have *laid* the book down.
INTRANSITIVE	I *sit* down.	I *sat* down.	I have *sat* down.
TRANSITIVE	I *set* my watch.	I *set* my watch.	I have *set* my watch.

Practice A: Identifying transitive and intransitive verbs   In each of the following sentences, underline transitive verbs once and intransitive verbs twice. The answers are listed at the end of this section.

Ask any parent what he or she wants a child to be when the child grows up. For generations, the ultimate profession has been the physician's for all Americans. In our society doctors, with their intimate knowledge of life and death matters, represent power and prestige. And everyone knows that, of all professional groups, doctors make the most money. But they don't earn as much as most people think, since the average salary for doctors who completed three years of residency ranged from $27,000 to $31,000. And just think—that rewards four years of college, four years of medical school with its demanding work, a year of internship, and a year or more of residency, during which a doctor specializes in a particular field of medicine. And don't forget that tuition at some medical schools can run as high as $16,000. Doctors earn less than popular mythology teaches, and they invest more in their profession than any of us know.

A **linking verb** joins the subject of a sentence to its complement, the predicate adjective that describes the subject or the predicate noun that renames the subject. A linking verb expresses a condition, frequently acting as an equals sign. For example, *the apples are ripe* means the same as *apples* = *ripe*. Because a linking verb does not convey action from a subject to an object, it can never have an object.

The most common linking verbs are forms of *be, become, seem, appear, feel, look, smell, taste,* and *sound.* Verbs pertaining to the five senses can be either linking or transitive, depending on how they are used. Remember that a linking verb states a condition, but a transitive verb passes action to an object.

TRANSITIVE VERB	LINKING VERB
The cat *smells* a mouse.	The cat *smells* terrible since its fight with a skunk.
She *looked* her opponent straight in the eye.	Her opponent *looked* nervous.
He *sounds* the alarm.	His voice *sounds* hoarse.
Mother *felt* my forehead.	I *felt* faint and dizzy.
Taste the stew.	Does the stew *taste* too salty?

Practice B: Identifying linking verbs   *In each of the following sentences, underline the transitive verbs once and the linking verbs twice. The answers are listed at the end of this section.*

Many people believe the traditional roles of the sexes in the health professions are silly and outdated. Of the nearly 400,000 doctors in the United States, over ninety percent are men. Female enrollments in medical schools look promising. They are definitely on the rise. Women often felt frustrated by the attitudes of medical school professors and admissions committees in the past, but fortunately that is changing now. The other side of this change is that during the last few years many men became interested in nursing. Though most nurses are women, men have found the field challenging and rewarding. Male nurses appear to be sought after by employers; male nurses with graduate degrees are in great demand for nursing schools and for hospital administration positions.

Answers to Practice A   *Transitive:* wants, represents, knows, makes, earn, rewards,
forget, earn, invest   *Intransitive:* grows, has been, ranged, think, specializes,
run, know

Answers to Practice B   *Transitive:* believe, have found   *Linking:* are, are,
look, are felt, is, is, became, are, appear, are

EXERCISE 12-1, TRANSITIVE AND INTRANSITIVE VERBS   (4)

For each of the listed verbs, first write a sentence using it as a transitive verb, and then write another sentence using it as an intransitive verb. You may use the verb in any tense you wish.

Example   *begin*

(transitive) *I began the transfusion at eleven o'clock.*

(intransitive) *When does this lecture begin?*

1. *wind*

    (transitive) _____

    (intransitive) _____

2. *blow*

    (transitive) _____

    (intransitive) _____

3. *burst*

    (transitive) _____

    (intransitive) _____

4. *do*

    (transitive) _____

    (intransitive) _____

5. *draw*

    (transitive) _____

    (intransitive) _____

6. *drink*

    (transitive) _____

    (intransitive) _____

7. *flip*

    (transitive) _____

    (intransitive) _____

8. *freeze*

   (transitive) _____

   (intransitive) _____

9. *grow*

   (transitive) _____

   (intransitive) _____

10. *know*

    (transitive) _____

    (intransitive) _____

11. *lay*

    (transitive) _____

    (intransitive) _____

12. *lead*

    (transitive) _____

    (intransitive) _____

13. *return*

    (transitive) _____

    (intransitive) _____

14. *run*

    (transitive) _____

    (intransitive) _____

15. *swim*

    (transitive) _____

    (intransitive) _____

Name _____ Date _____ Score _____

EXERCISE 12-2, TRANSITIVE, INTRANSITIVE, AND LINKING VERBS   (4)

In each of the following sentences, select the correct verb from the choices in parentheses, and cross out the incorrect choice.

Example   I believe I'll (sit / ~~set~~) down and write an answer now.

1. An aspiring physician should (set / sit) his or her goals early.

2. Many medical schools (sit / set) their admissions standards very high.

3. You can't take one science course and then (sit / set) back to rest.

4. In all health professions, the schools (lie / lay) great importance upon a student's aptitude in science.

5. However, a doctor or nurse doesn't (sit / set) and study science all day.

6. In fact, the futures of very few health professionals (lie / lay) in research.

7. Many schools have (sit / set) the goal of producing health professionals who can communicate well with patients.

8. They have decided to (sit / set) almost equal value on a student's ability to communicate, for example.

9. You should (set / sit) a schedule that allows for liberal arts courses and electives.

10. You can't just (lie / lay) around.

For each of the listed verbs, first write a sentence using it as a linking verb, and then write another sentence using it as a transitive verb. You may use the verb in any tense you wish.

Example   *feel*

(linking) *I feel unprepared for this task.*
(transitive) *I felt the rust on the electrodes.*

11. *become*

(linking) _____

(transitive) _____

12. *grow*

(linking) _____

(transitive) _____

13. *act*

(linking) _____

(transitive) _____

14. *taste*

(linking) _____

(transitive) _____

15. *smell*

(linking) _____

(transitive) _____

16. *prove*

(linking) _____

(transitive) _____

17. *appear*

(linking) _____

(transitive) _____

18. *turn*

(linking) _____

(transitive) _____

19. *look*

(linking) _____

(transitive) _____

20. *sound*

(linking) _____

(transitive) _____

13

ACTIVE AND PASSIVE VOICE VERBS   (5)

Transitive verbs can have either an active voice or a passive voice. An **active voice verb** indicates that the subject performs the action, transmits it to an object: *The worried parents called the doctor.* A **passive voice verb** indicates that the subject receives the action performed by someone or something else: *The doctor was called by the worried parents.*

Passive voice verbs enable us to emphasize the receiver of the action rather than the performer, or agent, of the action. For example, in the sentence *The nurse checked the patient's chart,* the subject is *nurse.* The emphasis is upon what the nurse is doing. In the sentence *The patient's chart was checked by the nurse,* however, the subject is *chart.* The emphasis is not upon the nurse—the agent—but upon what happened to the chart. Sometimes the agent in a passive voice sentence is not even identified: *The patient's chart was checked.*

The passive voice is formed by using the past participle of the main verb with the appropriate form of the verb *be* to indicate tenses. Like active voice verbs, passive voice verbs also have perfect and progressive forms. The following table lists, explains, and illustrates the various passive voice verb forms.

TENSE	TIME	EXAMPLE
Present	Present or habitual action	I *am called* to the telephone.
Present perfect	Completed action in the immediate past	I *have been called* to the telephone.
Present progressive	Present action continuing or in progress	I *am being called* to the telephone now.
Present perfect progressive	Continuing action occurring up to but not including the present	I *have been being called* to the telephone all morning.
Past	Completed past action	I *was called* to the telephone.
Past perfect	Past action completed before another past action	I *had been called* to the telephone, so I ran down the stairs.
Past progressive	Continuing action that occurred in the past	I *was being called* to the telephone when I tripped.
Past perfect progressive	Continuing past action that occurred before another past action	I *had been being* urgently *called* to the telephone, until I shouted that I had fallen down.
Future	Future action	I *shall/will be called* to the telephone no more.
Future perfect	Future action completed before another future time	I *shall/will have been called* at home by my boss tomorrow, however.
Future progressive	Action in progress at a future time	In fact, I *shall/will be being called daily* for progress reports.

67

TENSE	TIME	EXAMPLE
Future perfect progressive	Continuing future action that leads up to another future time.	I *shall/will have been being called* for weeks by the time my broken leg heals.

Obviously, we do not often need to write sentences using passive voice perfect progressive verb forms. Nevertheless, the other passive voice forms are widely used in writing, particularly for technical and scientific subjects where the receiver of an action is more important than the agent: *The results of the survey were tabulated, and the findings were reported to the review board.*

Keep in mind, however, that a sentence in the passive voice is longer and less forceful than a sentence in the active voice. Passive voice requires the addition of at least one helping verb, and a prepositional phrase if you identify the agent of the action. Active voice sentences are more direct, more economical, and more forceful, as the following comparison shows.

PASSIVE VOICE	The meeting was called to order by the president.
ACTIVE VOICE	The president called the meeting to order.

When you write, be aware of verb voice so that you select verbs in the voice that best achieves the emphasis you want.

Practice: Identifying passive voice verbs   Underline all the passive voice verb phrases in the following sentences. The answers are listed at the end of this section.

[1] Midwives are women who oversee and assist when babies are born. [2] In ancient Greece and Rome, midwives were required to have formal training. [3] Later, during the sixteenth century, European medical science flourished, and midwifery was largely absorbed into doctors' practices. [4] However, professional schools of midwifery were established for the training and licensing of midwives. [5] Although professional midwives are fairly common in Europe today, fewer of them can be found in the United States. [6] Recently, however, U.S. midwifery has received renewed interest and respect.

Answers to the Practice   [1] are born   [2] were required   [3] was absorbed   [4] were established   [5] can be found   [6] has received

EXERCISE 13, ACTIVE AND PASSIVE VOICE VERBS   (5)

Rewrite the following sentences, changing the passive voice verbs to active voice verbs. Try to retain the verb tense of the original sentence. If an agent is not supplied in the original sentence, provide an appropriate one in your revision.

Example   Laboratory tests are performed by medical technologists.

Medical technologists perform laboratory tests.

1. A bachelor's degree in medical technology and passing the licensing test are required for certification by the Registry of Medical Technologists.

   _____

2. As new specialties are explored by researchers, the demand for these vital technologists will increase.

   _____

3. Patients with disabilities have been taught new skills by occupational therapists.

   _____

4. Educational, vocational, and recreational activities will have been planned by the occupational therapist for his or her patients.

   _____

5. Jobs will be found in hospitals, clinics, community centers, and camps.

   _____

6. Actual physical treatment for disabilities will have been applied by a physical therapist.

   _____

7. Exercise, massage, machines, or mechanical devices may be used by a physical therapist.

   _____

8. Most physical therapists are hired by hospitals or nursing homes, but some are self-employed.

   _____

9. A bachelor's degree is necessary, but certification may be gained with a sixteen-month training program after a bachelor's degree in another field has been received.

   _____

10. Routine tasks such as simple examinations, sample collection, and bandaging are completed by physician's assistants.

_____

11. In this way, doctors are freed to concentrate on more demanding jobs.

_____

12. Since we have been experiencing a shortage of doctors for years, a physician's assistant plays a vital role.

_____

13. Acceptance has been being gained by physician's assistants for the last ten years.

_____

14. This field has been dominated by men, since many assistants are veterans who were trained as medical corpsmen.

_____

15. Requirements for this very new field have not been settled.

_____

16. Not only patience but extensive training as well is demanded of speech pathologists.

_____

17. Speech problems, whatever their cause, are diagnosed by the speech pathologist.

_____

18. A treatment program is developed and prescribed.

_____

19. Salaries are earned by pathologists that are quite comparable to those of physicians.

_____

20. Master's degrees in speech pathology and licensing exams are required by most states.

_____

14

MOOD (5d-f)

English has three moods. The **indicative mood** expresses a statement: *I will go.* The **imperative mood** expresses a direct command or request: *Go do what I told you.* In sentences in the imperative mood, the understood subject is always *you.* The **subjunctive mood** is now mainly used to express wishes and conditions contrary to fact: *I wish that I were at home. If I were you, I would leave now.* The subjunctive should also be used in *that* clauses that express formal demands, resolutions, recommendations, requests, or motions: *He moved that the motion be tabled.*

The subjunctive mood uses special forms in several tenses, persons, and numbers of the verb *be* and in the third person singular, present, and past perfect tenses of all verbs. The following tables pinpoint these variations.

Subjunctive Mood: *To Be*

	SINGULAR	PLURAL
PRESENT TENSE	I *be* [not *am*] you *be* [not *are*] he *be* [not *is*]	we *be* [not *are*] you *be* [not *are*] they *be* [not *are*]
PAST TENSE	I *were* [not *was*] you were he *were* [not *was*]	we were you were they were
PRESENT PERFECT TENSE	I have been you have been he *have* been [not *has*]	we have been you have been they have been
PAST PERFECT TENSE	had been (all persons and numbers)	

Subjunctive Mood: *To Speak*

	SINGULAR	PLURAL
PRESENT TENSE	I speak you speak he *speak* [not *speaks*]	we speak you speak they speak
PAST TENSE	I spoke you spoke he spoke	we spoke you spoke they spoke
PRESENT PERFECT TENSE	I have spoken you have spoken he *have* spoken [not *has* spoken]	we have spoken you have spoken they have spoken
PAST PERFECT TENSE	had spoken (all persons and numbers)	

The following sentences illustrate the correct use of the subjunctive:

I demand that this defendant *be found* guilty.

My lawyer has insisted that the judge *have delivered* her opinion by tomorrow morning.

If this woman *be* a citizen, as she claims, why have we found no public record of her existence?

They would not have asked that we *be* consulted if they *were* not interested in our opinions.

If Fargo *were* a Republican, he could not have been elected.

The subjunctive mood also survives in a few idiomatic expressions.

Far be it from me	Long live the king!
Suffice it to say	Come what may
Heaven help us!	Be that as it may
The devil take the hindmost.	Glory be to God!

EXERCISE 14, MOOD   (5)

Select the correct verb from the choices in parentheses, and cross out each incorrect choice.

Example   I wish I (~~was~~ / were) already working.

1. Some hospitals insist that an admitting officer (is / be) trained as a nurse.

2. If the officer (was / were) trained in sociology or psychology, that would also be helpful.

3. A knowledge of medical vocabulary (is / be) also necessary.

4. An admitting officer (arrange / arranges) for all the patients' care.

5. (Be it / It is) resolved that our hospital (require / requires) a business degree for our admitting officer.

6. We recommend that this officer (explains / explain) all hospital rules.

7. We further think it possible that he or she (obtain / obtains) all necessary signatures.

8. Medical records administrators (are / be) in great demand.

9. I cannot overemphasize the requirement that medical records (are / be) accurate.

10. For years, a bachelor's degree (has been / have been) required.

11. Is it still essential that a medical records administrator (hold / holds) a degree in that field?

12. No, a person (has / have) the option of one year's postgraduate training as well.

13. Every applicant please (inform / informs) us of any computer experience you may have.

14. We require that our administrator (has / have) instant access to all records.

15. Most important is the necessity that all records (be / are) in consistent terminology.

Write sentences using the mood indicated for each of the verbs listed below.

Example   (*be,* formal demand, subjunctive) _Be it recorded that we adjourned._

(*be,* condition, subjunctive) _If he be there, I'll find him._

(*give,* imperative) _Give me that syringe._

(*be,* wishes, subjunctive) _all I want is that you be well again._

16. (*jump,* imperative) _____

17. (*love,* indicative) _____

18. (*succeed,* subjunctive) _____

19. (*meet,* formal demand, subjunctive) _____

20. (*watch,* imperative) _____

21. (*discover,* condition, subjunctive) _____

22. (*complete,* formal demand, subjunctive) _____

23. (*finish,* imperative) _____

24. (*see,* condition, subjunctive) _____

25. (*choose,* wishes, subjunctive) _____

The following sentences are in the indicative mood. Rewrite them, using the subjunctive or imperative mood appropriately.

Example   What if the hospital needs no records?

What if the hospital were to need no records?

26. We asked the hospital administrator to explain her job.

_____

27. The hospital expects her to be responsible for the entire operation.

_____

28. She ensures that all functions of the hospital function in a businesslike way.

_____

29. Most governing boards require that the administrator has a graduate degree in health services administration.

_____

30. Large hospitals prefer that the chief administrator obtains experience first in smaller operations.

_____

15 BASIC GRAMMAR REVIEW (1-5)

For each of the following sentences, write in the blank the correct form of the word listed at the left. Note that verbs may require a change in tense, voice, or mood, or the addition of auxiliaries to be correct.

	Example	*be*	Everyone wishes he or she ___*were*___ a millionaire.

1. *who / whom*   There are over a half million Americans _____ are millionaires.

2. *Them / Their*   _____ reporting their incomes is strictly voluntary.

3. *quiet / quietly*   Some would probably prefer to remain _____ about money.

4. *bad / badly*   Many people want that status _____ .

5. *rise*   The number of millionaires has _____ sharply recently.

6. *drive*   I would _____ by a chauffeur in a limousine.

7. *lie*   I would spend all day _____ around the house.

8. *I / me*   Nothing would be too good for my friends and _____.

9. *inherit*   In the past, most millionaires _____ their wealth.

10. *whoever / whomever*   I'll give this proof to _____ comes to claim it.

11. *different*   Life must seem very _____ after an event like that.

12. *decrease*   The number of "hereditary" millionaires has _____ .

13. *begin*   Many new millionaires _____ with nothing, only a few years ago.

14. *found*   Some _____ their own businesses.

15. *produce*   The computer business has _____ many in the new class of wealthy people.

16. *who / whom*   People _____ start these businesses sometimes sell them and achieve instant wealth.

17. *make*   Others found that the sale of stock had _____ them rich.

18. *we / us*   Two of _____ in the investment club own that stock.

19. *had / have*   One fellow _____ worked at a company only a month when his stock's value topped $1 million.

20. *I / me*   What would make him luckier than _____ ?

21. *sly / slyly*   He picked his career _____ .

22. *sure / surely*   He _____ did.

23. *good*   That had to be the _____ choice he ever made.

24. *He / His*   _____ choosing that wasn't pure luck.

25. *sit / set*   Some career counselors advise you to _____ your eye on a growing industry

26. *slow / slowly*   Other founders have been _____ to follow this route.

27. *they*   Successful people are reluctant to leave the scene of

    _____ success.

28. *sell*   I insist that he _____ .

29. *move*   Many new millionaires _____ to California and Massachusetts recently.

30. *more*   These states are the _____ popular for high-technology companies.

31. *easy*   Officers in top corporations can _____ become millionaires.

32. *good*   The _____ lawyers and doctors earn fees high enough to make them millionaires in a few years.

33. *soar*   The value of land _____ in the last few years.

34. *find*   Many farmers _____ themselves suddenly wealthy.

16

SENTENCE FRAGMENTS   (6)

A sentence fragment lacks either a subject or a predicate or both and is not a complete statement. Usually, a fragment occurs because the writer has mistaken a phrase or subordinate clause (see Sections 6 and 7) for a complete sentence. Consequently, fragments can often be corrected by attaching them to an adjacent sentence.

> People sometimes find they are entrepreneurs. [Complete statement: independent clause]
> Almost before they're aware they are in business. [Fragment: subordinate clause]
> People sometimes find they are entrepreneurs almost before they're aware they are in business. [Complete statement: complex sentence]

Sometimes a comma is required to attach the fragment to an adjacent sentence.

> A product or service attracts interest. *Especially if no one else is supplying it.*
> A product or service attracts interest, *especially if no one else is supplying it.*
> *If your idea answers an unfulfilled need.* You may have something worth marketing.
> *If your idea answers an unfulfilled need,* you may have something worth marketing.

By reading a sentence aloud, you can usually tell if a comma is needed or not.

Another way to correct a sentence fragment is to rewrite the fragment as a complete sentence, containing both a subject and a verb.

> A chemistry professor I know began building specialized instruments for his lab. *Attracting the interest of other chemists.*
> A chemistry professor I know began building specialized instruments for his lab. *They attracted the interest of other chemists.*

Remember, to be a sentence a group of words must have a subject and a predicate and must not be introduced by a subordinating conjunction. Prepositional phrases, verbal phrases, appositives renaming or explaining nouns or noun substitutes, and other word groups lacking a subject or a verb are not sentences. The following examples show these types of fragments and suitable revisions:

PREPOSITIONAL PHRASE	The chemist could not carry out his research. *With the instruments then available.*
REVISION	The chemist could not carry out his research *with the instruments then available.*
VERBAL PHRASE	He needed special analytical equipment. *To complete some experiments.*
REVISION	He needed special analytical equipment *to complete some experiments.*
SUBORDINATE CLAUSE	He decided to build his own instruments. *Since no one manufactured what he needed.*
REVISION	He decided to build his own instruments, *since no one manufactured what he needed.*

APPOSITIVE	Soon he discovered there was a market for his new instruments. *Other chemists doing similar research.*
REVISION	Soon he discovered there was a market for his new instruments, *other chemists doing similar research.*
COMPOUND PREDICATE	He set up his own manufacturing company. *And found ready customers among industrial, governmental, and university scientists.*
REVISION	He set up his own manufacturing company *and found ready customers among industrial, governmental, and university scientists.*

Practice: Identifying sentence fragments　　　Underline all the sentence fragments in the following paragraph. The answers are listed at the end of this section.

[1] Have you ever wondered. [2] What to do with your plants. [3] When you go on vacation? [4] Boarding the dog can be expensive. [5] If your vacation is a long one. [6] Other people have similar problems. [7] Seeing an opportunity. [8] Several women in our town started a new business. [9] Caring for vacationers' plants, animals, and homes. [10] For a fee they will visit your home each day, check things, bring in the mail. [11] And feed and exercise your pets. [12] They chose an appropriate name for their business. [13] House-Sitters, Inc.

Answers to the Practice　　　The following items are fragments: 1, 2, 3, 5, 7, 9, 11, 13

EXERCISE 16, SENTENCE FRAGMENTS (6)

Revise the following word groups, eliminating fragments in two ways: (1) by joining
the groups to form one complete sentence, and (b) by rewording them as necessary to
form two separate sentences.

Example America is uniquely hospitable to entrepreneurs. Who often are
responsible for moving our economy ahead of other countries'.

a. *America is uniquely hospitable to entrepreneurs, who are often responsible for moving our economy ahead of other countries'.*

b. *America is uniquely hospitable to entrepreneurs. They are often responsible for moving our economy ahead of other countries'.*

1. Phil Knight started Nike, Inc. in 1958 when he was an undergraduate. Now selling
    $500 million worth of running shoes every year.

    a. _____

    b. _____

2. Federal Express posted $60 million in profits for Frederick W. Smith. Who had written
    a term paper proposing an airline to carry only freight.

    a. _____

    b. _____

3. Nolan Bushnell invented the video game Pong. Which became the basis for the Atari
    Company.

    a. _____

    b. _____

4. Founded by a 33-year-old broker. Charles Schwab and Co. was one of the first
    discount brokerage houses.

    a. _____

    b. _____

5. One of the main sources of computer software is VisiCorp. Started in 1978 as a project
    for a Harvard marketing course.

    a. _____

    b. _____

6. Apple Computers once was located in the garage of the chairman of the board's parents. And in six years grew to dominate the minicomputer market.

a. _____

b. _____

7. Henry Kloss founded Acoustic Research, the manufacturer of stereo speakers. At the ripe old age of 22.

a. _____

b. _____

8. Kloss has begun three more companies. Including Kloss Video, which makes projection television sets.

a. _____

b. _____

9. These small, adventurous companies are often built around one new or innovative idea. Which explains their risky nature.

a. _____

b. _____

10. Last year almost 600,000 small businesses were started. More than in any previous year.

a. _____

b. _____

Revise the following paragraph, eliminating sentence fragments. You may join groups of words to form a complete sentence, or you may reword fragments, adding missing subjects and predicates to form complete sentences. Write out your revision on your own paper.

Starting your own business may be one of the oldest parts of the American Dream. Dating from the early days in the Colonies. When immigrants from the Old World came to America to make their fortunes. America has a long tradition of entrepreneurship. Which may help explain the country's rapid growth from a colonial outpost. To a major economic leader. For example, the invention of the modern textile factory in 1813 by Francis Cabot Lowell. This made New England a manufacturing center. George Westinghouse was 22 years old. When he invented the airbrake. He used the profits from the airbrake to develop the first industrial-scale generators and transformers. And produced alternating current. To allow wide use of electricity. Edwin Land developed a new kind of camera. Which other people thought was just a novelty. So he sold it with the backing of his own lens-making company. Which he had named Polaroid Corporation.

17

COMMA SPLICES AND FUSED SENTENCES   (7)

A **comma splice** occurs when two main clauses are joined by a comma without a coordinating conjunction. A **fused sentence** (also called a **run-on sentence**) occurs when two main clauses are run together without any punctuation.

COMMA SPLICE	Our environment is relatively fragile, it must be protected.
FUSED SENTENCE	Our environment is relatively fragile it must be protected.

Comma splices and fused sentences are similar types of errors, and they have similar solutions. In both cases, the independent clauses require clear signals to tell the readers where one complete thought stops and another begins.

The conventions of written English provide only two such signals: the period and the semicolon. Two other alternatives are also acceptable. The thoughts may be coordinated, joined by a comma and coordinating conjunction (*and, but, or, nor, for, so, yet*), or one thought may be subordinated to the other and joined by a subordinating conjunction. The following sentences illustrate these four solutions for the comma splice and fused sentence.

PERIOD	Our environment is relatively fragile. It must be protected.
SEMICOLON	Our environment is relatively fragile; it must be protected.
COORDINATION	Our environment is relatively fragile, and it must be protected.
	Our environment is relatively fragile and must be protected.
SUBORDINATION	Because our environment is relatively fragile, it must be protected.

Notice that when the subordinate clause precedes the main clause, a comma joins the two. You may be wondering why a comma is acceptable in the middle of *Because our environment is relatively fragile, it must be protected* but not in *Our environment is relatively fragile, it must be protected.* Remember, the issue is not where the comma appears so much as *why* it appears.

In the first instance, one idea is subordinate and functions as a modifier of the main clause. The comma helps to signal the subordinate relationship and marks the beginning of the main clause. In the second instance, the ideas are not subordinate and consequently are expressed in independent clauses. A comma used between them would be a false signal, indicating a connection that does not grammatically exist.

Why is the comma in *Our environment is relatively fragile, and it must be protected* acceptable? The coordinating conjunction *and* grammatically establishes the connection between the two complete thoughts. The comma signals that relationship.

Practice: Identifying comma splices and fused sentences Decide which of the
following sentences contain comma splices and which are fused. The answers are listed
at the end of this section.

[1] The ecology movement started in the 1960's it hasn't ended yet. [2] In fact, its
effects are just now beginning to be felt, in government and in business, protection of
the environment has become a major concern. [3] The pollution of our environment and
the use of our natural resources are now controlled by law the movement helped
create and foster this awareness. [4] These laws, with their complicated enforcement and
refinement, have created a job market for scientists who study the environment.

REVISING SENTENCES WITH MULTIPLE ERRORS

When a sentence contains more than two fused independent clauses, more than one comma
splice, or both comma splices and fused independent clauses, a combination of remedies is
usually needed. Rewriting a sentence using only periods, only semicolons, or only coordinating conjunctions is likely to result in a choppy, awkward, and illogical or unfocused revision.

FAULTY SENTENCE	Battles concerning the environment are common, environmental issues confront commercial interests a territorial fight usually ensues.
POOR REVISION	Battles concerning the environment are common; environmental issues confront commercial interests; a territorial fight usually ensues.
BETTER REVISION	Battles concerning the environment are common; when environmental issues confront commercial interests, a territorial fight usually ensues.

Unless fused or spliced sentence elements are parallel—that is, of equal rank and therefore expressed in parallel grammatical form—repeating the same punctuation or conjunction
does not create an effective revision. Notice that the final revision above focuses the ideas,
clarifying the time sequence and the cause-effect logic by means of the subordinating conjunction *when*.

Similarly, in the revision of the following example, a relative pronoun is used to subordinate less important information. To avoid awkward length and to handle two relatively
independent ideas, the clauses have been divided into two separate sentences.

FAULTY SENTENCE	Florida real estate developers are battling marine biologists they say the beaches cannot survive continued condominium building, delicate ecosystems could be destroyed.
EFFECTIVE REVISION	Florida real estate developers are battling marine biologists who say the beaches cannot survive continued condominium building. Delicate ecosystems could be destroyed.

Answers to the Practice [1] fused   [2] comma splice   [3] fused
[4] correct sentence

82

EXERCISE 17-1, COMMA SPLICES AND FUSED SENTENCES   (7)

Revise each of the following faulty sentences in four ways to correct the spliced or fused independent clauses: (a) use a period to form two separate sentences; (b) use a semicolon between independent clauses; (c) use a coordinating conjunction and comma to form a compound sentence; and (d) use a subordinating conjunction or relative pronoun (with any necessary commas) to form a complex sentence.

Example   Most ecological research is performed by Ph.D.'s, people with bachelor's or master's degrees perform lab and field work.

a. *Most ecological research is performed by Ph. D's. People with bachelor's or master's degrees perform lab and field work.*

b. *Most ecological research is performed by Ph. D's; people with bachelor's or master's degrees perform lab and field work.*

c. *Most ecological research is performed by Ph. D's, but people with bachelor's or master's degrees perform lab and field work.*

d. *Although most ecological research is performed by Ph. D's, people with bachelor's or master's degrees perform lab and field work.*

1. Geologists study the structure of the earth's crust they often look for valuable deposits of oil or minerals.

    a. _____

    b. _____

    c. _____

    d. _____

2. Almost half of America's geologists work in private industry, most of the rest work with the Interior Department.

    a. _____

    b. _____

    c. _____

    d. _____

3. Geologists not only apply geology they also must know physics and mathematics.

    a. _____

    b. _____

c. _____

d. _____

4. The geophysicist is similar, this scientist works with heat flow, vibrations, and solar radiation.

a. _____

b. _____

c. _____

d. _____

5. Minerals, petroleum, and natural gas become scarce, geophysicists are in demand.

a. _____

b. _____

c. _____

d. _____

6. Most geophysicists work in oil and gas exploration they are very well paid.

a. _____

b. _____

c. _____

d. _____

7. Meteorologists study weather and climate conditions, they also study air pollution now.

a. _____

b. _____

c. _____

d. _____

8. Almost all meteorologists are government employees, NOAA and the armed forces employ most.

a. _____

b. _____

c. _____

d. _____

EXERCISE 17-2, COMMA SPLICES AND FUSED SENTENCES   (7)

The following sentences contain comma splices, fused independent clauses, or both. Revise them, correcting the errors and clarifying the logic. You may omit or rearrange some words to achieve an effective revision.

Example   Few television weather announcers are really meteorologists, some are.

Few television weather announcers are really meteorologists, though some are.

1.   Rachel Carson published *Silent Spring* in 1962 it focused public attention on ecology.

_____

2.   All ocean life is studied by oceanographers, they work at sea and in labs.

_____

3.   There are several branches of this science, biological, chemical, physical, and geological oceanography are some of them.

_____

4.   One-third of all oceanographers work at colleges or universities, one-third work at private companies, one-third of all oceanographers work for the federal government.

_____

5.   They work in desalinization programs, ocean protection programs, they work in programs to use tides to create electric power.

_____

6.   Agriculture is important soil scientists work to increase farmers' yields.

_____

7.   They also study the effects of agricultural chemicals they hope to protect the soil from harmful build-up of toxins.

_____

8.   Many different kinds of scientists perform environmental research, such specialties as agronomy, biology, nutrition, and many others have roles to play.

_____

9.   These scientists study the effects of pollution on plant and animal life, they also work to develop nonpolluting agricultural chemicals.

_____

10. New breeds of plants and selective breeding of animals protect both from pollution scientists work to produce both.

_____

11. Many engineers now work in environmental affairs they work sometimes more directly to control pollution.

_____

12. These engineers develop waste-disposal systems, water-treatment systems are another example of their work.

_____

13. Engineers work closely with research scientists to develop solutions is their primary task.

_____

14. Their work is creating still more new jobs with each new solution a facility is created that must then be operated.

_____

15. There are many state and federal agencies that are concerned with environmental affairs, each needs administrators, writers, public relations people, and even lawyers.

_____

18

SUBJECT AND VERB AGREEMENT   (8a)

When subjects and verbs do not agree, readers are likely to misunderstand a writer's message. Suppose you have written *The first two quarters of the game was exciting* in a letter to a friend. Reading the sentence, your friend understands that the game was exciting but doesn't quite know what the first two quarters have to do with it. Your reader has perceived the subject of the sentence to be *game.* Because *game* is a singular noun and *was* is a singular verb, the two fit together. If you had written *The first two quarters of the game were exciting,* your friend would quickly see that *quarters* is the subject because it fits the plural verb *were.* Your reader would understand the message correctly: you found half the game exciting, not necessarily all of it.

Subjects and verbs should agree in **person** and **number. Agreement in person** is achieved if the verb form corresponds to the first, second, or third person pronoun form of the subject. For example, *She buy new sneakers* is a faulty sentence because the third person pronoun *she* does not agree with the verb *buy.* In the present tense, the *-s* form of the verb is required for third person singular pronouns and all singular nouns: *she buys.* Agreement in person causes relatively few problems for writers because the *-s* form is the only exceptional verb form requiring special attention (see Special Problems with Verb Tenses, Section 11).

Agreement in number between subjects and verbs, however, can be more troublesome. Most writers are well aware that a singular subject requires a singular verb and a plural subject requires a plural verb. Agreement errors most often arise when the writer is uncertain about whether a subject is singular or plural or when intervening words obscure the real subject. The following guidelines will help you avoid subject-verb agreement errors.

1. If words or phrases come between the subject and the verb, be sure the verb agrees with the subject, not with an intervening noun or pronoun.

FAULTY	The final miles of the race was grueling.
CORRECT	The final *miles* of the race *were* grueling.

Singular subjects followed by expressions such as *with, along with, together with,* and *as well as* take singular verbs, even though they suggest a plural meaning. These expressions are not considered part of the subject.

FAULTY	Joan, together with her sisters, play in the semifinals tonight.
CORRECT	*Joan,* together with her sisters, *plays* in the semifinals tonight.

2. If the subject is an indefinite pronoun such as *everyone, somebody, another, each, either,* and *neither,* use a singular verb.

FAULTY	Everybody are here, but neither of the judges have arrived yet.
CORRECT	*Everybody is* here, but *neither* of the judges *has* arrived yet.

The indefinite pronouns *all, any, most, more, none,* and *some* take either a singular or a plural verb, depending on whether the noun to which the pronoun refers is singular or plural.

SINGULAR	*All* the *soap is* gone.
PLURAL	*All* my *socks are* dirty.

3. If two or more subjects are joined by *and,* use a plural verb.

| FAULTY | Football and rugby is only for the hearty. |
| CORRECT | *Football and rugby are* only for the hearty. |

However, if the parts of a compound subject refer to the same person or thing, use a singular verb. Also use a singular verb if a compound subject is understood to be a unit.

| SINGLE REFERENT | The play's *star and inspiration has stormed* off the stage. |
| SINGLE UNIT | *Macaroni and cheese was* his favorite lunch. |

4. If two or more subjects are joined by *or* or *nor,* the verb should agree with the nearest subject.

FAULTY	My assistants or my secretary have the keys to the lockers.
CORRECT	My assistants or my *secretary has* the keys to the lockers.
FAULTY	My secretary or my assistants has the keys to the lockers.
CORRECT	My secretary or my *assistants have* the keys to the lockers.

5. If an expletive (such as *there* or *it*) precedes the verb, locate the true subject and make sure the verb agrees with it, not with the expletive.

| FAULTY | There is many reasons for his success. |
| CORRECT | There *are* many *reasons* for his success. |

6. If the subject is a singular collective noun (such as *assembly, audience, jury, flock*), use a singular verb when the group is acting as a unit. Use a plural verb when the members of the group are acting separately.

| AS A UNIT | The *subcommittee addresses* the issue tomorrow. |
| AS INDIVIDUALS | The *staff take* turns answering the director's questions. |

7. If the sentence contains a predicate noun, the verb should agree with the subject, not with the predicate noun.

| FAULTY | Material things is a prime necessity with you. |
| CORRECT | Material *things are* a prime necessity with you. |

8. If a relative pronoun (*who, which, that*) is used as the subject, the verb should agree with the pronoun's antecedent.

| SINGULAR ANTECEDENT | They will release *one* of the men *who has* been injured. [Antecedent of *who* is *one.* The information *has been injured* is intended to describe only the one man.] |
| PLURAL ANTECEDENT | Here is one of the *shoes that were* missing. [Antecedent of *that* is *shoes.* The information *were missing* is intended to describe all the shoes.] |

9. If a subject is plural in form but singular in meaning (such as *news, physics, linguistics*), use a singular verb. Similarly, titles of novels, plays, songs, and the like take singular verbs, even if their form is plural. Subjects indicating sums or quantities also usually take singular verbs.

College *athletics is* big business these days.
Wales and Nightingales was a popular record album.
Ten years is a long career in professional sports.

EXERCISE 18-1, SUBJECT AND VERB AGREEMENT   (8)

Select the correct verb from the choices in parentheses, and cross out the incorrect form.

Example   The media (depend / ~~depends~~) on graphics.

1.   Artists and designers usually (work / works) in a studio with others.

2.   Everybody (think / thinks) of the artist as a lonely figure.

3.   But most (earn / earns) a living illustrating books or ads.

4.   Like actors, a painter first (creates / create) demand for his or her work.

5.   Until then, an artist or designer (have / has) to make a living like all of us.

6.   Commercial designers (design / designs) products from furniture to cars.

7.   In fact, almost everything around you (have / has) been designed by an artist.

8.   Illustrations in children's books (are / is) prepared by commercial artists.

9.   An art student (prepare / prepares) a portfolio of samples of his or her work.

10.   Then he or she (arrange / arranges) interviews with art directors of publishing companies.

11.   Free-lance artists (solicit / solicits) work in these interviews.

12.   Art directors who work for publishing firms (know / knows) every facet of illustration.

13.   Neither designing layouts nor illustration (comprise / comprises) the total job.

14.   One of the most demanding careers in the arts (is / are) medical illustration.

15.   It is also one of the few art careers that (pay / pays) well immediately.

16.   The training of most medical illustrators (include / includes) a year of medical school.

17.   There (is / are) many specializations among commercial artists.

18.   Among fashion illustrators, for example, there (is / are) some who draw only shoes.

19.   Every illustrator (have / has) to develop a specialty.

20.   Drawing animated cartoons (was / were) a popular field at one time.

21.   Hollywood (produce / produces) very few cartoons now.

22.   Much of the drawing for cartoons (is / are) performed in Europe.

23.   There (is / are) also a computer that (produce / produces) animation.

24.   Working on a free-lance basis (require / requires) self-discipline.

25.   Graphic designers are the people who (put / puts) print and pictures together.

26.   Text, headlines, illustrations, and border (balance / balances) on a well-designed page.

27. Graphic design, one of the largest art fields, (employ / employs) huge numbers of artists.

28. Newspapers, magazines, and direct mail advertisers (needs / need) graphic designers.

29. Every poster you see and every advertisement in a store window (was / were) designed by a graphic designer.

30. One of the most stable areas of commercial art (is / are) graphic design.

31. Publishers also (need / needs) these designers to design texts and covers.

32. Many designers (begin / begins) their careers in print shops.

33. A lithographer (transfer / transfers) the design to a printing plate.

34. Anything that has been designed usually (has / have) to be printed.

35. Besides the printer and compositor, engravers and silkscreen printers also (work / works) in printing plants.

36. Etchers and photoengravers (ply / plies) their trade there, too.

37. There (is / are) dozens of specialized jobs common to printing plants.

38. Printing is an art that (allow / allows) an artist to live just about anywhere.

39. There (is / are) printing plants in large and small cities.

40. Degrees in these specialties (is / are) offered by many schools.

EXERCISE 18-2, SUBJECT AND VERB AGREEMENT (8)

Write sentences that contain appropriate forms of the given verbs and that use the called-for forms of other words.

Example   (*Organization,* appropriate form of verb *be*)

Our organization is sensitive to its employees'
needs.

1. (*Airplanes and trains,* present tense form of *provide*)

    _____

2. (*There, kinds*)

    _____

3. (*Assembly* [acting as a unit], appropriate form of *be*)

    _____

4. (*Neither the sergeant nor the privates,* present tense form of verb *believe*)

    _____

5. (*Girl, with blue eyes,* present tense form of *appear*)

    _____

6. (*Justifications,* present tense form of *involve, an essential matter*)

    _____

7. (*Everybody,* present tense form of *know*)

    _____

8. (*Here, options,* appropriate form of *be*)

    _____

9. (*Motivations,* present tense form of *comprise, essential* [adjective])

    _____

10. (*Nobody,* present tense form of *see*)

    _____

11. (*Hope* [noun], *desires* [noun], *neither, nor,* appropriate form of *be*)

    _____

12. (*Foremost causes of failure,* appropriate form of *be*)

_____

13. (*There, disasters,* appropriate form of *be*)

_____

14. (*One, horses, that,* appropriate form of *be*)

_____

15. (*Committee* [individuals in group acting separately], present tense form of *arrive*)

_____

16. (*Motivation and persistence,* present tense form of *result*)

_____

17. (*There,* appropriate form of *be, decisions*)

_____

18. (*Either you or one of the others,* present tense form of *be*)

_____

19. (*Algebra, trigonometry,* appropriate form of *be*)

_____

20. (*Fifty dollars,* appropriate form of *be, high price*)

_____

21. (*Cable television,* present tense form of *have*)

_____

22. (*Some of the news,* present tense form of *seem*)

_____

23. (*None of the flock,* appropriate form of *be*)

_____

24. (*Bread and butter,* present tense form of *taste*)

_____

25. (*Printers and designers,* present tense form of *cooperate*)

_____

19

PRONOUN AND ANTECEDENT AGREEMENT   (8b-c)

Pronouns should agree with their antecedents in number. If the **antecedent**, the word or words for which the pronoun stands, is singular, the pronoun should be singular; if the antecedent is plural, the pronoun should be plural.

SINGULAR ANTECEDENT	The dog wanted its nightly run.
PLURAL ANTECEDENT	The dogs wanted their nightly run.

Antecedents such as *anyone, anybody, someone, somebody, each, every, everyone,* and *everybody* are singular and require singular pronouns. Collective nouns, such as *band, assembly, organization, mob, army, family, team, class,* and *brigade,* require singular pronouns when the group is being considered as a unit and plural pronouns when the individual members of the group are being considered separately.

GROUP AS A UNIT	The crew has finished its work.
MEMBERS OF GROUP CONSIDERED SEPARATELY	The crew have decided to quit their work.

A plural pronoun is used to refer to two or more antecedents joined by *and.* A singular pronoun is used to refer to a singular antecedent joined by *or* or *nor.* If one of the antecedents is singular and the other is plural, the pronoun should agree in number with the antecedent that is nearer.

ANTECEDENTS JOINED BY *AND*	Artists and artisans know their stuff.
SINGULAR ANTECEDENTS JOINED BY *OR* OR *NOR*	Either Jack or Joe must have missed his connecting flight.
COMBINATION OF SINGULAR AND PLURAL ANTECEDENTS	Neither the coach nor the players flagged in their desire.

The demonstrative adjectives *this, that, these,* and *those* agree in number with the nouns they modify. In constructions with *kind of* and *sort of,* the demonstrative adjective modifies *kind* and *sort,* and the following noun should be singular, not plural.

INCORRECT	These kind of situation are bad.
CORRECT	This kind of situation is bad.
	These kinds of situations are bad.

Historically, masculine pronoun forms (*he, him, his*) have been used to refer to antecedents such as *one, none, everybody,* and other indefinite pronouns, as well as to antecedent nouns of indeterminate gender. In recent years, this "common gender" use of masculine pronouns has been recognized as imprecise at best, at worst discriminatory.

Unless all the members of a group are known to be male, it is inappropriate to use a masculine pronoun when referring to them. For example, to write *every employee should fill out his time card correctly* is inaccurate if some of the employees are women. By the same token, not all secretaries, librarians, and nurses are female. Be equally careful about the blanket use of feminine pronouns if the antecedent refers to men as well.

If you wish to avoid common gender when referring to antecedents that include both males and females, you can use one of the following methods:

INSTEAD OF	*Each job applicant must submit his resumé.*
USE BOTH MASCULINE AND FEMININE PRONOUNS	*Each job applicant* must submit *his or her resumé.*
USE THE PLURAL FOR BOTH ANTECEDENT AND PRONOUN	*All job applicants* must submit *their* resumés.
RECAST THE SENTENCE TO REMOVE THE PRONOUN	Each job applicant must submit a resumé.

Practice: Avoiding inappropriate common-gender pronouns   In which of the following sentences is the use of common-gender pronouns inappropriate? The answers are listed at the end of this section. Your instructor may ask you to revise those sentences that use pronouns inappropriately.

[1] The term "free lance" means one who sells his services without a long-term commitment to any employer. [2] In the Middle Ages, a free-lance knight hired himself out as a mercenary to any lord willing to pay the right price. [3] Literally, his lance was free to do battle for the highest bidder. [4] Today's free-lance artist lives by her pen and brush rather than a sword. [5] Whether an artist, writer, or photographer, a free-lance will tell you he likes independence and variety.

Answers to the Practice   Sentences 1, 4, and 5 should be revised to avoid common-gender pronouns because the persons to whom they refer can be either women or men.

EXERCISE 19-1, PRONOUN AND ANTECEDENT AGREEMENT (8)

In each of the following sentences, select the correct form of the pronoun from the choices in parentheses and cross out the incorrect choice.

Example   Free-lance designers do (~~his~~ / their) work at home.

1.   Working at home allows (these / this) designer free time in the studio.
2.   Illustrators and mechanical artists spend (their / his) time at the office.
3.   A company maintains a small staff to do (its / their) retouching work.
4.   Good art schools give (its / their) students practice at these skills as well.
5.   A beginner should try for (his / his or her) start at any of these jobs.
6.   (These sorts / This sort) of jobs allow quick advancement.
7.   Designers with talent find (themselves / himself) moving up rapidly.
8.   Fortunately, a good designer's salary reflects (his / his or her) creativity and responsibility.
9.   Beginners at ad agencies find (himself / themselves) assigned to paste-up work.
10. The lettering artists are proud of (his or her / their) skills.
11. A lettering artist must have a full knowledge of type faces at (his or her / their) command.
12. He must know how the elements of (his / their) art combine.
13. Some type faces are beautiful by (itself / themselves) but do not look good in combinations with other typefaces.
14. One kind of type may lend (itself / themselves) to use, while others may not.
15. (This / These) artists do very little hand lettering in modern agencies.
16. (This / These) job is done with type or photo lettering.
17. "Sketch men" are really men and women who draw the agency's ads; (he or she / they) must be fast and accurate.
18. (These / This) kind of artist must be able to work in all media.
19. Art directors and supervisors are paid to spend (his / their) day thinking.
20. They are experienced at all (this / these) jobs.
21. They may not perform the work (himself / themselves).
22. (These / This) field is very popular among women trained as artists.
23. They help manage the studio by supervising all (its / their) work.
24. For these jobs and the jobs higher above (it / them), creative thinking is necessary, in addition to graphic skills.

25. No one at these levels is paid for drawing; (he / they) are paid for ideas.

26. An agency has (its / their) own philosophy.

27. (Their / Its) employees must understand this philosophy.

28. The directors of the agency want (this / these) philosophy reflected in their ads.

29. The studio managers make sure (his or her / their) projects conform.

30. Most studios are organized this way, whether (they / it) work in advertising, publishing, or another medium.

EXERCISE 19-2, PRONOUN-ANTECEDENT
AND SUBJECT-VERB AGREEMENT   (8)

Revise the following sentences, correcting errors of pronoun-antecedent and subject-verb agreement. Revise to avoid common-gender pronouns where their use is inappropriate.

Example   A photographer finds their skills frequently in demand.

A photographer finds his or her skills frequently in demand.

1.   Like artists, a photographer prepares their portfolio for interviews.

   _____

2.   Photographers performs almost all their work on a free-lance basis.

   _____

3.   Some of the highest-paid photographers hires agents to obtain work for them.

   _____

4.   The photographer's agent takes a 20-percent commission on each of their jobs.

   _____

5.   An agency art director give the free-lance photographer the details for each job.

   _____

6.   The photographer arranges the hiring of models and the renting of props and costumes for each assignment they are given.

   _____

7.   The advertising photographer also discovers that lighting is their responsibility, as well.

   _____

8.   Once a photographer's work is known, he may be approached to photograph ads, brochures, and general illustrations for packages.

   _____

9.   Sometimes photographers think that he is best suited to still-life photography.

   _____

10.   Technical skill with all sizes of cameras are required.

   _____

11. A sense of composition and appreciation of lighting is also helpful.

_____

12. You must also be able to find the right model and work with them.

_____

13. A good photographer handles their models like a director handles actors.

_____

14. In some ways, this jobs are similar.

_____

15. There's many specialized careers possible in photography.

_____

16. Frequently, a good photographer specializes in another field that interests her.

_____

17. Photographers who are interested in technical matters sometimes specializes in industrial subjects.

_____

18. Architectural photographers provide illustrative material for architectural firms, helping it with annual reports and sales presentations.

_____

19. One of the most lucrative specialties have been fashion photography.

_____

20. Sometimes a photographer finds themselves hired to provide illustrative material for one company's brochures and reports.

_____

21. This staff jobs are secure, but sometimes the pay is low.

_____

22. Frequently, a staff photographer is free to find themselves free-lance work as well.

_____

23. A theatrical photographer photograph theatrical productions.

_____

24. Photographers also specializes in portraits, ecology, news or sports, or art photographs.

_____

20

REFERENCE OF PRONOUNS   (9)

Pronouns conveniently spare us the awkwardness of having to repeat nouns monotonously in our writing. However, pronouns are more general and less precise than their antecedents, the names of people, places, and things. Consequently, writers must be careful to make pronoun references very clear. If the reader is unsure what antecedent a pronoun refers to, the pronoun becomes a source of confusion.

Pronoun reference problems usually result from vague usage. The following discussion addresses the most common usage problems.

1. A pronoun should clearly refer to only one antecedent, and that antecedent should be located as near to the pronoun as possible. Don't make the reader search for and choose among remote antecedents.

VAGUE

When Ray told his father about the accident, *he* was calm.

Who was calm, Ray or his father? Readers are used to associating a pronoun with the noun that most closely precedes it, in this case *father*. However, *Ray* and *he* are both subjects of their clauses, so the parallel positions of the two words suggest Ray was calm. The reader cannot be sure which noun is really the intended antecedent.

CLEAR REVISIONS

Ray was calm when he told his father about the accident.

His father was calm when Ray told him about the accident.

When Ray told his father about the accident, his father was calm.

VAGUE

The neighbors decided to celebrate the Fourth of July with a block party. The morning was sunny, but by late afternoon rain began to fall. Clearing out a garage, *they* moved the picnic tables under its roof.

Neighbors is the only sensible antecedent for *they,* but because the pronoun is several sentences away from its antecedent, the reader must back-track to find the correct reference.

CLEAR REVISIONS

. . . Clearing out a garage, the neighbors moved the picnic tables under its roof.

When rain interrupted their Fourth of July block party, the neighbors cleared out a garage and moved the picnic tables under its roof.

2. The pronouns *this, that,* and *which* should not be used to refer to the general idea of a preceding clause or sentence. A specific antecedent must always be supplied.

VAGUE USE
OF *WHICH*
AND *THIS*

The dog slipped his leash but did not run away, *which* showed his training. *This* resulted from his going to obedience school.

What showed the dog's training, that he slipped his leash or that he did not run away? Was slipping the leash, not running away, or showing training the result of obedience school?

CLEAR	The dog slipped his leash, but the fact that he did not run away showed his training. This training resulted from his going to obedience school.

3. Although we commonly use *it* and *they* for general, indefinite references in informal speech, nouns should be used in writing for exactness and clarity. *You,* used in speech to mean people in general, should be replaced by nouns such as *people, person,* or the pronoun *one. You* is correct, however, when used as the subject in writing directions or where the context is clearly *you, the reader* (as in *You should sand the surface before painting it*).

VAGUE USE OF *IT, THEY,* AND *YOU*	*It* says in the newspaper that *you* can still get tickets because *they* have added two more performances.
CLEAR	The newspaper says people can still get tickets because the theater has added two more performances.

4. A sentence containing two or more different uses of the pronoun *it* can be confusing. Especially when *it* is used as an idiom in one place in a sentence (as in *it is cold*) and as a definite pronoun referring to a specific noun in another place, the reader may have trouble keeping the uses straight.

CONFUSING	My wife and I were hiking along the mountain trail when *it* began to snow, but we decided *it* was time to turn back in case *it* drifted shut.
CLEAR	When the snow began to fall, my wife and I were hiking along the mountain trail, but we decided to turn back in case it drifted shut.

5. A pronoun should refer to a noun that is actually expressed, not to one that is merely implied. For example, a pronoun should not refer to a noun that functions as an adjective or to a word whose form does not correspond to that of the pronoun.

VAGUE	Joan's form was excellent when *she* played on the college golf team, but now she has no time for *it*.

The possessive *Joan's* implies but does not express *Joan,* the correct antecedent for *she.* Neither the adjective *golf,* nor the verb *played,* nor the nouns *form* or *team* provide an appropriate antecedent for *it.*

CLEAR	When Joan played on the college golf team, her form was excellent, but now she has no time for golf.

EXERCISE 20-1, REFERENCE OF PRONOUNS   (9)

Revise the following sentences, correcting vague, remote, and implied pronoun references.

Example   It says in this book they need people in the media.

This book says people are needed for jobs in the media.

1. They say all the jobs in the media are glamorous and exciting.

    _____

2. The speaker told Jim that his ideas might all be wrong.

    _____

3. Most entry-level jobs involve difficult, almost menial work. This always is a surprise to graduates.

    _____

4. Many jobs in the media are staffed by English majors, as well as media arts majors. They are well-suited for creative work.

    _____

5. More and more, business degrees are welcome; it is becoming more technical and businesslike.

    _____

6. You can learn production techniques on one of your first jobs.

    _____

7. Media arts programs are popular, which teaches you the specifics of production or writing.

    _____

8. Announcing positions are the entry positions in broadcasting. The average station has five of them.

    _____

9. A small television or radio station may assign many varied duties to announcers. This gives them experience quickly.

    _____

10. Station managers value versatility in announcers. They would be wise to emphasize this.

_____

11. At small stations, announcers speak on the air, write scripts, choose programming, operate the control board, and even sell ads, who want to learn the business.

_____

12. A traffic manager schedules commercials and programs. These are needed to keep the station's "personality" consistent.

_____

13. A continuity writer revises all scripts to keep the station's style consistent, which the traffic manager establishes.

_____

14. Newswriters write the script and choose news items to cover, and it is sometimes also performed by the announcer.

_____

15. Script readers review scripts to see that they follow station and FCC policies; it cannot be vulgar, misleading, or biased.

_____

16. All commercial programs for television are on film or tape, so the tape or film editor, who edits them, is an important person.

_____

17. You also have to load and cue all the film or tape about to go on the air.

_____

18. Dozens of people work in operating studios; they need them to be efficient.

_____

19. Designers, sound technicians, camera operators, and teleprompter operators are all necessary to run them.

_____

20. As in the theater, you aspire to the most prestigious job, the director's.

_____

EXERCISE 20-2, PRONOUN REVIEW   (2, 8–9)

Revise the following sentences, correcting errors in pronoun case, pronoun-antecedent agreement, and vague pronoun reference.

Example   They say 115 million people watch television every night.

One research study claims that 115 million people watch television every night.

1. There are 8,000 radio stations in this country; it is on 18 to 24 hours per day.

   _____

2. Americans own 400 million radios; huge numbers of people listen to it.

   _____

3. Felicia and me are fascinated by the electronic media.

   _____

4. Us two have grown up completely surrounded by movies, television, and radio.

   _____

5. That has attracted us to the media as students and, we hope, professionals.

   _____

6. Our discussion with a station manager gave Felicia and I a new way of looking at the media.

   _____

7. People are attracted by the glamorous personalities on television; he forgets that the media are profit-oriented businesses.

   _____

8. A station manager isn't interested in glamor; they want to know that hiring you will help the station be more efficient.

   _____

9. So, the broader your education and experience, the more one has to offer a media employer.

   _____

10. One fellow told the manager he wanted a job so he could learn about the media, which caused the manager to lose interest immediately.

    _____

11. The greatest need at radio stations everywhere is for salespeople who can sell time on it.

_____

12. The best advice for a student wanting to break into the media is that they should take any job available.

_____

13. It's very similar to the movie industry.

_____

14. They know the clerks at MGM don't want to be clerks forever.

_____

15. People in these kind of job are available first when other jobs open.

_____

16. The second piece of advice he gave to we students was to start at a small station first.

_____

17. Professor Bird teaches a great course in camera technology, and this is a skill I hope to learn.

_____

18. People in the media have to be very mobile, and this is disconcerting to some students.

_____

19. Seniority is very important within the station itself, so they move from station to station to advance rapidly.

_____

20. Satellites and cable have revolutionized television; it is responsible for opening up thousands of new technical positions.

_____

21. My father is in television, so I want to be one, too.

_____

22. In many of these technical positions, you have union membership to obtain first.

_____

23. Cable companies have expanded so rapidly that it is primarily staffed by technical people.

_____

24. This cable franchises are eager to hire marketing and business graduates.

_____

21

SHIFTS IN POINT OF VIEW   (10)

Point of view in a sentence is the vantage point or focus the writer provides for the reader. Unless grammar or meaning necessitates changing that focus, a sentence's subjects, verb tenses, mood, and voice, and pronoun person and number should work together to maintain a consistent point of view.

Most needless shifts occur in compound and complex sentences. The writer may begin with one focus but carelessly change to another in midsentence. The shift in point of view can distract and confuse the reader, as the following example shows.

Terry wanted to be a musician, but piano lessons were boring. [Subject changes from *Terry* to *lessons;* voice changes from active to passive.]

The sentence focuses on Terry at the beginning, suggesting that he, his activities, or his interests are going to be emphasized. But when the sentence's subject shifts to *lessons* in the second clause, the reader's initial assumptions are disturbed. What happened to Terry? The reader is left wondering just what the real focus of the sentence is. The sentence below illustrates a consistent point of view.

Terry wanted to be a musician, but *he* found piano lessons boring.

Sometimes the meaning of a sentence requires a shift in point of view. A change from one subject to another or a change in time, number, or person may be needed to keep the reader's attention in the right place and to convey the intended meaning clearly. For example, the sentence *I will wash the dishes while the cupcakes are baking* contains shifts in subject, tense, voice, and number (first person, singular pronoun subject *I* to third person, plural noun subject *cupcakes;* active future tense verb *will wash* to passive present progressive tense verb *are baking*). These shifts are natural and necessary for conveying the ideas in the sentence. *Needless* shifts in point of view, like those that follow, can make writing confusing and unfocused.

NEEDLESS SHIFT OF SUBJECT	She hated to study and, as a result, the grades she received were bad. [Subject changes from *she* to *grades.*]
REVISION	She hated to study and, as a result, she received bad grades.
NEEDLESS SHIFT OF VOICE	After a great deal of time had been spent in preparation, they started on their journey. [Voice changes from passive to active.]
REVISION	After they had spent a great deal of time in preparation, they started on their journey.
NEEDLESS SHIFT OF PERSON	When a person becomes ill, you should see a doctor. [Person changes from third, *a person,* to second, *you.*]
REVISION	When a person becomes ill, he or she should see a doctor.
NEEDLESS SHIFT OF NUMBER	If one tries hard, they will succeed. [Number changes from singular to plural.]
REVISION	If one tries hard, he will succeed.
NEEDLESS SHIFT OF TENSE	The mechanic first adjusts the carburetor and then set the points. [Tense changes from present to past.]

REVISION	The mechanic first adjusted the carburetor and then set the points.
NEEDLESS SHIFT OF MOOD	You must be careful; take no chances. [Mood changes from indicative to imperative.]
REVISION	Be careful; take no chances.

Another type of shift, from indirect to direct quotation (called a **shift of discourse**), is also particularly annoying to readers. Shifts from indirect to direct quotation usually involve a shift of verb tense and the omission of quotation marks.

NEEDLESS SHIFT OF DISCOURSE	The accompanist asked Claire if she had considered an opera career or does she just sing for enjoyment.
REVISION	The accompanist asked Claire if she had considered an opera career or just sang for enjoyment.
	The accompanist asked Claire, "Have you considered an opera career, or do you just sing for enjoyment?"

EXERCISE 21-1, SHIFTS IN POINT OF VIEW   (10)

The sentences below contain shifts in point of view. For each, indicate the type of shift by writing the appropriate abbreviation—*s* (subject), *v* (voice), *t* (tense), *m* (mood), *p* (person), *n* (number), or *d* (discourse)—at the end of the sentence. Then revise the sentence to eliminate the shifts.

Example   For students who want careers as performing musicians, you may want to attend a conservatory after high school. *p*

If you want a career as a performing musician, you may want to attend a conservatory after high school.

1. I wanted to be a performing musician, so the routes to that sort of career were familiar to me.

   _____

2. After a great deal of time has been invested in practice, many aspiring musicians still cannot make the leap to professional status.

   _____

3. When a musician has to ask if he should be a pro, you know you lack the necessary confidence.

   _____

4. If a musician has talent and is willing to sacrifice, they will eventually succeed.

   _____

5. There were many ways that are available for a musician to play professionally.

   _____

6. The dean asked me whether I knew about military bands and was I interested in becoming a church musician.

   _____

7. A good pianist can get themselves steady work as an accompanist.

   _____

8. Be flexible; an accompanist must be ready to play many different kinds of music.

   _____

9. Free-lance musicians may work one day at a wedding and then be asked the next day to play in an orchestra for a ballet.

   _____

10. Studio work has always been a sideline for the best artists; "session" players made very good salaries.

_____

11. A session player must be able to read music quickly and be familiar with all styles of music; sometimes, improvising ability is even demanded.

_____

12. If a musician doesn't want a performing career, they might consider tuning, building, repairing, or selling musical instruments.

_____

13. Piano tuners have very steady incomes, and training of three to five years is required.

_____

14. It's a complicated job, since most pianos had about 8,000 parts.

_____

15. Many schools that teach piano technology have closed recently, since students were not interested in learning the craft.

_____

16. But pianos were one of the most popular musical instruments, so the demand for tuner-technicians is very solid.

_____

17. Arts managers are the people who handle the business matters for musicians; arranging performances is generally the task of an arts manager.

_____

18. An arts manager might be museum directors, symphony managers, talent agents, or managers of concert halls.

_____

19. If one has a talent for both business and music, they should consider becoming an arts manager.

_____

20. Many managers are entrepreneurs in the sense that their jobs, titles, and sources of income were created by them.

_____

EXERCISE 21-2, SHIFTS IN POINT OF VIEW   (10)

The following paragraphs illustrate just how confusing and distracting shifts in point of view can be to a reader trying to follow a writer's train of thought. After reading the paragraphs, use your own paper to write revisions that eliminate the shifts.

Professional dancers are the smallest group of professionals making their living in one branch of the performing arts. Look at any of the other arts, and people will see more artists actually able to support themselves by working at their art. A government study was performed in 1974 and discovered that only some 7,000 people worked as professional dancers that year. One private study was performed in that same year to study the organization of performing arts groups with large budgets. Ninety-one symphonies have budgets over $100,000; thirty-one operas and twenty-seven theater groups have budgets that size. Many more people may dance as amateurs, or made a career of dance teaching, but there were very few professional openings. The career of a dancer is as short as that of most other athletes, as well, since they begin to lose strength and stamina after their mid-thirties. If one wants to continue a dancing career, teaching and choreography are possibilities for you. Many people have an interest in dance when young, but the dedication, ability, and confidence needed for a successful career seem to desert them in their late teens. The turning point seems to be the question of whether you can continue the discipline and training of a dancer or do you simply think of dance as recreation or exercise. You must be aware of the competition in the dance world; but if you are dedicated to the art, go out and dance.

Dance has always been popular with a small segment of the American population, but recently one sees more general interest in this performing art. We found this interest expressing itself in various ways. While not just anyone could be professional dancers themselves, many people have been dancing for fun and for exercise. Take, for example, the growing enrollments in aerobic dance classes. When our university offered a non-credit aerobic dance class at 5:30 in the afternoon, the first meeting was attended by more than 150 students, secretaries, faculty members, and most of the varsity basketball team. Many people said the after-work or after-class exercise really appeals to them as a good way to get rid of the day's tension. The basketball players have been sent by their coach to improve their coordination and flexibility.

We have to wonder if the interest in dance hadn't also been influenced by the television program *Fame.* By showing students at a high school for the performing arts, viewers can see that these kids are ordinary teenagers with the usual teenage problems. The main difference was that the students excel at music, drama, or dance rather than at math, English, or biology. As one viewer put it, the students' focus isn't on whether the football team will win but does everybody have their number ready for the talent show. The kids on *Fame* act out your favorite fantasy: most of us secretly believe that all the world's a stage, and, if the music was just right, you can dance through life as if it was one big production number.

Dance was an ancient art form, and it has its roots in prehistoric tribal rituals.If we look at tribal cultures still existing today, many ancient dance elements can be seen. The rain dance performed by some American Indian tribes are good examples. This dance acts as an invocation, a prayer for rain, and was not just an opportunity for exercise. Many ritual dances were serious business rather than the participants mainly taking time out for entertainment. As cultures changed, you will notice changes also occurred in their dances. Rituals become obscure, and perhaps only a vague notion of a dance's original purpose remained. At this stage a ritual dance can evolve into a folk dance whose main goal really is just to have fun. Still, if one studies a folk dance closely, we can often detect their roots in rituals such as harvest celebrations, court-ship, and marriage ceremonies. Folk dance elements have been borrowed by ballet: the ballets *Rodeo* and *Appalachian Spring,* choreographed for composer Aaron Copland's music, contains portions based on American folk tunes and folk dances. A few critics claimed folk dance polluted ballet's "classical" nature and it does not seem appropriate. But it is found to be well-suited to the ethnic American flavor of Copland's music by most people.

22

MISPLACED PARTS: MODIFIERS   (11)

As a general rule, modifiers should be positioned as close as possible to the words they modify. Word order is crucial to meaning in English; readers depend on word order to follow a writer's train of thought. The sentence below illustrates what happens when a modifier is misplaced, violating the principle of word order.

She gave the fish hook to her brother baited with a worm.

After a moment's thought, the reader can untangle the sentence, being reasonably certain it is not the brother but the hook that is baited with a worm.
However, the following sentence cannot be untangled so easily.

The bartender handed a glass to the customer that was half full.

In this case, either the customer or the glass may be half full. Only the writer knows for sure.
Modifiers should be positioned so that the writer's intended meaning is unambiguous. The following discussion identifies some of the more common problems caused by misplaced sentence parts.
1. Adverbial modifiers such as *almost, even, hardly, just, merely, only, nearly,* and *scarcely* should be placed immediately before the words they modify.

AMBIGUOUS MODIFIER	He had only a face a mother could love. [Is his face all of him a mother could love?]
REVISION	He had a face only a mother could love. [*Only* placed thus conveys the idea the writer intends, that no one but a mother could love that face.]

2. Modifying phrases and clauses should refer clearly to the words they modify. The **squinting modifier** is an ambiguous construction so located that it can modify what precedes it and what follows it.

UNCLEAR MODIFYING PHRASE	It is the car that won the race which has yellow wheels.
REVISION	It is the car which has yellow wheels that won the race.
UNCLEAR MODIFYING PHRASE	She had a meal in a restaurant that was low in price.
REVISION	She had a meal that was low in price in a restaurant.
SQUINTING MODIFIER	The cow he was milking irritatedly switched her tail.
REVISIONS	The cow he was irritatedly milking switched her tail.
	The cow he was milking switched her tail irritatedly.

3. As a general rule, infinitives should not be split. An infinitive is split when an adverbial modifier is positioned between the *to* and the verb: *to not go.* It is not always incorrect to split an infinitive; sometimes a sentence sounds more awkward when the writer attempts to avoid a split. But usually a split infinitive registers in the reader's mind as unharmonious. Consequently, avoid splitting infinitives if possible.

AWKWARD	I want to, if I can, leave the office early.
REVISION	I want to leave the office early, if I can.

4. Generally speaking, sentence parts such as subject and verb, verb and object, and parts of verb phrases should not be separated unless the result of the separation adds greatly to the effectiveness of the sentence.

AWKWARD SEPARATION	He realized, after many hours, that his course of action was wrong.
REVISION TO REMOVE AWKWARDNESS	After many hours, he realized that his course of action was wrong.
EFFECTIVE SEPARATION	The squad leader, sensing that the enemy was near, ordered the platoon to take up defensive positions.

Practice: Identifying misplaced parts   *In the following sentences, underline the misplaced words that make the sentences unclear or awkward. The answers are listed at the end of this section.*

[1] Architecture is more than making buildings attractive merely. [2] It is not a succession of arbitrary styles meant to for the moment show casual trends or decorative fads. [3] Good architecture both responds to the needs and to new construction methods that people express. [4] Climate, methods of labor, available materials, and economic factors provide the impetus for new architectural styles as well as good looks.

Answers to the Practice   [1] merely   [2] for the moment   [3] both, that people express   [4] as well as good looks

EXERCISE 22-1, MISPLACED WORDS, PHRASES, AND CLAUSES   (11)

Revise the following sentences, placing the adverbs so that the relationship to the words they modify is clear and the meaning is unambiguous.

Example   Architecture is the most known of the design arts widely.

Architecture is the most widely known of the design arts.

1.   Architecture in ancient times was considered the highest art form.

_____

2.   Merely painting and sculpture were considered decorative.

_____

3.   Architecture only combined all the lesser arts in the design of buildings.

_____

4.   Really environmental design is a difficult concept to comprehend.

_____

5.   Mainly architects design the building itself.

_____

6.   Architects are asked to build entire complexes of buildings in modern times.

_____

7.   Interior designers only are concerned with the smaller spaces of single rooms.

_____

8.   Landscape architects design the usually open spaces around or between buildings.

_____

9.   We can afford scarcely to ignore how all these buildings will fit together.

_____

10. Like pieces in a puzzle, urban and regional planners design larger patterns.

_____

11. Nearly tearing down and rebuilding is a constant process.

_____

12. Always people's needs in housing are changing.

_____

13. A hundred years ago, a town that might have been comfortable would have to be changed to suit modern people's needs.

_____

14. All kinds of environmental designers are needed to make these changes badly.

_____

15. Homes would need modernizing with plumbing and electricity desperately.

_____

16. Underground parking and widened streets for cars carefully would have to be installed.

_____

17. Constantly structures weakened with age must be replaced or repaired.

_____

18. We lost almost the beauty of many towns by rebuilding haphazardly.

_____

19. We must try carefully to preserve the beauty of our cities.

_____

20. No one scarcely wants to see the environment made ugly.

_____

Revise the following sentences, relocating words, phrases, and clauses so the relationship to the words they modify is clear and the meaning is unambiguous.

Example   Suburban land was once cheap that was empty.

Suburban land that was empty was once cheap.

21. When land was cheap, houses were designed by architects that sat on separate lots.

_____

22. Now houses share a common yard that land is so expensive.

_____

23. Entire towns are being designed by architects that save land by "clustered" housing.

_____

24. Stores once were popular with their own, separate buildings.

_____

25. Under one roof, it is cheaper to put several stores.

_____

26. These shopping centers are more popular with the public with easy parking.

_____

27. People like where they can walk from store to store protected from the weather to shop.

_____

28. Custom-built homes now that building costs are so high are not as popular as they were.

_____

29. Architects now with prefabricated sections are building and designing homes.

_____

30. Sometimes the differences are very unclear between these design professions.

_____

31. There are fewer architects than you might expect employed in this country.

_____

32. By architects only about one-tenth of all buildings are designed.

_____

33. By contractors or developers most buildings are designed.

_____

34. This fact by any future architect should be considered.

_____

35. From which they work, most architects maintain an office.

_____

36. To hire an architect for the job, they convince a client by persuasion or reputation.

_____

37. They sketch designs of the proposed building that are preliminary.

_____

38. They choose the building materials for the project and mechanical systems.

_____

39. A written plan is prepared by the architect that provides detailed plans.

_____

40. Sometimes in his search for building sites an architect helps the client.

_____

41. They choose contractors for the client who will do the actual building.

_____

42. They supervise the work of the contractor for the client involved in the actual building.

_____

43. The architect's work is more business than art for his or her client.

_____

44. An architect's job is described as part salesperson, part artist, part businessperson by people in the business.

_____

45. Finances must be considered which determine the size and finish of the building.

_____

46. The climate must also play a part which determines much of the design of the building.

_____

47. Local building codes must be considered that regulate building standards by the architect.

_____

48. The designer that determines where a building may be built must follow zoning laws.

_____

49. The most important thing that actually determines the building's structure sometimes to be taken into account is the geology of the building site.

_____

50. Give any job to an architect that is complicated in the least way.

_____

EXERCISE 22-2, SPLIT INFINITIVES AND SEPARATED SENTENCE PARTS (11)

Revise the following sentences, correcting awkwardly split infinitives.

Example   Most architecture students want to eventually open their own practice.

Most architecture students want to open their own practice eventually.

1. Clients hire architects to professionally solve building problems.

   _____

2. They may want the architect to quickly design a building for them.

   _____

3. Newer firms try to innovatively offer new services.

   _____

4. These companies employ many kinds of designers to conveniently offer any service.

   _____

5. Engineers, planners, architects, and landscape architects consult to efficiently plan the client's projects.

   _____

6. Government agencies hire architects to competently supervise their buildings.

   _____

7. Some restaurant and hotel chains employ architects to constantly plan their expansion.

   _____

8. The kind of work an architect is hired to usually perform depends on his or her company.

   _____

9. In a small company, a designer is asked to often design every phase of the project.

   _____

10. He or she might be expected to constantly find clients.

    _____

11. He or she might be asked to intermittently supervise construction.

    _____

12. Large companies can be expected to usually be divided into departments.

_____

13. The designers in each department are assigned to generally perform a specific task.

_____

14. A client gives a project to the whole firm to together work on.

_____

15. The project can be expected to smoothly flow from one department to the next.

_____

16. The architects are not encouraged to individually work on a design.

_____

17. They are expected to cooperatively work in teams.

_____

18. A senior architect is assigned to usually direct the team's work.

_____

19. The work a designer is assigned to generally perform also depends on the firm's specialty.

_____

20. Some firms try to always design the same types of structures.

_____

Revise the following sentences, eliminating awkward separation of sentence parts. If a sentence is satisfactory without revision, write *Satisfactory* in the blank below it.

Example   An architect may, with time, inclination, practice, and schooling, develop his or her own specialization.

With time, inclination, practice, and schooling, an architect may develop his or her own specialization.

21. Architects can never, if they want to get ahead, have sloppy work habits.

_____

22. Architecture is not, though attractive, a very stable line of work.

_____

23. Some designers choose to concentrate because so many skills are involved on one skill.

_____

24. However, some specialists earn, such as draftspeople or specification writers, lower salaries.

_____

25. Architects who work in government agencies frequently earn, since their responsibilities are smaller, lower salaries.

_____

26. The entire construction industry is directly by the economy affected.

_____

27. When interest rates are high, architects, because building slows, are first to feel the pinch.

_____

28. Builders can when money is short build without an architect.

_____

29. Some, short-sightedly since the environment suffers, do.

_____

30. Many architects, looking to the future, envision great changes in the technology of their field.

_____

31. Architects must in every state be licensed.

_____

32. An aspiring architect must first of all earn a bachelor's degree in the field.

_____

33. Then an architect serves, after graduating, a three-year internship.

_____

34. The intern serves during this internship under a professional's supervision.

_____

35. The intern usually, drafting and helping senior architects, does the routine tasks.

_____

36. The architect takes after the internship the state licensing exam.

_____

37. Many architects prefer to start after several years of experience their own firm.

_____

38. Some branch, for example teaching, into related fields of work.

_____

39. Another field, landscape architecture, is popular as a related specialty.

_____

40. Landscape architects work, as architects work with metal and glass, with trees, grass, and rocks.

_____

41. Landscape architecture is, with the elements of nature, the design of natural environments.

_____

42. They work to, with other designers, create parks, gardens, and other open, public spaces.

_____

43. These designers have not had, unlike architects, to go through such rigorous training and licensing requirements.

_____

44. But that in many states is changing.

_____

45. Some states do now require a licensing exam for landscape architects.

_____

23

DANGLING MODIFIERS   (12)

A **dangling modifier** does not logically modify anything in a sentence. Sometimes it seems to modify a certain word but cannot because such a relationship does not make sense. In other instances, there is nothing it could possibly modify.

One type of dangling modifier is the **dangling participle**. Because it functions as an adjective, a participle or participial phrase must have a substantive (noun or noun substitute) to relate to. If the substantive is not present, the participle has nothing to modify. One remedy for a dangling participle is to supply a word it can logically modify. Another solution is to expand the dangling modifier into a full subordinate clause.

DANGLING PARTICIPLE	*Tied to the mast,* the storm lashed at him.
REVISION	Tied to the mast, he was lashed by the storm. [Making *he* the expressed subject supplies the appropriate word for the participial phrase to modify.]
DANGLING PARTICIPLE	*Running in a race,* the finish is hardest.
REVISION INTO SUBORDINATE CLAUSE	When you are running in a race, the finish is hardest.

Dangling gerund phrases, like dangling participles, lack a word they can logically modify. These dangling constructions are usually prepositional phrases with the gerund serving as the object of the preposition. To correct a dangling gerund phrase, you must supply a word that the phrase can modify. Another solution is to recast the sentence so that the gerund is no longer part of a modifying phrase but is instead the subject or object of the verb.

DANGLING GERUND	*After mowing the lawn,* the lemonade tasted very good.
REVISION BY SUPPLYING SUBJECT	After mowing the lawn, I decided that the lemonade tasted very good.
REVISION BY RECASTING SENTENCE	Mowing the lawn made the lemonade taste very good to me.

A **dangling infinitive** also must have a word to modify logically. Like a gerund, an infinitive can substitute for a noun, so an alternative method for correcting a dangling infinitive is to recast the infinitive as a noun substitute rather than a modifier.

DANGLING INFINITIVE	*To win at tennis,* practice is required.
REVISION	To win at tennis, one must practice.
	To win at tennis requires practice.

As with other types of modifiers, participles, gerunds, and infinitives can also be misplaced: they can be situated near nouns with which they have no connection instead of near nouns they logically modify.

MISPLACED PARTICIPLE	*Fleeing down the alley,* the police caught the thief.
REVISION	The police caught the thief fleeing down the alley.
MISPLACED GERUND	*Playing with the symphony,* she loved her job.
REVISION	She loved her job playing with the symphony.

MISPLACED INFINITIVE	*To stick to a diet*, her doctor told her she needed will power.
REVISION	Her doctor told her she needed will power to stick to a diet.

An **elliptical clause** is one that has an implied or understood, rather than a stated, subject or verb: for example, *While tying his shoes, he broke a lace.* In the example sentence, the subject and auxiliary verb (*he was*) of the subordinate clause are implied. An elliptical clause dangles if its implied subject is not the same as the subject of the main clause. The remedy for a dangling elliptical clause is to be sure the objects of both clauses agree or to supply the omitted subject or verb.

DANGLING ELLIPTICAL CLAUSE	*While eating our supper*, the rain began to fall.
REVISION	While eating our supper, we noticed that the rain had begun to fall.
	While we were eating our supper, the rain began to fall.

Practice: Identifying dangling and elliptical modifiers   In the following sentences, underline the dangling or elliptical modifiers. Answers are listed at the end of this section.

[1] Having found gardening enjoyable, a career in landscape design and architecture might be rewarding. [2] Designed as either a two-year or a four-year curriculum, students in this program take geography, forestry, botany, agriculture, and even engineering and psychology. [3] A course in mechanical drawing is also usually required to be a landscape designer. [4] Constantly shrinking, landscape designers help make the most of our cities' green spaces.

Answers to the Practice   [1] Having found gardening enjoyable   [2] Designed as either a two-year or a four-year curriculum   [3] to be a landscape designer   [4] Constantly shrinking

EXERCISE 23-1, DANGLING PARTICIPLES AND GERUNDS   (12)

Revise the following sentences to eliminate all dangling or misplaced participles and gerunds. Write the word *Satisfactory* in the blank if the sentence requires no revision.

Example   Designed by F. L. Olmstead, New York boasts Central Park in its center.

Designed by F. L. Olmstead, Central Park is in the center of New York.

1. Designed in the nineteenth century, the most famous landscape in America is Central Park.

    _____

2. Remaining the country's most famous landscape designer, the reputation of Olmstead is still secure.

    _____

3. Left as pasture land, Olmstead found most of New York undeveloped.

    _____

4. Predicting the need for a large park, most people were surprised by Olmstead's ideas.

    _____

5. Crowded into the city, space for recreation is more precious for city dwellers.

    _____

6. Growing quickly, he realized New York would soon have no open spaces.

    _____

7. Offering relief to people tired of city life, the people could turn to Central Park.

    _____

8. Olmstead knew just any piece of land wouldn't make a park trained as a landscape designer.

    _____

9. Designed for a specific purpose, Olmstead carefully planned every square foot of the park.

    _____

10. For boating, Olmstead included huge lakes.

    _____

11. Designed purely for beauty, Olmstead built fountains and gardens.

   _____

12. Catering to the favorite recreations of the day, playing fields and bandstands are included.

   _____

13. Using the natural terrain, flat meadows and granite "cliffs" were created.

   _____

14. Harmonizing with the terrain, Olmstead installed bridges and tunnels.

   _____

15. Helping pedestrian traffic, shortcuts are made possible by these additions.

   _____

16. Left essentially as he designed it, Olmstead's park is still used daily by New Yorkers.

   _____

17. Having finished the plans for Central Park, Olmstead's fame spread.

   _____

18. While working throughout the East, parks were designed in many different states by Olmstead.

   _____

19. Lake Olmstead in Augusta, Georgia, was designed by Olmstead, working at the height of his fame.

   _____

20. Merely by meeting the needs of people, his work with environmental design made Olmstead famous.

   _____

EXERCISE 23-2, DANGLING INFINITIVES AND ELLIPTICAL CLAUSES   (12)

Revise the following sentences to eliminate dangling or misplaced infinitives and elliptical clauses. Write the word *Satisfactory* if the sentence requires no revision.

Example   To solve the problems of our cities, urban planners are needed.

Urban planners are needed to solve the
problems of our cities.

1.   To make buildings safe, urban planners create building codes.

    _____

2.   To ensure vegetation such as trees, environmental codes are used.

    _____

3.   When creating or modifying traffic systems, streets are designed to allow traffic flow.

    _____

4.   When planning public transportation systems, people must be able to travel con-
     veniently.

    _____

5.   To create parking areas off the street, housing patterns must be modified.

    _____

6.   To divide business areas from residential areas, urban planners help plan zoning laws.

    _____

7.   To allow land for public parks, free spaces must be left in the city plan.

    _____

8.   While designing water and sewer systems, care must be taken to avoid pollution.

    _____

9.   While preventing pollution and disease, the sewer system must not deplete the water
     supply unnecessarily.

    _____

10. While planning the street system, wide streets must be planned.

    _____

11. To allow business and industrial expansion, industrial areas must be carefully designed.

    _____

12. To ensure that the city is a unified whole, the planner must work with a more complex and larger design than the architect or landscape designer.

_____

13. When preparing for the field of urban planning, geology, geography, sociology, and economics may be studied.

_____

14. When planning urban areas, art is less important than problem solving.

_____

15. To plan urban areas, no single area of study is best.

_____

16. While learning the techniques, most urban planners take graduate work in urban planning.

_____

17. While undergraduates, urban planners may study many different fields.

_____

18. By combining areas of study, planners are more likely to understand the problems of cities.

_____

19. To prepare urban planners, many schools offer graduate degrees in the field.

_____

20. When investigating the field of urban planning, I found very few schools that offered undergraduate degrees in the field.

_____

24

OMISSIONS (13)

Omissions in sentences may occur because of the writer's haste, carelessness, or lack of proof-reading. A few types of omissions occur, however, because the writer is not fully aware that certain omissions common in speech can be very confusing in writing. Omissions of this sort typically fall into three categories: omitted prepositions and verbs, omissions in compound constructions, and incomplete comparisons.

1. Be sure to proofread carefully. Proofreading is difficult for almost everyone. When we have written a sentence or paragraph, we have trouble seeing our own omissions because we tend to "fill in" anything that is missing. We listen to our thoughts rather than see what is actually written on the page. Keep a list of errors you have difficulty seeing when you are proofreading. You may notice an emerging pattern that will help you to spot mistakes more easily in the future. When you proofread, do it slowly and do it some time after you have finished the final draft—when the words will be less familiar to you. Read a line at a time, using a ruler or sheet of blank paper under each line as you read it. This technique will help to isolate the line on which you are concentrating and eliminate distractions from other sentences on the page.

Careless omissions usually involve the little words our minds fill in but our pens fail to record: articles and prepositions.

CARELESS OMISSION	The car was little, green one.
REVISION	The car was *a* little, green one.
CARELESS OMISSION	I saw it parked next the gas pump.
REVISION	I saw it parked next *to* the gas pump.

2. Be sure to write out relationships that are merely implied in speech. In casual speech we may say *This type motorcycle is very powerful* or *We were roommates last semester,* but in writing you need to supply the prepositions.

OMISSION	Gasoline consumption the last few years has decreased.
REVISION	Gasoline consumption *during* the last few years has decreased.

3. Be sure compound constructions are complete. Check the verbs and prepositions in particular. When we connect two items of the same kind with a conjunction, we frequently omit words that unnecessarily duplicate each other; however, these omitted words must in fact be the same as words that do appear in the sentence: *She can* [*climb*] *and will climb the mountain.* Too often, omitted words are not duplicates of stated ones, and the result is an illogical sentence.

OMISSION	She is interested and experienced at mountain climbing.
REVISION	She is interested *in* and experienced at mountain climbing.
OMISSION	On the other hand, I never have and never will go mountain climbing.
REVISION	On the other hand, I never have *gone* and never will go mountain climbing.

Sometimes duplicate words should be repeated in a compound construction. Otherwise the expressed meaning may be illogical.

OMISSION
: They lost the game because of a lack of speed and good blocking. [It is doubtful that the game was lost because of good blocking, but the reader might understand that to be the case.]

REVISION
: They lost the game because of a lack of speed and *a lack of* good blocking.

4. Be sure all comparisons are clear, complete, and logical. Avoid illogical use of *than any of* or *any of.* Do not compare items that are logically not comparable. Make sure not only that comparisons are complete but also that both terms of the comparison are given and that the basis of the comparison is stated. The sentences below illustrate omissions that create illogical comparisons.

ILLOGICAL USE OF *THAN ANY OF*
: She is the best player than any of them.

REVISION
: She is the best player *on the team.*

ILLOGICAL COMPARISON
: The vegetables here are as high in price as any other region.

REVISION
: The vegetables here are as high in price as *those in* any other region.

GRAMMATICALLY INCOMPLETE COMPARISON
: This horse is as fast, if not faster than, the other.

REVISION
: This horse is as fast *as,* if not faster than, the other horse.

TERMS OF COMPARISON INCOMPLETE
: I like biology more than Jan.

REVISION
: I like biology more than Jan *does.*

BASIS OF COMPARISON NOT STATED
: This brand costs less.

REVISION
: This brand costs less *than other popular brands.*

EXERCISE 24, OMISSIONS (13)

Revise the following sentences, correcting omissions and comparisons that are illogical or incomplete. Write the word *Satisfactory* if the sentence requires no revision.

Example   Interior design requires the least education than any design career.

Interior design requires the least education of any design career.

1. Many schools offer four-year degrees in interior design and some two.

_____

2. A combination education and experience is probably the most common background.

_____

3. At one time, creative person could get one these jobs with no training.

_____

4. Now an untrained designer is unlikely to get any type job.

_____

5. Urban planners aren't all that different than interior design.

_____

6. The difference is mainly of scale.

_____

7. An urban planner's "canvas" is a neighborhood or city and an interior designer a room.

_____

8. A good sense color is a prerequisite for an interior designer.

_____

9. No one can teach to be creative.

_____

10. You must create a sense trust in your clients.

_____

11. After all, you'll be spending their money, just as they.

_____

12. The more projects and the larger the projects, more money an interior designer makes.

_____

13. A designer hopes to contract a job for important client.

_____

14. Another method of advancement is get pictures of your work published.

_____

15. Designers specializing in residential work generally make less money than designers for hotels and restaurants.

_____

16. Some designers design settings for department stores furniture stores.

_____

17. Designers make sketches of rooms and show samples fabric to their clients.

_____

18. They supervise contractors just as an architect.

_____

19. Some designers expand designing their own furniture lines.

_____

20. Sometimes designing a room's renovation requires services of an architect.

_____

21. Remodeling is likely to involve moving a wall as changing the wallpaper.

_____

22. This design field is as rewarding, if not more rewarding than, the other fields.

_____

23. Some designers specialize in theatrical work.

_____

24. The sets of theatrical productions are likely to have been professionally designed than any other rooms you ever see.

_____

25. When the economy is slow, people spend less money than when economic conditions are better.

_____

25

AWKWARD AND CONFUSED SENTENCES   (14)

Sometimes sentences are clumsy, meaningless, or, in some instances, absurd. Often it is difficult to determine exactly which violation of grammar is involved. The reason may be a combination of violations or simply a heavy-handed or vague and illogical manner of saying something. However, awkwardness may be the result of faulty predication or mixed construction—sentence faults that occur when a sentence begins with one kind of construction but ends with another, incompatible one.

Faulty predication results if the verb or complement is not appropriate to the subject of a sentence.

INAPPROPRIATE VERB	The data make several errors.
REVISION	The data contain several errors.
INAPPROPRIATE COMPLEMENT	His daughter is the reason he stayed at home today.
REVISION	His daughter's illness is the reason he stayed at home today.

In the first faulty sentence above, action is illogically attributed to the subject, *data*. In the second faulty sentence, the linking verb *is* joins a subject and complement that are not equal. Because the verb *to be* in its various forms equates what precedes and follows it, the two sides of such an "equation" must be logically compatible. *His daughter is the reason* makes no sense.

Another common cause of faulty predication is the construction of definitions and explanations that use *is when, is where, is what,* or *is because.* Remember that the linking verb *is* functions as an equals sign between the subject and the words that rename or define it; equivalent terms must be used on both sides.

ILLOGICAL USE OF *WHEN*	A hurricane is when the winds in a tropical storm exceed 75 miles per hour.
CORRECTED SENTENCE	A hurricane occurs when the winds in a tropical storm exceed 75 miles per hour.
ILLOGICAL USE OF *WHERE*	Skydiving is where people jump from airplanes into free-fall.
CORRECTED SENTENCE	Skydiving is jumping from an airplane into free-fall.
ILLOGICAL USE OF *WHAT*	The direct object is what receives the action of the verb.
CORRECTED SENTENCE	The direct object receives the action of the verb.
ILLOGICAL USE OF *BECAUSE*	The reason she laughed is because the joke was funny.
CORRECTED SENTENCE	The reason she laughed is that the joke was funny.

To avoid a **mixed construction**, attempt to maintain throughout a sentence the type of construction you establish in the first part of the sentence. Frequently, mixed constructions are caused by unnecessary shifts between active and passive voice verbs within a sentence, as the following example illustrates.

| MIXED CONSTRUCTION | Although he had the best intentions, many errors were made. |
| SMOOTH CONSTRUCTION | Although he had the best intentions, he made many errors. |

Sometimes mixed constructions occur when the writer forgets the true subject of a sentence and constructs a predicate that fits a word in a modifying phrase or clause.

MIXED CONSTRUCTION	By eating sensibly and exercising regularly will protect your health and prolong your life.
REVISION	Eating sensibly and exercising regularly will protect your health and prolong your life.
	By eating sensibly and exercising regularly, you will protect your health and prolong your life.

The best way to avoid writing awkward, confused, or mixed constructions is to evaluate each statement critically. Is it clear? Is it precise? Is it logical? Is it sensible? Is it to the point?

EXERCISE 25, AWKWARD SENTENCES AND MIXED CONSTRUCTIONS   (14)

Revise the following sentences, correcting awkward, confused, and mixed constructions. Write the word *Satisfactory* if the sentence requires no revision.

Example   The pharmaceutical industry is where they make prescription medications.

The pharmaceutical industry makes prescription medications.

1. By spending so much money on research makes this industry hire scientists from many varied disciplines.

   _____

2. Great strides were discovered in medicine in the twentieth century.

   _____

3. The reason for the increase in life expectancy is because of better medical care.

   _____

4. Although some new drugs were discovered by researchers at universities, the pharmaceutical industry discovered most of them.

   _____

5. The pharmaceutical industry is also what produces most medical devices.

   _____

6. Like microcircuitry, the latest technology is used in these devices.

   _____

7. Examples of the latest developments illustrate artificial heart valves and pacemakers.

   _____

8. This huge industry employs over 300,000 workers which half are production workers for.

   _____

9. The Northeast, the Midwest, and California is where most of the companies are located.

   _____

10. There are pharmaceutical offices and facilities positioned throughout the world.

   _____

11. Animal toxicity studies are where drugs are tested in animal systems.

_____

12. By sending these results to the Food and Drug Administration, it allows for research to continue with human subjects.

_____

13. By evaluating the drug in humans, the developers learn such critical matters as dosage and tolerance.

_____

14. A New Drug Application is where the firm applies for permission to market the drug.

_____

15. These trials are because extreme caution is necessary with new drugs.

_____

16. These experiments and trials can make up as many as ten years.

_____

17. By taking so long and being so careful, public health is protected.

_____

18. During the development stage is also when the final form of the drug is determined.

_____

19. In an average year, the pharmaceutical industry screens almost 200,000 chemicals.

_____

20. Although many chemicals are tested by the industry, only 1,000 ever prove to have medical benefits.

_____

21. As an approved medicine, only about 10 to 20 chemicals ever make it.

_____

22. This extreme care is what makes so many scientists and technologists welcome in the pharmaceutical industry.

_____

23. All the life sciences, medical sciences, engineering, and mathematics are jobs in this important industry.

_____

26

SENTENCE FAULTS REVIEW   (6-14)

Revise the following sentences, correcting fragments, fused sentences, comma splices, faulty agreement, faulty reference of pronouns, unnecessary shifts, misplaced and dangling modifiers, omissions, and awkward constructions.

Example   Everyone in our culture share a misconception about writers.

Everyone in our culture shares a misconception about writers.

1.   We tend to think of writers as someone who lives a glamorous, celebrity's life.

_____

2.   Or a starving artist in a garret apartment.

_____

3.   Interested in writing, teaching English becomes the career of many students.

_____

4.   Anyone who have tried to earn a living as a writer can tell you how difficult it is.

_____

5.   However, everyone who has done this has enjoyed their career.

_____

6.   Huge advances for novels are really rare the publicity about them is misleading.

_____

7.   While they work on that one great novel or screenplay or biography.

_____

8.   Many writers work at other jobs, they work at writing only part of the time.

_____

9.   If one has an independent income, you might be able to write full time.

_____

10.   There's many jobs that allow you to write some involve free-lance work, and some involve working for a company.

_____

11. Of course, the entertainment media, the news media, and advertising are a field with constant demand for good writers.

_____

12. The government employs writers as public relations people, and technical writers are also hired by the government.

_____

13. To write and edit reports, brochures, and correspondence, many businesses and industries employ staff writers.

_____

14. Free-lance writers who work only with local companies may find themselves with more work than they can handle.

_____

15. Local clubs and associations produce newsletters and bulletins, free-lance writers are hired to write and edit them.

_____

16. Reviewing books or writing columns for local papers are often rewarding.

_____

17. Not all publishers are in New York, some publishing jobs, such as proofreading and indexing, can be done at home.

_____

18. It's not really a writing job but this will keep you involved in writing.

_____

19. Many institutions, such as colleges and universities, employ writers to write or edit its publications.

_____

20. Any organizations involved in fund raising, a group which may include schools, museums, hospitals, churches, hires writers to produce their materials.

_____

21. One type writer specializes in producing grant applications and proposals for these sorts institutions.

_____

22. Job hunters to have a resumé or application letter prepared turn to professional writers.

_____

23. Some writers have begun his or her resumé-writing services.

_____

24. For local industries, they also provide temporary technical writers.

_____

25. One market that is surprisingly large are politicians, who need speeches written for them.

_____

Ten incomplete statements follow. Replace the dots with your own words, creating complete sentences from the fragments.

Example   Jodie likes . . . better . . .

Jodie likes writing better than she likes reading.

26. Neither fame nor riches . . . necessary . . .

_____

27. Stuck in the mud . . .

_____

28. This brand . . . costs about the same . . .

_____

29. . . . drank more . . .

_____

30. Someone will bring in your mail if you give . . . your key.

_____

31. The committee . . . cast . . . votes by secret ballot.

_____

32. . . . flying through the air . . .

_____

33. Overtime . . . when the game continues because the score is tied.

_____

34. I served . . . covered with whipped cream.

_____

35. . . . nearly . . .

_____

Revise the following sentences to make plural subjects and verbs singular and singular subjects and verbs plural. Be sure that the subjects and verbs agree in number in each of your revisions. Also, be sure that you have changed pronouns and the articles *a, an,* and *the* where necessary, so that they agree with the nouns to which they refer.

Example   Many writers have begun their careers writing for newspapers.

Many a writer has begun his or her career writing for newspapers.

36. A reporter may have a specific kind of news he or she must cover.

_____

37. This specific responsibility is called the reporter's "beat."

_____

38. While checking on his beat continually, a reporter may also be given other assignments.

_____

39. A good reporter must have a "nose for news."

_____

40. Newspaper writers must be able to recognize news stories or to find them.

_____

41. Their entire day is spent on gathering the facts about stories, sometimes several stories at once.

_____

42. Reporters really spend more time out looking for facts than they spend writing.

_____

43. A "rewrite" specialist stays in the office and writes more than reporters do.

_____

44. The rewriter takes stories from several reporters, combines it with research or the result of a phone call for information, and writes a story.

_____

45. Rewriters also check the accuracy of facts and sources.

_____

27

NUMBERS, ABBREVIATIONS, AND SYLLABICATION   (16-18)

In writing for general readers, **numbers** are usually spelled out if they can be expressed in one or two words and are less than one hundred: *four, ninety-nine, fifteen*. Scientific and technical writing, however, tends to favor figures over spelled-out numbers, especially if numbers are used extensively, because figures are clearer and less time-consuming to read. Often scientific and technical writers use the "rule of ten": isolated numbers of ten or less are spelled out, whereas numbers greater than ten are written as figures. For example, *The machine took two years to design and 12 years to be accepted by the industry.*

A good rule of thumb for writing numbers is to follow the conventions of the field to which your readers belong. (You can find these conventions in the style manual for that field.) The most important thing is to be consistent in your use of numbers. The following guidelines explain the prevalent conventions for general, nontechnical writing.

1. Spell out numbers or amounts less than one hundred: otherwise, use figures.

My son is *twelve*.   We saw *thirty-five* horses.   The mountain is *15,000* feet high.

2. Use figures for dates and addresses.

July 4, 1776   1914–1918   908 B.C.   1426 Homer Avenue
Route 2   P.O. Box 606

3. The suffixes *-st, -nd, -rd,* and *-th* should not be used after dates if the year is given.

May 1, 1985   May 1st of last year

4. Figures are ordinarily used in the following situations:

DECIMALS	2.67 3.14159
PERCENTAGES	45% *or* 45 percent
MIXED NUMBERS AND FRACTIONS	10½
SCORES AND STATISTICS	The vote was 67–24 against the plan.
IDENTIFICATION NUMBERS	Flight 457 Channel 6
VOLUME AND CHAPTER NUMBERS	Volume 2 Chapter 3 page 17
ACT, SCENE, AND LINE NUMBERS	Act IV, Scene 1, lines 10–11
NUMBERS FOLLOWED BY SYMBOLS	8" × 10" 55 mph 89°
EXACT AMOUNTS OF MONEY	$35.79
TIMES	9:30 P.M. 2:45 A.M. 11:00 A.M.
BUT	quarter to three, eleven o'clock

5. Except in legal or commercial writing, a number that has been spelled out should not be repeated as a figure in parentheses.

LEGAL	The easement is twenty (20) feet wide.
STANDARD	The ladder is twenty feet long.

6. Numbers that begin sentences should always be spelled out. If such a number is long or falls into a category of numbers usually expressed in figures (e.g., 40,000; 33 1/3), recast the sentence to eliminate its beginning with a number.

One thousand five hundred refugees stepped off the boat.
Off the boat stepped 1500 refugees.

Abbreviations should generally be avoided in writing, with a few standard exceptions. These exceptions and other conventions governing the use of abbreviations include:

1. The abbreviations *Mr., Mrs., Ms.,* and *Dr.* are appropriate only before surnames, as in *Mr. Brown, Mrs. Sanchez, Ms. Trent, Dr. Jacobson.*

2. Abbreviations such as *Hon., Rev., Prof., Sen.,* and *Gen.* are appropriate only when both the surnames and given names or initials are given, as the *Rev. Oscar Smith.*

3. The abbreviations *Jr., Sr., Esq., M.D., D.D., J.D., LL.D.,* and *Ph.D.* are used only when a name is given, as in *John Roberts, Jr. is the new district manager.* Academic degrees are usually used in abbreviated form, as in *Gloria Jones received her M.A. last year and is now working toward her Ph.D. in economics,* in all but the most formal writing situations.

4. The abbreviations *B.C.* (before Christ), *A.D.* (*anno Domini,* after Christ), *A.M.* or *a.m.* (*ante meridiem,* before noon), *P.M.* or *p.m.* (*post merediem,* after noon), *Vol.* or *vol.* (volume), *No.* or *no.* (number), and *$* are used only when specific dates, times, and figures are given, as in *12 B.C., No. 4, $50.00.* The twentieth century's two world wars are abbreviated—*World War I* and *World War II; WW I* and *WW II* should not be used.

5. Latin abbreviations such as *i.e.* (that is), *e.g.* (for example), and *etc.* (and so forth) are appropriate in most contexts. *Etc.,* however, should be avoided in formal writing and should not be used as a catch-all in any type of writing. Instead of saying, for example, *I like seafood such as shrimp, clams, etc.,* say *I like such seafood as shrimp and clams.*

6. Personal names and names of countries, states, months, days of the week, and courses of instruction should be spelled out. For example, *On September 17 we studied Germany and France in our history class,* instead of *On Sept. 17 we studied Ger. and Fr. in our hist. class.* Three exceptions are the District of Columbia, abbreviated *D.C.* when it follows the city name, Washington; the United States, abbreviated *U.S.A.* or *USA* or *U.S.*); Soviet Russia, abbreviated *U.S.S.R.* (or *USSR*). The names of states may of course be abbreviated when they are parts of addresses.

7. Names of agencies, organizations, corporations, and persons commonly referred to by initials need not be spelled out unless you believe your reader will be unfamiliar with them. In that case, spell out the name the first time you use it and place the abbreviation in parentheses. Thereafter you may use the abbreviation by itself: *The president of the United Auto Workers (UAW) refused to comment on the UAW's negotiations with Ford.*

Use abbreviations such as *Inc., Co., Bros.,* or *&* (for *and*) only if they are part of a firm's official title, as in *MacLaren Power & Paper Co.*

8. The words *street* and *avenue* should be spelled out. References to a subject, volume, chapter, or page should also be spelled out. The only exceptions are special contexts such as addresses and footnotes.

Syllabication, or word division, at the end of a line properly occurs only between syllables. If you are in doubt about where a word's syllable breaks occur, consult your dictionary. When you must divide a word between one line and the next, place the hyphen, which indicates the break, after the first part of the divided word, not before the remainder of the word at the beginning of the next line: *inter- esting,* not *inter -esting.*

Dictionaries indicate syllabication by means of dots: in·ter·est·ing. However, not every syllable division is an appropriate place to break a word at the end of a line. Three general rules govern word division at ends of lines.

1. Do not divide one-syllable words or words pronounced as one syllable (*thrust, blanched, stream*).

2. Do not divide a word so that a single letter stands alone on a line. If necessary, leave the line short and carry the whole word over to the next line.

INCORRECT	The neighbors moved a-way.	CORRECT	The neighbors moved away.

3. Divide hyphenated compound words at the hyphen only, to avoid awkwardness.

AWKWARD	The committee re-ex-amined the issue.	IMPROVED	The committee re-examined the issue.

EXERCISE 27-1, NUMBERS AND ABBREVIATIONS   (16–17)

Assume an audience of general readers. Cross out incorrectly expressed numbers in the following sentences, then write the correct forms in the blanks at the right.

Example   I graduated on June ~~20th~~, 1981,   *20*
             at the age of 22.   _____

1.   25 candidates reported for the interviews.   _____

2.   She will arrive in thirty (30) days.   _____
3.   On April nineteenth, we observe our
      anniversary.   _____
4.   I am 6 feet tall and weigh two hundred
      pounds.   _____
5.   Their address is forty-three One Hundred
      Twenty-third Street.   _____
6.   They saved $2,500 and spent one hundred
      fifty-nine dollars and seventy cents of it on
      advertising.   _____

7.   Reduce your bid by fifteen percent.   _____
8.   I ran the one-hundred-yard dash in nine and
      two-fifths seconds.   _____
9.   The assignment is on page two hundred
      forty-nine of Chapter 11.   _____
10.   We arrived at eleven twenty A.M. and left
      at ten P.M.   _____
11.   Buy 10 gallons of gas, 1 quart of oil, and
      2 new tires.   _____
12.   The radius was twenty six-hundredths of
      an inch.   _____
13.   Phone me at five seven two 3 one nine one
      at 7 o'clock.   _____

14.   25 times 25 equals 625.   _____
15.   His grade point average for the term was two
      point nine.   _____
16.   Physics three hundred thirty-two is the last of
      the twelve physics courses offered.   _____
17.   They will arrive at three fifteen A.M. on
      track seven.   _____

18.   I was driving fifty mph when the hose burst.   _____
19.   We drive 2 miles Monday through Friday and
      5 miles on Saturday.   _____
20.   At half-time the score was tied at fourteen to
      fourteen.   _____

Cross out inappropriate abbreviations in the following sentences, and then write the corrections in the blanks at the right.

Example   ~~Wm.~~, a ~~bio~~ major, has a
                  high average.   *William biology*

21. The fruits lemons, oranges, etc. are grown in FL. _____

22. Her office is on Westview St. _____

23. She was the Sr. member of the faculty. _____

24. This is going to cost us many $, I believe. _____

25. He has previously worked in Ger. and Eng. _____
26. John Werdt, Sr., and John Werdt, Junior are
certainly highly dissimilar persons. _____
27. Walter Cronkite retired from the CBS eve.
news in 1981. _____

28. I don't know whether the Dr. will approve. _____
29. The Lamson Co. manufactures hardware
specialties. _____
30. I like the month of Aug. better than I do
the month of Feb. _____
31. Rev. McIntoch preached an inspiring sermon
on greed. _____

32. The No. is either four dollars or five $. _____

33. He drove his new Cad. to the Co. meeting. _____

34. They love the Blue Ridge Mtns. of Va. _____
35. Span. is an easier language than Fren. or
Ger. _____
36. Ms. Jare could not find the answer in vol. 9
of the encyclopedia. _____
37. Hon. George Dorain will address the meeting
at 121 Birch Ave. _____
38. The Jr. looked a great deal like his father,
Matt Brown, Sr. _____
39. The boss told Sandy to bring his wife with
him to the office New Yrs. Eve party. _____
40. Way back in B.C., Gen. Julius Caesar won some
important Roman victories. _____

EXERCISE 27–2, SYLLABICATION   (18)

Some of the following word groups contain errors in word division or hyphenation. In the blank to the right, show by means of a slash where the word should be divided. If the word cannot be divided, write *ND* (no division) and then write out the whole word. If the word division is acceptable, copy the word as it is given. For each word in question, indicate each of its syllable points with a dot. Indicate any hyphens with a dash.

Example	know- ledgeable	*knowl/edge·able*	pe- rt	*ND pert*	
	a- ble	*ND a·ble*	sis- ter-in-law	*sis·ter -/in - law*	

1. a-
cute _____

2. e-
rupt _____

3. trimm-
ing _____

4. longwind-
ed _____

5. hind-
rance _____

6. non-
support _____

7. in-
flation _____

8. high-
strung _____

9. malig-
nant _____

10. barb-
aric _____

11. pre-
medical _____

12. pre-
judice _____

13. court-
martial _____

14. ver-
y _____

15. post-
office _____

16. re-en-
actment _____

17. coll-
ective _____

18. e-
qual _____

19. pre-his-
toric _____

20. inacc-
essible _____

21. exh-
ibition _____

22. learn-
ed [adjective] _____

23. defi-
nite _____

24. re-
al _____

143

25. *pre-*
    sent [adjective] _____

26. *int-*
    elligent _____

27. *guil-*
    ty _____

28. *undou-*
    btedly _____

29. *pre-*
    sented [verb] _____

30. *o-*
    pen _____

31. *yearn-*
    ed _____

32. *re-en-*
    list _____

33. *twe-*
    lve _____

34. *leth-*
    al _____

28

MANUSCRIPT MECHANICS REVIEW   (16-18)

The following sentences contain errors involving numbers, abbreviations, and word division. Assume a general audience and rewrite the sentences, correcting the errors.

Example   I was 23 years old before I found out the placement center's location.

I was twenty-three years old before I found out the placement center's location.

1.   It is a mistaken idea to wait until you are a Sr. to begin researching the job mkt.

_____

2.   Students might be able to choose majors more carefully if they knew more about the job market.

_____

3.   While it may be an error to begin a 4-year cou-
rse of study to prepare for a particular job, researching the labor market can provide useful information.

_____

4.   The *College Placement Annual* lists one thousand two hundred employers.

_____

5.   About two hundred and 50 ads provide further information about these employers.

_____

6.   The annual is published each year by the College Placement Counc., Inc.

_____

7.   The annual lists the personnel needs of e-
mployers who normally recruit college graduates.

_____

8.   Copies of the annual are available at most placement ofc.

_____

9.   400,000 students read the annual every year.

_____

145

10. Copies can also be bought directly from the Council, for about $ ten each.

_____

11. Their office is in Pa.

_____

12. Most placement offices offer this and similar vols.

_____

13. Natl. and local directories, mag., newspapers, journals will all be gathered there in one convenient place.

_____

14. Many U.S. Dept. of Labor publications offer valuable facts.

_____

15. This info. is useful to stu-
dents who have not made up their minds, since it may
help suggest an area of study.

_____

16. The information is probably equall-
y useful for a student whose mind is
made up.

_____

17. The variety of careers listed in
these guides might help by sugges
-ting alternatives.

_____

29

END PUNCTUATION   (19)

Three punctuation marks signal the end of a sentence: the period, the question mark, and the exclamation point. The **period** signals the end of an assertion or a mild command. It is also used at the end of an indirect question.

ASSERTION	She mailed the letter.
MILD COMMAND	Please mail the letter.
INDIRECT QUESTION	He asked if she had mailed the letter.

A period is also used for abbreviations: for example, *Jr., Ms., Mr., Mrs., Ph.D., C.P.A.* Omit the period in abbreviations that serve as names of organizations or government agencies: *NAACP, UNESCO, NCTE, NSF, AMA, USAF, IBM.*

The **question mark** signals the end of a direct question. It is also used to indicate doubt or uncertainty about the correctness of a statement. When used to express uncertainty, the question mark is placed in parentheses. A good substitute for (*?*) is simply to say *about*.

DIRECT QUESTION	Have you paid the bills?
EXPRESSION OF UNCERTAINTY	This house is 150 (?) years old. This house is about 150 years old.

A polite request phrased as a direct question is usually followed by a period rather than a question mark. Phrasing a request as a question rather than as a command is considered to be courteous and tactful, but the underlying intention of such statements is not interrogative.

POLITE REQUEST	Will you please mail your payment as soon as possible.

A period rather than a question mark is used for indirect questions because such statements imply a question but do not actually ask one. Although the idea expressed is interrogative, the actual phrasing is not.

DIRECT QUESTION	Had he turned off the water?
INDIRECT QUESTION	He wondered whether he had turned off the water.

The **exclamation point** signals the end of an emphatic or exclamatory statement. It is also used for emphatic commands and for interjections. Interjections are exclamatory words and phrases capable of standing alone: *Oh!, Ouch!, My goodness!,* and so forth.

EXCLAMATORY STATEMENT	Help! I'm drowning!
INTERJECTION WITH EMPHATIC COMMAND	Ouch! Stop pinching me!

Be careful not to overuse exclamation points in your writing. Inexperienced writers tend to use exclamation points for indicating everything from mild excitement to full-scale disaster. While exclamation points used sparingly can provide genuine emphasis, too many of them will make the tone of your writing seem hysterical. Furthermore, your reader may begin to distrust you; like the boy in the fable who falsely cried "Wolf!" too often, you will not be able to attract your reader's attention with an exclamation point if you have previously misused it.

Practice: Using end punctuation   *Supply the missing end punctuation in the following paragraph. The answers are listed at the end of this section.*

[1] How many people still think money will make them happy   [2] Even millionaires have their problems, though   [3] They need help meeting women [4] A club in New York has been formed for men who are millionaires and women who are beautiful   [5] A man has to answer the club's single qualifying test to join [6] "Are you a millionaire   "   [7] The members, men and women, are invited to lavish penthouse parties   [8] Why would such parties appeal to these people [9] The parties are efficient ways to meet people, apparently, for busy rich folks [10] *The Wall Street Journal* sent a reporter to ask some of the club members why they had joined   [11] Some said, "To meet a better class of people   "   [12] As one member said, "A million dollars is practically middle class these days   "

Answers to the Practice   [1] happy?   [2] though.   [3] women. [4] beautiful.   [5] join.   [6] millionaire?"   [7] parties.   [8] people? [9] folks.   [10] joined.   [11] people."   [12] days!" *or* days."

EXERCISE 29, END PUNCTUATION   (19)

Circle any errors involving the use of periods, question marks, or exclamation points in the following sentences; then write the correct forms in the blanks at the right. If the punctuation is correct, write *Correct* in the blank.

Example   He asked if I had taken any of the
newer tests⟨?⟩   _*tests .*_____

1.   Dozens of tests are designed to measure your
interests.   _____

2.   Do they ask about specific tasks or jobs.   _____
3.   They test only preferences, such as whether
you prefer to work in a group effort or alone.   _____
4.   Some people may have misunderstood their
real purpose!   _____
5.   One psychologist wondered if the tests were
really valid?   _____
6.   In fact, the tests should not be used as
absolute or foolproof measures?   _____
7.   Quite often, the tests don't even agree with
other tests!   _____
8.   If they can't predict a perfect career for you,
then why bother to take these tests at all.   _____
9.   As you grow older, the tests do become
more reliable?   _____
10. Most importantly, the tests ask you questions
you probably wouldn't ask yourself?   _____

Punctuate each of the following sentences as indicated, changing the wording if necessary so the sentence will be appropriate to the end punctuation requested.

Example   Time, according to the old adage, waits for no one.
(question) _*Does time, as the old adage says, wait for no one?*_
(exclamation) _*Time waits for no one !*_

11. I wonder, like many other people, if this will prove worthwhile.

(question) _____

(exclamation) _____

12. He asked if we had seen the new computerized tests.

(question) _____

(exclamation) _____

13. What a great idea!

(period) _____

(question) _____

14. Doesn't that take a long time to finish?

(exclamation) _____

(period) _____

15. She questioned my authority to give the order.

(question) _____

(exclamation) _____

Write sentences with end punctuation appropriate to the instructions given below.

Example   (expression of uncertainty) _Mugwumps (?) were Republicans who voted for Grover Cleveland._

16. (indirect question)

    _____

17. (polite request phrased as question)

    _____

18. (mild command)

    _____

19. (direct question)

    _____

20. (assertion)

    _____

21. (interjection with assertion)

    _____

22. (expression of uncertainty)

    _____

23. (emphatic command)

    _____

The **comma** is an internal punctuation mark that indicates relationships between sentence elements. It is the most frequently used (and misused) punctuation mark, in fact. A principal function of the comma is to signal relationships between clauses. (See also Sections 7 and 17).

1. A comma separates main clauses (independent clauses) joined by the coordinating conjunctions *and, but, or, nor, for, so,* and *yet.* The comma always precedes the coordinating conjunction.

> She was a good student, and she was also a good athlete.

Be sure when you use a comma with a coordinating conjunction that the conjunction introduces an independent clause and not just a compound sentence part. For example, no comma is necessary before a conjunction linking compound predicate nouns (see Section 5).

INCORRECT	She was a good student, and also a good athlete.
CORRECT	She was a good student and also a good athlete.

If two main clauses are not joined by a coordinating conjunction, use a semicolon between them (see also Section 33).

> She was a good student; she was also a good athlete.

A semicolon may also be used before the coordinating conjunction when one or both of the main clauses are very long or are internally punctuated with commas.

> She was a good student, getting nearly all *A*'s in even the most difficult courses; and she was also a good athlete, with many conference records to her credit.

2. A comma separates introductory words, phrases, or subordinate clauses from the main clause. Such introductory elements function as modifiers—either adverbial modifiers qualifying the verb or the whole main clause or adjectival modifiers qualifying the subject of the main clause. The comma following a modifying word, phrase, or clause signals the reader that the main clause is about to begin.

INTRODUCTORY PARTICIPLE	Depressed, George thought about all his unpaid bills.
INTRODUCTORY PREPOSITIONAL PHRASE	Without enough money for his tuition, he looked for a part-time job.
INTRODUCTORY SUBORDINATE CLAUSE	Because he could type well, he found work as a temporary secretary.

Be sure not to confuse modifying verbal phrases with verbals used as subjects. An introductory verbal modifier needs a comma; a verbal used as a subject does not.

INTRODUCTORY VERBAL MODIFIER	Having learned to type in high school, he now put his skill to use.

VERBAL AS SUBJECT	Having learned to type in high school was a blessing now that he needed to earn money for tuition.

3. The commas may be omitted after very short introductory clauses or phrases if there is no chance the reader will misunderstand your meaning. Remember that your use of a comma may be your reader's only clue to the exact meaning you intend. Note, for example, the following sentence: *Watching my sister Barbara was no fun.* The sentence might mean that Barbara is my sister. On the other hand, it might mean that Barbara was watching my sister.

CLEAR	Watching my sister, Barbara was no fun.
CONFUSING	After rolling the ball fell into the hole.
CLEAR	After rolling, the ball fell into the hole.
CONFUSING	In case of fire escape down the stairs instead of using the elevator.
CLEAR	In case of fire, escape down the stairs instead of using the elevator.
CLEAR	Before breakfast we went for a walk.
CLEAR	Next Tuesday my vacation begins.

The decision to use a comma after short introductory elements is sometimes a matter of emphasis. If, when you say a sentence aloud, you find yourself pausing for emphasis, a comma is probably desirable so that the reader will distinguish the same emphasis.

CLEAR	Unfortunately my daughter's teeth need braces.
COMMA USED FOR EMPHASIS	Unfortunately, my daughter's teeth need braces.

EXERCISE 30-1, PUNCTUATION BETWEEN CLAUSES (20a–b)

Insert a caret (∧) to show where punctuation should be placed between main clauses or between an introductory element and the main clause in each of the following sentences. Then indicate whether the sentence requires a comma (,) or a semicolon (;) by writing the correct punctuation mark in the blank at the right. If the sentence needs no additional punctuation, write *NP* in the blank.

Example   Dentists were once figures of fear in popular literature.   *NP*

In the last three decades ∧ all that has changed.   )

1. Dentists locate and fill cavities in the teeth and extract teeth when necessary. _____
2. At one time dentists' primary service was the extraction of teeth but that is no longer the case. _____
3. Dentists now also treat mouth and gum diseases they also straighten teeth and build dentures. _____
4. Most dentists own their own private practice but some work in industry or in institutions. _____
5. Dentistry is the second most highly paid profession in America and the preparation for a career in dentistry doesn't take as long as you might expect. _____
6. After taking science classes in high school most would-be dentists complete four years of college. _____
7. Most students begin dental school with a four-year degree but the dental schools themselves require only two or three years of college. _____
8. If he or she doesn't specialize a dentist can be practicing six years after high school. _____
9. Most successful dentists specialize their further training and education can add four more years to their four years of dental school. _____
10. Some dentists specialize in pedodontics or oral surgery others specialize in orthodontics or periodontics. _____
11. Pedodontists work with children orthodontists straighten teeth. _____
12. Periodontists treat gum diseases and endodontists specialize in root-canal therapy. _____
13. A dental student must have a strong science background but the most important prerequisite of all is manual dexterity. _____
14. Because most dentists work directly with patients all day a pleasant personality and a working knowledge of psychology also help. _____
15. Dental schools require applicants to take the Dental Admissions Test and admission is very competitive. _____
16. Dentistry is a rewarding field for women yet only two out of every 100 U.S. dentists are women. _____
17. In contrast to our situation in Finland 80 percent of all dentists are women. _____

18. Preventive dentistry and dental education have succeeded in their goals many dentists find that their practices have shrunk or changed in the last few years. _____

19. The government continues to predict a shortage of dentists their skills are needed for continuing the techniques of preventive dentistry. _____

20. In most dental practices preventive services and dental education are provided by dental hygienists. _____

21. Dental hygienists need the same high school background and personal skills as dentists, but their career preparation may take less time. _____

22. Universities and colleges offer two-year programs for hygienists who want to practice and four-year programs for those going into research or teaching. _____

23. Most dental hygienists are women and many of them work part time. _____

24. Most hygienists work in dentists' offices but one-fourth of the hygienists in America work for public health departments or school systems. _____

25. As the population and the need for dental education increase demand for dental hygienists should remain strong. _____

26. Because so many of their patients are children hygienists must be pleasant and have a delicate touch. _____

27. The hygienist takes and records dental histories and he or she also takes and develops X-rays. _____

28. The primary job of most hygienists in private practice is removing stains and calcium deposits from patients' teeth. _____

29. Because so much of a hygienist's work involves this delicate process he or she must have excellent vision. _____

30. Some dentists and hygienists are now developing a new specialty "dental phobia" clinics are springing up to help relax unwilling patients. _____

EXERCISE 30-2, PUNCTUATION BETWEEN CLAUSES (20a–b)

Expand each of the core sentences in the following ways: first, by adding another main clause; second, by adding an introductory subordinate clause; third, by adding an introductory phrase. Use appropriate internal punctuation.

Example   My favorite possession is my old car.

(main clause) *My favorite possession is my old car, and I'll never trade it.*

(subordinate clause) *Because I built it myself, my favorite possession is my old car.*

(phrase) *In the first place, my favorite possession is my old car.*

1. The women shook hands.

   (main clause) _____

   (subordinate clause) _____

   (phrase) _____

2. The day finally ended.

   (main clause) _____

   (subordinate clause) _____

   (phrase) _____

3. People are funny animals.

   (main clause) _____

   (subordinate clause) _____

   (phrase) _____

4. She would not share her notes.

   (main clause) _____

   (subordinate clause) _____

   (phrase) _____

5. You have ruined your suit.

   (main clause) _____

   (subordinate clause) _____

   (phrase) _____

6. Swimming is good exercise.

   (main clause) _____

   (subordinate clause) _____

   (phrase) _____

7. I hate dogs.

   (main clause) _____

   (subordinate clause) _____

   (phrase) _____

8. I visit my dentist twice a year.

   (main clause) _____

   (subordinate clause) _____

   (phrase) _____

9. He learned to type in high school.

   (main clause) _____

   (subordinate clause) _____

   (phrase) _____

10. Inez bought her tickets last week.

   (main clause) _____

   (subordinate clause) _____

   (phrase) _____

31

COMMAS: NONRESTRICTIVE AND RESTRICTIVE SENTENCE ELEMENTS   (20c-f)

Nonrestrictive elements are nonessential modifying words, phrases, or clauses that add useful but incidental information to a sentence. **Restrictive elements** are essential modifying words, phrases, or clauses that affect a sentence's basic meaning. Nonrestrictive sentence elements are set off with commas; restrictive elements are not.

We noted previously in Section 30 that commas can be crucial to the reader's understanding of the writer's meaning. In the case of nonrestrictive and restrictive elements, the presence or absence of commas is particularly important because the meaning can be quite different, depending upon their use. A simple example will illustrate the difference.

NONRESTRICTIVE	Children, *who hate vegetables,* should take vitamins.
RESTRICTIVE	Children *who hate vegetables* should take vitamins.

In the first sentence above, the subordinate clause *who hate vegetables* can be removed without changing the sentence's basic message: *all* children ought to take vitamins. The subordinate clause adds the incidental information that all children also dislike vegetables.

The second sentence says something very different. Its meaning is that the *only* children who ought to take vitamins are those who hate vegetables. In this sentence, the subordinate clause *restricts* the category, children, to those hating vegetables.

This is the crucial point: readers have no way of knowing whether the writer intends the category to be all-inclusive (nonrestrictive) or limited (restrictive) unless the commas are used (or omitted) correctly. The words are identical in both sentences.

A reader can occasionally distinguish whether a sentence element is restrictive or nonrestrictive even though the writer has misused commas.

RESTRICTIVE BUT INCORRECTLY PUNCTUATED	A waiter, *who gives good service,* gets generous tips.
NONRESTRICTIVE BUT INCORRECTLY PUNCTUATED	Max *who gives good service* gets generous tips.

If the reader follows the signals provided by the faulty punctuation in the first sentence and interprets the basic message to be *a waiter gets generous tips,* he or she will recognize this as a false statement. Generally, waiters do not get generous tips unless they give good service. The subordinate clause is essential to the meaning because it *restricts* the category of generously tipped waiters to those who give good service. The clause *should not* be set off with commas.

Conversely, the subject of the second sentence designates a particular waiter who gets generous tips. The proper noun *Max* restricts the category to one individual. The subordinate clause merely supplies additional but nonessential information. Consequently, the clause *should be* set off with commas.

CORRECT (RESTRICTIVE)	A waiter *who gives good service* gets generous tips.
CORRECT (NONRESTRICTIVE)	Max, *who gives good service,* gets generous tips.

157

As you can see, a reader may eventually be able to figure out the meaning in spite of faulty comma usage. Nevertheless, writers who fail to follow the punctuation conventions that signal whether a sentence element is restrictive or nonrestrictive run the risk of confusing their readers—or, at the very least, annoying them and thus detracting from the content of the message.

Now analyze the preceding sentence, containing the subordinate clause *who fail to follow . . .* , and decide why that clause is restrictive (not set off by commas). If you determined that without the clause (i.e., *writers run the risk of confusing their readers*) we won't know *which* writers—and surely not *all* writers confuse their readers—then you are well on your way toward understanding the difference between nonrestrictive and restrictive elements.

Be sure to use *two* commas to set off a nonrestrictive element unless it begins or ends a sentence.

NOT	That restaurant, specializing in Cuban cooking is one of my favorites.
BUT	That restaurant, specializing in Cuban cooking, is one of my favorites.
OR	Specializing in Cuban cooking, that restaurant is one of my favorites.

Typical nonrestrictive sentence elements are clauses, prepositional, verbal, and absolute phrases, appositives, and elements that slightly interrupt the structure of a sentence. Of these, clauses, prepositional and verbal phrases, and appositives may also be restrictive.

NONRESTRICTIVE CLAUSE	Food, *which I adore,* is big business in this country.
RESTRICTIVE CLAUSE	The foods *which I like best* usually cost the most.
NONRESTRICTIVE PREPOSITIONAL PHRASE	Lobster, *without question,* is outrageously expensive.
RESTRICTIVE PREPOSITIONAL PHRASE	Lobster *with drawn butter* simply melts in one's mouth.
NONRESTRICTIVE VERBAL PHRASE	Americans, *too busy to cook,* eat out an average of three times a week.
RESTRICTIVE VERBAL PHRASE	Women *employed outside the home* have boosted fast-food sales.
NONRESTRICTIVE APPOSITIVE	Restaurant management, *a popular major,* attracts many students.
RESTRICTIVE APPOSITIVE	The words *"We do it all for you"* really sell hamburgers!

An **appositive**, shown in the last two examples above, is a noun or a group of words functioning as a noun substitute. An appositive renames another noun and usually follows immediately after the noun. Most appositives of more than a word or two are nonrestrictive. Restrictive appositives, like other restrictive sentence elements, limit, define, or designate the noun they follow in such a way that their absence would change the basic meaning of the sentence.

Absolute phrases are always nonrestrictive, providing explanatory detail rather than essential information. An absolute phrase is a noun or pronoun followed by a present participle or past participle verb form. The phrase modifies the entire main clause rather than specific words in the clause. Because they are nonessential and therefore nonrestrictive, absolute phrases are always set off by commas.

Business schools even use cases about the restaurant industry, *case writers having studied its management problems.*

Interrupting expressions—words, phrases, or clauses that slightly disrupt the flow of a sentence—are sometimes called **parenthetical elements**. These elements should be set off by commas because they are not integral to the grammatical structure of the sentence. Words of direct address, mild interjections, transitional words and expressions, phrases expressing contrast, and words such as *yes* and *no* are usually considered interrupting expressions.

Other sentence elements also fall into the category of interrupting expressions if they are inserted out of their normal grammatical order. When they disrupt a sentence's grammatical flow (see Section 5), they require commas.

DIRECT ADDRESS	You may have noticed, *folks,* that fast food is pretty salty.
MILD INTERJECTION	*Well,* I suppose the salt masks the bland taste.
TRANSITIONAL WORD	So much salt, *however,* is unhealthy for many people.
CONTRASTED ELEMENTS	Home-cooked meals, *unlike fast food,* usually contain much less sodium.
DISRUPTED SENTENCE	Sodium, *many doctors warn,* aggravates high blood pressure.
	Hyperactivity in children, *until recently a puzzle,* has been linked to food additives.

One final category of sentence elements needs to be discussed: clauses and phrases that follow the main clause. In Section 30, we examined punctuation for introductory subordinate clauses and phrases that precede the main clause. These usually require a comma to prevent misreading and to signal the start of the main clause. But what about a subordinate clause or lengthy phrase that follows the main clause? Here, again, you must decide whether the information provided by the clause or phrase is restrictive or nonrestrictive.

If the information is essential to the meaning of the main clause, then the sentence element is restrictive and does not need a comma. If the information is nonessential and does not restrict the main clause's meaning, then the sentence element is nonrestrictive and should be separated from the main clause by a comma. Such phrases and clauses usually explain, amplify, or offer a contrast to the main clause, but the main clause does not depend on them for its meaning. Consider the following examples:

RESTRICTIVE	We don't know what's in processed food *unless the package label tells us.*
NONRESTRICTIVE	I like to know exactly what I'm eating, *preferably before I've eaten it.*

In the first example, the subordinate clause presents a condition for acquiring knowledge. The meaning of the main clause depends upon the qualification presented in the dependent clause. In the second example, the subordinate adverbial clause adds a kind of afterthought—an explanation, but not a condition that is essential to the meaning of the main clause. Consequently, a comma is necessary in the second sentence, but not in the first.

Usually subordinate clauses and phrases that follow the main clause are so closely tied to its meaning that they are considered restrictive. Using a comma after the main clause is generally the exception rather than the norm.

A good guide to whether or not a clause, phrase, or other sentence element is restrictive is the pitch and pause of your voice when you read a sentence. If your voice dips and hesitates before and after reading an expression, the element is likely to be nonrestrictive and require commas. If you read the sentence fairly even-toned and even-paced, the element is probably restrictive and does not need commas.

Remember that your readers will pause where you insert commas. Readers depend on you to provide the appropriate signals for meaning and emphasis.

Practice: Punctuating restrictive and nonrestrictive sentence elements   *Some of the following sentences use commas correctly; some do not. Examine the sentences and determine whether they are correct or incorrect as punctuated. The answers are listed at the end of this section.*

[1] Hamburgers, with all the trimmings, are known as "burgers with the works" at the local drive-in. [2] This drive-in unlike the typical fast-food restaurant is not part of a nationwide franchise. [3] The food, rather than tasting mass-produced, tastes home-cooked. [4] In fact almost everything served there is made from scratch even the hamburger buns. [5] The family, who runs the drive-in, has owned it for more than forty years. [6] Grandpa Joiner the original owner turned the business over to his daughter in 1970. [7] She and her husband, Fred, do all the cooking. [8] My father home on army leave during World War II couldn't wait to get to Joiners' drive-in. [9] He remembers, craving one of their hamburgers, more than my grandmother's succulent Sunday pot roast. [10] My own children, obviously taking after their grandfather, head straight for the drive-in when they come home from college.

Answers to the Practice   [1] incorrect   [2] incorrect   [3] correct
[4] incorrect   [5] incorrect   [6] incorrect   [7] correct   [8] incorrect
[9] incorrect   [10] correct

160

EXERCISE 31-1, COMMAS: NONRESTRICTIVE AND RESTRICTIVE SENTENCE ELEMENTS   (20c–f)

Although the following sentences are not punctuated to indicate the presence of nonrestrictive elements, many of them should be. In the blanks following the sentences, indicate whether the expressions set off or preceded by asterisks are restrictive or nonrestrictive.

Example   Those of us * on diets * stayed to hear the speaker.   *restrictive*

Ms. Grey * who spoke to the group * seemed well-prepared.   *nonrestrictive*

1. There are three ways * of becoming a practicing dietitian.   _____

2. Some students * studying for the field * pursue a coordinated program.   _____

3. The coordinated program * the quickest of the three methods * combines classroom work and an internship in four years.   _____

4. The 71 internship programs * which are all in clinical settings * are recommended by the American Dietetic Association.   _____

5. Some dietitians * having earned a bachelor's degree in another subject * go on to study in a certificate program.   _____

6. The certificate programs * that are best * combine clinical work with graduate courses in nutrition.   _____

7. The third way is first to earn a bachelor's degree * usually in home economics, food management, or nutrition.   _____

8. The graduate then begins an internship * which lasts anywhere from ten to twelve months.   _____

9. The internship * always in a setting approved by the ADA * combines hard work with practical learning.   _____

10. There are 45,000 full-time dietitians * in the United States.   _____

11. Ninety percent * of U.S. dietitians * are women.   _____

12. About 50 percent of all American dietitians work * in hospitals.   _____

13. Almost all * of the other 50 percent * work at cafeterias in educational institutions.   _____

14. The remaining few work in cafeterias * in large companies * or in the Armed Forces.   _____

15. Dietitians also plan menus for patients * who need special diets.   _____

16. They also are frequently called on to instruct patients * about their nutritional needs after returning home.   _____

17. Some dietitians teach courses * for hospital personnel. _____

18. Nutrition * a field that has captured the interest of many Americans * is also a favorite subject for publishers. _____

19. Diet books * a category of publishing that has produced hundreds of best sellers * are often written by dietitians. _____

20. Some dietitians * who feel their expertise is needed badly by the public * have opened their own offices. _____

Expand each of the following core sentences with nonrestrictive and restrictive clauses or phrases, using commas correctly.

Example All employees may leave early.

(nonrestrictive) *All employees who have finished may leave early.*

(restrictive) *All employees, a group including all of us, may leave early*

21. The rain came down unceasingly.

(nonrestrictive) _____

(restrictive) _____

22. The answer was correct.

(nonrestrictive) _____

(restrictive) _____

23. The insurance business is good nowadays.

(nonrestrictive) _____

(restrictive) _____

24. An unpopular decision was made by the President.

(nonrestrictive) _____

(restrictive) _____

25. I've just gone on a diet.

(nonrestrictive) _____

(restrictive) _____

EXERCISE 31-2, COMMAS: NONRESTRICTIVE AND RESTRICTIVE SENTENCE ELEMENTS (20c–f)

Insert commas when they are needed for nonrestrictive elements or interrupting expressions in the following sentences. If a sentence contains a restrictive element and needs no additional punctuation, write *NP* after it.

Example   For years , people have thought the U.S. consisted of separate economic regions.

1. Moreover the popular idea has been that one area might be depressed and another prosperous.

2. The truth is in fact quite different from the popular idea.

3. Instead of the vast differences people expect similarity between the major regions is an economic fact.

4. The common myth of the last few years was that the Northeast has lost jobs and industries.

5. As the North supposedly has suffered the South has prospered.

6. However studies have indicated none of this is true.

7. Figures from the Commerce Department break the United States into five geographical areas.

8. Two of the areas are the Northeast including New England and the Middle Atlantic States and the North Central area from Ohio west to the Dakotas.

9. Two more areas studied are the Pacific States and the South.

10. The most interesting area was the Mountain States which stretch from Arizona north to Montana.

11. Per capita income in each of these areas is actually becoming more similar each year.

12. The North Central area per capita income has remained precisely the national average since 1960.

13. Both the Pacific and Northeast regions have higher income averages just as people have thought.

14. However since 1960 the averages of these regions have dropped toward the North Central region average the average of the entire country.

15. The averages of the South and the Mountain States in similar fashion have risen toward the figures for the North Central region.

16. Workers tend to move into areas with high income averages increasing the supply of labor in these areas.

17. An increase in labor supply will in turn depress wage increases.

18. Furthermore it is easier for people to enter the labor pool in areas where wages are lower.

19. As one would expect one finds a corresponding rise in average incomes.

20. Thus while specific local areas may show great prosperity or depression the larger geographical units are becoming very similar at least in economic terms.

As you have seen from the text and exercises in Section 31, nonrestrictive and restrictive sentence elements are modifiers used to expand core sentences with additional information. At each number below, write a core sentence. Then expand that core sentence by adding modifying words—subordinate clauses, phrases, and interrupting elements. Make sure that at least two of your expanded sentences contain nonrestrictive modifying elements and at least two contain restrictive modifying elements. Set off nonrestrictive or interrupting elements appropriately with commas. Be ready to explain why you consider the modifying elements you have added restrictive or nonrestrictive.

Example   (core sentence) *I want to move to a warmer climate.*
I want to move to a warmer climate, one with more sunny days.

26. (core sentence) _____

_____

27. (core sentence) _____

_____

28. (core sentence) _____

_____

29. (core sentence) _____

_____

32

COMMAS: ITEMS IN SERIES   (20g-i)

Commas are used to separate **three or more coordinate words, phrases, or clauses in a series**. Such items in a series are coordinate if they are of approximately equal grammatical rank or importance.

> What do *the women's movement of the 1970's, the Massachusetts Institute of Technology, and home economics* have in common? [Three noun phrases]
>
> They all owe a debt to Ellen Henrietta Swallow Richards, an *enthusiastic, dedicated, knowledgeable* woman. [Three adjectives]

You have probably seen sentences in newspapers and magazines that omit the comma before the final element in a series: *The candidate offered a platform that Democrats, Republicans and Independents could support.* Although omitting the final comma is not incorrect, doing so can lead to confusion for the reader. Consider the following sentence, for example:

> Richards was born in 1842, graduated from Vassar and entered MIT in chemistry.

A reader may be unsure as to whether Richards majored in chemistry at both Vassar and MIT or whether the modifying prepositional phrase pertains only to MIT. To prevent such confusion, establish the habit of always using a comma to signal the final element in a series.

> Richards was born in 1842, graduated from Vassar, and entered MIT in chemistry; she was the first woman to attend MIT in any field.

Commas are used to separate coordinate adjectives in a series, but they are **not used between adjectives that are not coordinate**. Adjectives are coordinate if each one separately modifies the noun: that is, (1) if *and* can be placed between each of the adjectives without distorting the meaning and (2) if the order of the adjectives can be changed without distorting the meaning.

> She developed systematic, simplified, and scientific methods of housekeeping. (She developed systematic and simplified and scientific methods . . . She developed scientific, simplified, and systematic methods . . .)

Adjectives in a series are not always coordinate; sometimes they are cumulative, as the following sentence shows:

> An MIT instructor in sanitary chemistry until her death, Richards organized the modern home economics movement.

Clearly, the adjectives cannot be moved around without reducing the sentence to nonsense. *Home* modifies the noun *economics,* but we ordinarily use the two words together in such a way that they really constitute a single concept and function together as a compound noun— like *baseball* or *mailman.* What's more, in this case the two words function not as a compound noun but as a compound adjective, modifying *movement. Modern,* in fact, modifies the whole concept of the three words—*home economics movement*—taken together. Of the three words functioning as adjectives, *modern* is the most independent and loosely attached.

Coordinate adjectives are rather like the spokes of a wheel, each one focused on the noun at the hub, each one separated from the others by a spacing comma. Adjectives in series that are not coordinate are more like funnels tightly stacked one inside the other, each one often modifying a word or words ahead of it and the last one modifying the noun itself.

The same principles governing punctuation for adjectives in a series apply when only two modifiers precede the word being modified. If the two modifiers are coordinate but not joined by a conjunction, use a comma between them. If they are not coordinate, do not use a comma.

> Ellen Richards's aims were the systematic, scientific management of the home and the freeing of women for other worthwhile activities.

Commas are also used to set off **items in dates** following the series order month, day, and year. Commas are not used if just the month and year are given or if the series order is day, month, and year.

> The Home Economists Conference of June 18, 1982, met here.
> We selected the June 1984 conference site and voted to close registration on 6 December 1983.

Commas are used to set off **items in addresses and geographical names**. A comma should be placed after the last item if the geographical name or address appears within a sentence. No comma is used before a zip code.

ADDRESS	The area Home Economics Extension Office is at 634 Eagle Avenue, Crawfordsville, Indiana 47369.
GEOGRAPHICAL NAME	Conference participants came from as far away as Dallas, Texas, and Montreal, Canada.

Commas are also used to set off **titles that follow names**. In addition, commas are used in **numbers** to indicate thousands, but not in social security numbers, telephone numbers, zip codes, and so forth.

> According to Professor Mark Jones, Ph.D., the home economics school at Purdue was renamed the School of Consumer and Family Sciences in 1976 and has an enrollment of more than 1,600 students. For more information, phone: 555-1212.

EXERCISE 32-1, COMMAS: ITEMS IN SERIES (20g-i)

After each of the following sentences, write *C* if the sentence is punctuated correctly and *NC* if it is punctuated incorrectly.

Example　　　Home economics has been a traditional, popular, and useful area of study in large land-grant universities. *C*

Brigham Young, Colorado State and Penn State award more home economics degrees than any other schools. *NC*

1. Home economists improve products services, and practices used in the home.

2. They are concerned with the health, comfort, and safety of the family.

3. Home economics students are stereotyped as frivolous, prissy, provincial females.

4. In fact, home economics is rigorous, scientific and demanding.

5. Research, and education in home economics is methodical, painstaking, and finally rewarding.

6. You may specialize in child development, family relations, clothing and textiles, foods and nutrition or institutional management.

7. The American Home Economics Association has its offices at 2010 Massachusetts Avenue, Washington D. C. 20036.

8. There are almost 150000 home economists working in this country.

9. Half that number teach in high schools and colleges, almost one-third that number are dietitians, and the remainder work in government or private industry.

10. Many businesses hire home economists to test products, to prepare advertisements, and to present television and radio programs.

11. They make sure that a manufacturer's products are salable, useful, and safe.

12. Textile companies often hire clothing and textile specialists, as do dress pattern companies and interior designers.

13. County and state extension services hire home economists for urban and rural adult education programs.

14. There are still very few, male, home economists.

15. As the field expands, changes, and assumes different responsibilities, large numbers of men are becoming interested in home economics.

Insert commas at all points where they are required in the following sentences. (Use a pen or pencil that writes in a color other than black.)

Example   Larry Bryant , Associate Professor of Textile Studies , will speak tonight.

16. We don't just bake pies do laundry and sew curtains anymore.

17. There are many home economics career possibilities.

18. Some home economists even perform research for experimental outer space programs.

19. Hotels hospitals and restaurants need these professionals.

20. Many of these workers find themselves editing teaching researching or running businesses.

21. Experienced mature people are especially welcome.

22. In centers for children adults or the elderly home economists have many varied challenging responsibilities.

23. Nutrition budgeting and household or institutional management are typical assignments.

24. Consumer education money management and marketing are emerging areas of study and responsibility for home economists.

25. Extension workers conduct workshops forums discussion groups and make home visits.

26. They instruct families in food selection preparation safety and sanitation.

27. Pamphlets exhibits films and articles are prepared to use in this instruction.

28. Talents for speaking writing editing and demonstrating are important qualities for the home economist.

29. Many large metropolitan newspapers and many magazines employ home economists as food editors restaurant critics or consumer affairs editors.

30. It is interesting that established successful home economists emphasize the importance of practical experience in cooking doing laundry sewing and running a household.

EXERCISE 32-2, ALL KINDS OF COMMAS   (20)

Insert commas where they are required in the following sentences. (Use a pen or pencil that writes in a color other than black.)

Example   She was trying to decide among Alaska , Houston , and California.

1.   After settling on a career choice many graduates discover that their next choice is location.

2.   Many recruiters who hire college graduates expect the graduate to relocate to a new area.

3.   Of course this relocation should be as carefully thought out as any other career choice has been.

4.   No one of course will interview you on say April 18, 1983 and expect you to be in Atlanta Georgia on April 23, 1983.

5.   Before moving to Memphis Tennessee or Savannah Georgia you will want to learn as much as possible about these towns you're going to live in.

6.   In the past too many people moved to areas which were supposed to be "booming."

7.   A sudden influx of workers which tends to lower wages strains the social services of cities and towns.

8.   The cycles in regional prosperity are I think as difficult to predict.

9.   Just as for example the demand for engineers goes through cycles of scarcity and over-supply so does the demand for labor in a particular city.

10.   You are likely to arrive as many people have unfortunately learned too late to participate.

11.   Sociologists have found that people move to a town because of job or career possibilities but people stay in towns because of tangible and intangible benefits what we might call "quality of life."

12. Alaska experienced a sudden though expected demand for workers on the Alaska pipeline.

13. The workers many of whom migrated north along with their families created instant boom towns.

14. The sudden overwhelming influx of workers also created high prices housing shortages and critically strained public services.

15. Now that the pipeline construction is finished many of these workers have left.

16. While in Alaska they found the living very tough indeed.

17. Many workers particularly those who worked farthest north had no intentions of staying in the state.

18. Living in temporary company quarters they viewed their jobs logically enough as temporary too.

19. State officials expect another migration for a proposed gas pipeline but they expect to be better prepared this time.

20. The cycle of migration "boom" and exodus that accompanies sudden prosperity may be inescapable though.

21. Though the pipelines are the most recent examples there have been many other examples both in Alaska and the rest of the United States.

22. In the summer of 1898 three Swedes discovered gold in Nome Alaska which was then an Eskimo settlement of 200 people.

23. By the later months of 1900 there were 40000 miners living in a tent city that stretched for 25 miles.

24. Every month gold worth $1000000 was taken from Nome's rivers and creeks.

25. Soon after the tents were replaced by hotels banks theaters dance halls and bars.

26. The gold that could be easily mined was removed quickly and most of the miners left.

27. Only the corporations that could afford huge dredging machines remained and today there is only one corporation still active in Nome's gold fields.

33

SEMICOLONS (21)

A semicolon is used to separate main clauses not joined by a coordinating conjunction. (See also Sections 17 and 30.)

> In today's complex world, police departments and lawyers often rely on specialists; these people are called expert witnesses.

Like a period, a semicolon marks the end of a complete, grammatically independent statement. Although it can be substituted for a period, a semicolon is most effectively used between two independent clauses that are closely related in thought. Whereas a period is a "full stop," marking a complete break between sentences, the semicolon separates and stops but does not fully break the flow of thought between grammatically independent statements.

> Expert witnesses are authorities in their fields; they supply information and courtroom testimony.

This close relationship of thoughts is underscored by another of the semicolon's uses: to separate main clauses joined by a conjunctive adverb. Conjunctive adverbs, words such as *however, moreover, therefore,* and *consequently,* carry a thought from one main clause to the next. (See Section 7 for additional discussion of conjunctive adverbs and a more extensive list of them.)

> You cannot plan a career as an expert witness; *however,* you might be asked to give testimony some day if your occupation is a technical one.

Conjunctive adverbs are easy to distinguish from coordinating and subordinating conjunctions if you remember that, unlike the other connectives, they can be moved from the beginning of their main clauses without destroying the sense.

> Most jurors are not very familiar with mental illness; *consequently,* psychiatrists may testify if a defendant pleads innocent by reason of insanity.
> Most jurors are not very familiar with mental illness; psychiatrists, *consequently,* may testify if a defendant pleads innocent by reason of insanity.

Coordinating and subordinating conjunctions cannot be moved around in this way. *Most jurors are not very familiar with mental illness, so psychiatrists may testify* makes sense, but *Most jurors are not very familiar with mental illness, psychiatrists so may testify* does not have the same meaning at all.

Note that when a conjunctive adverb comes within the second main clause instead of at the beginning, the clauses still must be separated by a semicolon and the conjunctive adverb set off by a pair of commas.

A semicolon is also used to separate main clauses joined by a coordinating conjunction if the clauses are exceptionally long or contain internal commas. This use of the semicolon helps the reader see clearly where one main clause stops and another starts. When you compare the following sentences, you will appreciate a reader's relief at finding a semicolon among the welter of commas.

We frequently hear about physicians, psychiatrists, or ballistics experts who testify for the defense or the prosecution, but less glamourous professions, engineering or accounting, for example, also get opportunities.

We frequently hear about physicians, psychiatrists, or ballistics experts who testify for the defense or the prosecution; but less glamourous professions, engineering or accounting, for example, also get opportunities.

Similarly, semicolons are used in place of commas to separate items in a series if the items themselves contain internal commas.

An expert witness might be an accountant, who explains tax loopholes; an electrician, who examines a burglar alarm; or a trainer, who describes how a vicious dog could have been controlled.

Practice: Using semicolons   *The following sentences are punctuated with commas and periods. Underline those punctuation marks that you think could be replaced by semicolons. The answers are listed at the end of this section.*

[1] Women who have chosen careers as police officers have apparently won acceptance. [2] The original controversy has subsided. [3] Consequently, the percentage of female police officers has risen from 1.5 percent to 3.38 percent in the last ten years. [4] Skepticism about these officers' performance has subsided, too. [5] They are apparently performing well. [6] Some officials are still concerned over the ability of women to fire heavy handguns, and firearms courses have been developed to help women, who may have difficulty holding and firing a heavy gun, become more familiar with their .357 magnums and .38 specials. [7] No one is concerned any longer that women will not make good police officers. [8] More women are assigned to patrol duty, and some already hold administrative positions. [9] At least one city, Cannon Beach, Oregon, already boasts a woman as its chief of police.

Answers to the Practice   [2-3] subsided; consequently,   [4-5] too; they
[6-7] specials; no

EXERCISE 33, SEMICOLONS   (21)

Insert semicolons where they are needed in the following sentences. (Use a pen or pencil that writes in a color other than black.)

Example   Law schools usually do not emphasize a particular major for prospective applicants ; however, English courses are beneficial.

1. Courses in composition and speech are particularly helpful the essence of legal practice is the ability to communicate clearly.

2. An undergraduate can pursue almost any college major educators prefer that a student develop the skills and habits of legal reasoning rather than learn a particular subject.

3. A lawyer counsels clients about proposed actions in addition, a lawyer assists people in making wills, buying homes, and starting businesses.

4. Many practicing lawyers see the need for training in psychology, sociology, and economics they often find themselves giving personal as well as legal guidance.

5. Our courts are a place where irreconcilable points of view are presented hence, a lawyer often acts as an advocate for a client.

6. Thus, a lawyer may spend part of his or her working day doing research, sometimes in a law library and sometimes in a public library writing legal arguments, reports, and documents or conferring with clients.

7. Frequently, a lawyer might be in one court in the morning and in two courts in the afternoon then he or she might spend evenings in further research at home or working for the bar association.

8. The requirements for practicing law vary from state to state in Georgia, for example, law school is not strictly required.

9. You must pass the bar examination to practice law in this state it lasts two days and consists of an objective test and an essay examination.

10. Graduates of law schools are eligible to take the exam however, anyone who has

    completed two years of college and is enrolled in certain courses is also eligible to take

    the exam.

    Combine or repunctuate the sentences below, substituting semicolons for periods and commas where appropriate and changing capitalization if necessary.

    Example   First you must complete your studies. Then you must pass the bar
                     exam and be sworn in as an officer of the court. After paying the State
                     Bar Association dues, you will be eligible to practice law.

    *First you must complete your studies; then you must
    pass the bar exam and be sworn in as an officer
    of the court. After paying the State Bar Association dues,
    you will be eligible to practice law.*

11. The areas of practice for lawyers are many. Many lawyers set up their own practices or
    take salaried positions with large law firms.

    _____

    _____

12. Some judges hire recent graduates to help them research cases. Many other lawyers work
    in city, county, and state government agencies.

    _____

    _____

13. Legal aid assists low-income groups. Similarly, legal clinics aid middle-income people
    with their legal problems.

    _____

    _____

14. Lawyers also work in business and industry. Most of them work at the management
    level in manufacturing, banking, or insurance.

    _____

    _____

15. Most lawyers never appear in court. In fact, most of their time is spent conferring,
    writing, or researching.

    _____

    _____

16. The trial lawyer represents clients in civil and criminal cases. Trial lawyers are the smallest subgroup of specialized lawyers, but their specialty is the most publicized.

_____

_____

17. Lawyers advise businesses on contracts, mergers, the combining of businesses, acquisitions, the buying of businesses, and on taxes.

_____

_____

18. The Department of Labor predicts that demand for lawyers will grow moderately. The American Bar Association expects that the number of lawyers will double in this decade.

_____

_____

19. Law school enrollment is at an all-time high. Increased business activity is expected to create a growing need for legal advice.

_____

_____

20. Legal secretaries and paralegals assist lawyers in their duties. The paralegal assists with research and investigations, and legal secretaries aid lawyers by handling client relations and by completing standard forms and contracts.

_____

_____

21. Training programs for paralegals are growing in number. They are available in many settings, from community colleges to universities.

_____

_____

22. Attorneys interpret government regulations as well as law. Many represent clients before administrative agencies such as the Internal Revenue Service or the Environmental Protection Agency.

_____

_____

23. Legal training prepares people for other careers, as well. Most U.S. Senators are lawyers.

_____

_____

24. Many management positions in government agencies are held by lawyers. Many lobbyists for special-interest groups are also lawyers.

_____

_____

25. Average income figures reported for lawyers can be very misleading. Lawyers work in a variety of settings, and their income varies widely according to experience, location, and specialty.

_____

_____

34

COLONS, DASHES, AND PARENTHESES   (22-23)

The **colon** has some characteristics similar to the semicolon and some similar to the dash. In fact, from time to time you may be unsure about whether to use a colon or one of the other two punctuation marks. In this section, we examine the distinctions that will help you determine the appropriate punctuation to use.

Like a semicolon, a colon can be used between main clauses that lack a coordinating conjunction. However, whereas the semicolon indicates a stop, the colon indicates an addition or expectation. The colon separates main clauses, the second of which explains, illustrates, or amplifies the first.

> Stonecutting is not something you can learn in a day: it requires a four-year apprenticeship.

A colon can also be used to set off a long final appositive (words that rename a nearby noun or noun substitute) or to set off a long summary. A dash is used to set off a short final appositive or short summary.

LONG APPOSITIVE USING COLON	Medieval cathedrals were built by apprentices: young workers learning their trade under a master craftsman.
SHORT APPOSITIVE USING DASH	Medieval masters paid their apprentices not with money but with subsistence—food and lodging.
LONG SUMMARY USING COLON	The apprentices working on the Cathedral of St. John the Divine today are an unusual bunch: they have come from New York's ghetto to learn a medieval European craft.
SHORT SUMMARY USING DASH	They receive not only wages but a place in history for their work—a kind of immortality.

A colon can be used to introduce examples, a series, or a list. When it introduces a list, the colon may be preceded by the phrases *as follows* or *the following,* or these phrases may be only implied.

COLON PRECEDED BY *THE FOLLOWING*	Some of the world's great cathedrals are in the following cities: Chartres, Amiens, Canterbury, Cologne, Barcelona, and Milan.
COLON USED WHERE *AS FOLLOWS* IS IMPLIED	Two architectural styles dominate European cathedrals: the Romanesque and the Gothic.

It is not necessary to use a colon after the linking verb *are* or after the participle *including.*

> Several features distinguish Gothic cathedrals, including pointed arches, ribbed vaults, and buttresses.

A colon is used to introduce a formal quotation. Also, established convention requires a colon to separate items in biblical citations, titles with subtitles, and divisions of time.

FORMAL QUOTATION	In 1170 four knights murdered Archbishop Thomas à Becket in Canterbury Cathedral, acting upon the words of King Henry II: "Will no one rid me of this priest?"
BIBLICAL CITATION	Ecclesiastes 3:1–8
TITLE WITH SUBTITLE	*Poets and Pilgrims: Chaucer's Canterbury Tales*
DIVISION OF TIME	11:55 P.M.

The **dash** is best used for emphasis and clarity to indicate shifts in sentence structure or thought or to set off parenthetical elements that might be confusing if punctuated with commas.

SHIFT IN SENTENCE STRUCTURE	A cathedral in New York City—its presence seems almost an anachronism—sets a bit of the Old World down in the New World.
SHIFT IN THOUGHT	The stonecutters at St. John the Divine—the best will go to Bath, England, for special training—work from scale drawings of the structure.
EMPHASIS ON PARENTHETICAL ELEMENT	James Robert Bambridge—a master builder from England—is directing the construction of the cathedral's gallery and two towers.
INTRODUCTORY LIST OR SUMMARY	Measuring, marking, and chiseling—these are the steps in "tapping stone."
INTERRUPTION OR HESITATION IN SPEECH	"The feeling I get from working here is like—like soaring. It makes me want to—" "To sing," says another stonecutter, finishing the sentence for his friend.

The dash is also used for clarity to set off internally punctuated appositives. You will remember that a semicolon can be used between items in a series containing internal commas (see Section 33). Using dashes to set off an appositive made up of an internally punctuated series serves a similar clarifying purpose.

A cathedral's architectural elements, gables, turrets, pinnacles, and spires, reach heavenward, designed as a celebration of glory to God.
A cathedral's architectural elements—gables, turrets, pinnacles, and spires—reach heavenward, designed as a celebration of glory to God.

The dashes quickly signal to the reader that the words following *elements* are a series of appositives and that *elements* is not part of the series.

When typing a dash, use two hyphens with no space beside or between them.

Parentheses are used to set off nonrestrictive parenthetical information, explanation, or comment that is incidental to the main thought of a sentence. Parentheses used instead of dashes downplay the importance of the information, whereas dashes emphasize it. Parentheses are also used to enclose numerals or letters that label items listed within a sentence.

PARENTHETICAL INFORMATION	The Cathedral Church of St. John the Divine will take a great deal of money ($21 million) and thirty years to finish.
NUMBERED OR LETTERED ITEMS	Other modern cathedrals built according to medieval architectural styles are (1) St. Patrick's Cathedral in New York City, (2) the National Cathedral in Washington, D.C., and (3) the Anglican cathedral in Liverpool, England.

EXERCISE 34, COLONS, DASHES, AND PARENTHESES   (22-23)

Insert carets at the points in the following sentences where dashes or colons are required. Then write the dashes or colons above the line.

Example   He went to work for many reasons ∧ not for money alone.

1. She always had many hobbies art, music, sports, drama.

2. They seemed unrelated pursuits completely separate areas of her life until she studied recreation.

3. Financial considerations a lack of money made it necessary to return to work.

4. My friend has worked with a variety of groups businesspeople, schools, churches, and civic organizations.

5. Most but not all areas of specialization in recreation involve physical activity.

6. A bachelor's degree it must be in recreation is a prerequisite for professional positions in parks and recreation.

7. A master's degree may be required for the following types of jobs administrative positions, college teaching, and university teaching.

8. With an associate degree, many people prefer the two-year course a person may go to work immediately as a recreation leader.

9. Some new fields are emerging therapeutic recreation, special population recreation, and commercial recreation.

10. Without a specialization there may be little demand for your services there are too many general recreation and supervision workers already.

11. Many factors point, however, to great growth in the field increased leisure and incomes, earlier retirements, larger populations.

12. An increased interest in physical fitness this factor seems the most important to me.

13. Two decades ago, only a select few usually the very affluent skied at all.

14. Needle-craft once was associated with a small, select group grandmothers.

15. Now skiing is big business thousands of people crowd into high-priced classes.

16. Each new interest creates new jobs recreation leaders, teachers, and administrators.

17. Recreation jobs are located in many institutions camps, playgrounds, community centers, churches, industry, military bases and may be pursued full-time or part-time.

18. Hospitals, correctional institutions, and voluntary agencies these too employ recreation specialists.

19. Recreation specialists must be able to work flexible hours the job extends to days, nights, and weekends.

20. The ill, handicapped, or disabled these are the special populations served by the recreation therapist.

Insert carets at the points in the following sentences where dashes, colons, or parentheses are required. Then write the dashes, colons, or parentheses above the line.

Example   There were two applicants left $\wedge$ (out of ten $\wedge$) for our final choice.

21. The major youth agencies with voluntary support are these Scouts, YWCA, and YMCA.

22. Specific skills such as skills in sports, music, or crafts are often helpful.

23. Good judgment, creativity, and enthusiasm about recreational activities these are the qualities these agencies look for.

24. Only a few years ago 1978 there were 85,000 recreation specialists.

25. These are people who worked full time another 100,000 work part time.

26. Joseph B. Wolfe, M.D., says in *Recreation, Medine and the Humanities* "Many physicians prescribe forms of recreation for their patients."

27. And everyone knows this proverb "All work and no play makes Jack a dull boy."

28. Of course what we used to think was true only about Jack is now known to be true about Jill and the elderly and disabled, as well.

29. Some agencies for example, American Red Cross and USO provide recreation services for military personnel.

35

SUPERFLUOUS INTERNAL PUNCTUATION   (24)

If you have not provided enough internal punctuation to guide your readers, they may have to go over your sentences several times to understand the meaning. But too many internal punctuation marks can be just as confusing. If punctuation is inserted where it is not necessary, or if it separates words that belong together, readers will have to struggle to untangle your message. Punctuation should aid meaning, not detract from it. The guidelines below discuss some common instances of superfluous (unnecessary) internal punctuation.

1. Do not separate a single or final adjective from a noun.

INCORRECT	A snazzy, good-looking, suede, jacket
CORRECT	A snazzy, good-looking, suede jacket

2. Do not separate a subject from a verb unless there are intervening words that require punctuation.

INCORRECT	Men's fashions, receive too little attention.
CORRECT	Men's fashions receive too little attention.
	Men's fashions, unlike women's fashions, receive too little attention.

3. Do not separate a verb from a complement or an object unless there are intervening words that require punctuation.

INCORRECT	Women can buy, dozens of fashion magazines.
CORRECT	Women can buy dozens of fashion magazines.
	Men, on the other hand, can buy only a few.

4. Do not separate two words or phrases that are joined by a coordinating conjunction. It is true that a comma is used to separate independent clauses joined by a coordinating conjunction. However, if constructions other than independent clauses are involved, a comma does not precede the coordinating conjunction.

INCORRECT	Jon is a fashion retailing major, and works part time at a men's store.
CORRECT	Jon is a fashion retailing major and works part time at a men's store.

5. It is not necessary to separate an introductory word, brief phrase, or short clause unless such a separation is necessary for clarity or emphasis.

CORRECT	In my opinion, he has an excellent eye for style.
OR	In my opinion he has an excellent eye for style.
CORRECT	In short, pants and jackets he selects always look good together. [The comma is necessary after *In short* to prevent a momentary misreading.]

6. Do not separate a restrictive modifier from the main part of a sentence. (See Section 31.)

181

INCORRECT	Anyone, who likes clothes, might consider fashion retailing.
CORRECT	Anyone who likes clothes might consider fashion retailing.

7. Do not separate (a) indirect quotations or (b) single words or short phrases in quotation marks from the rest of the sentence.

INCORRECT	Jon said, he was taking a tailoring class.
CORRECT	Jon said he was taking a tailoring class.
INCORRECT	The blazer he made was voted, "best student project."
CORRECT	The blazer he made was voted "best student project."

8. Do not separate a preposition from its object with a comma.

INCORRECT	The tailoring class taught him about, the correct cut and fit of men's clothes.
CORRECT	The tailoring class taught him about the correct cut and fit of men's clothes.

9. Do not use a semicolon to separate a main clause from a subordinate clause, a phrase from a clause, or other parts of unequal grammatical rank.

INCORRECT	He did quite well; although he had never sewn before.
CORRECT	He did quite well although he had never sewn before.
INCORRECT	Jon chose retailing for his major; specializing in men's clothing.
CORRECT	Jon chose retailing for his major, specializing in men's clothing.
	Jon chose retailing for his major; he has specialized in men's clothing. [Equal rank: two main clauses.]

10. Do not use a semicolon before a direct quotation or before a list.

INCORRECT	He says; "Unfortunately, too many men ignore their clothes."
CORRECT	He says, "Unfortunately, too many men ignore their clothes."
INCORRECT	Fashion sense has rewards; improved self-esteem and a more successful image.
CORRECT	Fashion sense has rewards: improved self-esteem and a more successful image.

11. Do not use a colon between a verb and its object or complement or between a preposition and its object—even if the objects or complements are in series (see also Section 34).

INCORRECT	Publications featuring men's fashions include: *Dress for Success, Gentlemen's Quarterly,* and *Playboy.*
CORRECT	Publications featuring men's fashions include *Dress for Success, Gentlemen's Quarterly,* and *Playboy.*
INCORRECT	A well-dressed look results from: quality fabrics, good styling, and a careful fit.
CORRECT	A well-dressed look results from quality fabrics, good styling, and a careful fit.

182

EXERCISE 35, SUPERFLUOUS INTERNAL PUNCTUATION

Write out each of the following sentences, correcting any superfluous internal punctuation. If a sentence is correctly punctuated, write *Correct* in the blank.

Example   Retailing is, the transfer of goods.

Retailing is the transfer of goods.

1.   Retailing is the second, largest industry in the United States.

_____

2.   Seventy percent, of Americans' disposable income is spent on retail goods.

_____

3.   Disposable income is your income, after taxes.

_____

4.   In the United States, retail sales are worth over $350 billion annually.

_____

5.   Many experts say, that women find retailing a wide-open field.

_____

6.   Almost 60 percent, of the people working in the retail field, are women.

_____

7.   Forty percent of the executives in retailing are: women.

_____

8.   Half the buyers, in department stores are women.

_____

9.   Thousands of new retailing jobs are being created; because retail stores are moving to suburbs.

_____

10.   There is a higher percentage of executive positions in retailing, than in other fields.

_____

11.   You may ask; "What do I know about retailing?"

_____

12. Well, you have bought things, and listened to advertisements.

_____

13. You probably know many product lines very well; clothes, food, cars, or the supplies for some special hobby.

_____

14. There are five, major, job categories in retailing.

_____

15. Merchandising has, traditionally been the entry field for most people.

_____

16. The two vital functions of merchandising are; sales and buying.

_____

17. Buyers earn very good salaries, and deserve them.

_____

18. Buying requires, taste, timing, business sense, and a knowledge of the competition.

_____

19. Sales positions are excellent training for people, who move into top positions.

_____

20. Selling gives, a new worker a great deal of experience in a short time.

_____

21. Another key job in merchandising is, that of the fashion coordinator.

_____

22. Fashion coordinators see that the, "fashion style and tone" of the store is consistent.

_____

23. Other retailing job categories, include, promotion, personnel, finance, and store operations.

_____

24. Most large stores have their own promotion department rather than an outside ad agency; since their volume of advertising is so high.

_____

25. Store operations is composed of: stocking and warehouse operations, deliveries, and customer services.

_____

36

INTERNAL PUNCTUATION REVIEW I   (20-24)

Insert correct internal punctuation marks where they are needed in the sentences below.

Example   Art , fashion , or business courses are helpful in a fashion career.

1.   If you're interested in fashion you may find that your first job is a clerk's position.

2.   Although Los Angeles has a large fashion industry New York is still the center of the industry in America.

3.   Over 1000000 workers are employed in the clothing business most of them in New York New York.

4.   Fashion is a glamorous career but it is a very competitive career.

5.   Some of the top jobs in the field are the following fashion editor fashion designer publicity manager fashion illustrator and merchandising manager.

6.   A publicity manager may be employed by a major department store these positions are generally available only in larger cities.

7.   These key people plan fashion shows including fittings booking of models invitations and sometimes publicity.

8.   They often are responsible for arranging parties and they often do a lot of business entertainment sometimes at home.

9.   Retailing experience is an exceptionally good background almost a required background for a fashion career.

10.   There are of course many management positions available in an industry this large.

11.   Some of the jobs that you may not immediately think of as fashion careers are plant manager executive assistant time study analyst all the jobs associated with manufacturing.

12. Many large stores and large companies have advertising departments which offer much the same opportunities as independent advertising agencies.

13. However fashion writers and editors must know their field and the field of fashion thoroughly.

14. Salaries in this field are high but entry-level salaries generally are low.

15. For fashion designers as for any other artist the road to recognition can be long and tortuous.

16. Designers who must create the demand for their work must expect to work in one of the centers of fashion.

17. For serious designers the places to be are Paris Milan California and New York.

18. Galanos the American designer happily admits that a dress from Sears may be a better value than one of his.

19. To persuade people to buy a dress for $700 or $2000 takes real merchandising expertise.

20. Associating the designer's name with prestige and status the public is willing to pay the price asked.

21. As in any field of art investment or collecting rarity and exclusivity cost more money.

22. Slightly lower in prestige than the exclusive designers are the designers of ready-to-wear lines often referred to as "Seventh Avenue Design."

23. Exclusive designers design one dress for one customer Seventh Avenue designers design one piece that is reproduced thousands of times.

24. Representatives of the fashion world travel regularly to Paris where they see the latest designs of the most exclusive designers.

25. Twice a year the "high fashion" design houses in Paris show their new designs.

26. At one time it was assumed that whatever was shown in Paris was that season's fashion.

27. Now most people even the very rich ignore these designs except for an occasional purchase.

37

INTERNAL PUNCTUATION REVIEW II   (20-24)

Expand the following core sentences, adding the constructions that are indicated in parentheses. Be sure to use correct internal punctuation.

Example   The men reacted angrily.

(beginning participial phrase) *Seeing the ruined shipment, the men reacted angrily.*

(nonrestrictive appositive) *The men, all shippers, reacted angrily.*

(a brief introductory phrase) *Only last week, the men reacted angrily.*

(two independent clauses) *The men reacted angrily, but no one noticed.*

1.   The lecture had begun.

(appositive) _____

(items in series) _____

(two independent clauses) _____

(coordinating conjunction) _____

2.   The farmers hoped for a good year.

(subordinate clause) _____

(beginning participial phrase) _____

(nonrestrictive element) _____

(interrupting expression) _____

3.   The officers of the club met.

(expressions in series requiring commas) _____

(expressions in series requiring semicolons) _____

(a date and an address) _____

(short final summary) _____

4. He was a man for all seasons.

(long introductory expression) _____

(nonrestrictive modifier) _____

(long final appositive) _____

(two independent clauses) _____

5. The train rounded the curve.

(restrictive modifier) _____

(abrupt interruption of the sentence) _____

(items in series requiring no punctuation within items) _____

6. I graduate in June.

(beginning participial phrase) _____

(brief introductory phrase) _____

(two independent clauses) _____

7. He seems to be making progress.

(a date) _____

(long introductory expression) _____

(an appositive) _____

8. Margaret is an electrician.

(two independent clauses) _____

(coordinating conjunction) _____

(subordinate clause) _____

9. This car isn't expensive.

(nonrestrictive modifier) _____

(subordinate clause) _____

(two independent clauses) _____

(items in series requiring no punctuation within items) _____

(items in series requiring punctuation with semicolons) _____

38

QUOTATION MARKS, BRACKETS, AND ELLIPSIS MARKS   (25-26)

Quotation marks signal to the reader that you are writing someone else's words rather than your own. If you decide to insert your own words within a quotation, those words are set off with brackets to let the reader know they are not part of the original, quoted material. If you omit any of the quoted words, ellipsis marks are used to indicate the omission. These three types of punctuation marks enable the reader to distinguish between your words and those of another source.

Double quotation marks are used to enclose a direct quotation from either a written or a spoken source. Commas or periods that occur at the end of the quoted matter always are placed within the quotation marks. Colons and semicolons are always placed outside, after the quotation marks.

> She answered very shortly, "I don't want to."
> The boys' leader replied: "The driver of the yellow car was driving recklessly," and the others in the group agreed with him.
> He answered very shortly, "I don't want to"; this was not the answer we had expected.
> She said, "There are several reasons for my actions": one was that she was tired, a second was that she was bored, and a third was that she didn't play tennis.

A dash, question mark, or exclamation point belongs inside the quotation marks when it applies only to the quotation; it is placed outside the quotation marks when it applies to the entire statement.

> She asked, "When may I see you again?"
> Did she say, "I'll probably see you again"?

A comma is used to separate an opening quotation from the rest of the sentence unless the quotation ends in an exclamation point or a question mark.

> "This is the book I'm looking for," he said.
> "Drat it!" he roared.
> "When do we leave?" she asked.

When a quotation is broken to designate the speaker, a comma should be used after the first part of the quotation. The quotation following the interrupting construction should be punctuated as would any phrase or clause.

> "I don't believe," said Mr. Wicket, "that I understand you."
> "I don't believe it," said Mr. Wicket. "There are too many reasons why it can't be true."
> "I don't believe it," said Mr. Wicket; "you really can't mean it."

Although a comma ordinarily follows the designation of the speaker, as the foregoing examples show, the comma may be omitted if the quotation is grammatically closely related. When the quotation is fairly long or formally introduced, a colon may precede it.

CLOSELY RELATED: NO PUNCTUATION	He growled "Now you just wait a minute" and barred the door.
	I remember the words "Four score and seven years ago," but I can't remember the rest of the speech.
FORMAL INTRODUCTION: COLON	My mother's disciplinary lectures always began: "When I was your age, I had funny notions, too. But I outgrew them."

189

Quotation marks are used to set off poems and song titles and also to indicate titles of articles, short stories, and parts of longer works.

"The Death of the Hired Man" is one of Robert Frost's best poems.
Glenn Miller's theme song was "Moonlight Serenade."

Quotation marks can be used to set off words used in a special sense, but do not use them around common nicknames, slang, colloquialisms, trite expressions, or for emphasis or apology. If a word is appropriate, it will stand on its own.

	This is what I call a "foppish" metaphor.
	"Silly" means "stupid" or "foolish," according to the dictionary.
BUT NOT	In these supposedly "modern" times, I feel "out of it."

When words ordinarily placed within quotation marks appear within another quotation, use single quotation marks to set them off. Single quotation marks should never be used for anything but a quotation within a quotation.

	She told the class, "Please read 'The Tell-Tale Heart' for Monday."
BUT NOT	I said, 'Where did you put my notebook?'

A prose quotation more than four lines long should be displayed—that is, set off from your own words and each line indented from the left margin. A displayed quotation does not take quotation marks at its opening and close; setting it off serves to signal the reader that it is a quotation. If quotation marks occur within material you intend to use as a displayed quotation, include them as they appear in the original material.

As Hayes says in *The Crane Papers:*
> Part of the distinctly American tradition is a belief in the New World. America was the land fondly dreamed of as the New Eden, a second chance for men and women to begin again on virgin shores. They could build a new civilization—and this time do it right. It is this tradition that the poet Hart Crane inherits and expounds in his poem "The Bridge."[4]

Quoted poetry and song lyrics should be enclosed in quotation marks and run into the text if three or fewer lines are being quoted. Indicate the end of a run-in line of poetry with a slash mark (/).

Crane is sure unity is possible. He writes, "The stars have grooved our eyes with old persuasions / O, upward from the dead."

If you are quoting more than three lines of poetry, they should be displayed. Like displayed quotations of prose, displayed quotations of poetry do not take quotation marks at opening and close unless they occur in the original. Displayed lines of poetry are not run on and consequently do not need slash marks.

Brackets are used to set off editorial remarks in quoted material and to enclose *sic* ("thus it is") to indicate that a mistake in a quotation is that of the original writer and not that of the quoter.

"He [Tennyson] was poet laureate of England for several years."
The dispatch continued: "It was a climatic [*sic*] battle. The end is near."

Ellipsis marks (three spaced periods) show you have deliberately omitted a word or words from the material you are quoting. If you omit words at the end of a quotation, use four periods: the first is the usual sentence period, and the last three are the ellipses. The closing quotation mark encloses all the periods.

"Part of the distinctly American tradition is a belief in the New World. America was . . . the New Eden . . . a second chance to begin again. . . . "

EXERCISE 38-1, QUOTATION MARKS   (25)

Rewrite the following indirect quotations as direct quotations.

Example   Monica said that she was sorry about the yard.

Monica said, "I am sorry about the yard."

1. The client declared that he could not make up his mind about buying the Mills property.

    _____

2. She yelled angrily that she wouldn't do it.

    _____

3. He asked the salesman what the price of the property was.

    _____

4. [Make a split quotation out of the following.] She said it seemed to her that they had no real reason to complain.

    _____

5. Did she ask when he was coming to Maine again?

    _____

6. He said that the clients had postponed the date until tomorrow.

    _____

7. [Make a split quotation out of the following.] Grandfather said that when he was a boy they didn't have the conveniences we have today.

    _____

8. The owner answered very quickly that we should tell the salesman.

    _____

9. [Make a split quotation out of the following.] Sue said that she had thought it over and the house on Laurel Lane was her favorite.

    _____

10. The owners asked the sales force what the prospects were for profits the next year.

    _____

Rewrite the following sentences to punctuate each correctly. In addition to other changes, be sure to capitalize where necessary.

Example   Do you know what I think she asked I think you are crazy.

"Do you know what I think?" she asked. "I think you are crazy."

11. Houses said Margo are getting smaller all the time.

_____

12. One of my favorite poems is Geography of the House by W. H. Auden.

_____

13. He asked them three times are you ready to sell?

_____

14. The editorial read as follows the present board of realtors is wrong in doing away with competive sic bidding.

_____

15. During the season he said I never got to bed before midnight.

_____

16. Did you hear him say I'm not going to do it asked Jan.

_____

17. One of Woody Guthrie's most famous songs is This Land Is Your Land.

_____

18. I asked Rick do you have any smaller houses listed.

_____

19. None he said that you would be interested in.

_____

20. We'll go out again tomorrow Rick promised.

_____

EXERCISE 38-2, QUOTATION MARKS, BRACKETS, AND ELLIPSIS
MARKS   (25–26)

Punctuate the following sentences by inserting punctuation marks where they are necessary. Circle any letters that should be capitalized.

Example   " Where do you think you are going ? " the guard asked ,
"(t)his is private property. "

1.   We are on a field trip we explained to study real estate.

2.   This week we're studying the chapter How to Choose Your Best Buy in Lowry's *How You Can Become Financially Independent by Investing in Real Estate.*

3.   Our instructor quoted one authority as claiming there are over one and a half million licensed realtors.

4.   Mr. Buwell stated categorically no specific education is required to become a real-estate salesperson.

5.   Are you sure asked Vincent.

6.   The text I had read as follows correspondent sic courses are helpful.

7.   I know I said but no courses are required before taking the state license test.

8.   Adam Smith wrote the chapter entitled Why Houses Became More Than Houses in his book *Paper Money.*

9.   Our lecturer said authoritatively all salespeople hope to become brokers.

10.   A broker he explained is required to have more experience than a salesperson.

11.   I know brokers make more money but his idea seems overstated John maintained.

12.   The dictionary says the word realty means the same as the words real estate.

13.   I'm not interested in sales are there other jobs in real estate asked Susan.

14.   One saying that gives good advice is look before you leap another is he who hesitates is lost.

15.   Large realty companies he assured Susan hire appraisers and property managers.

16. He also remarked land development, leasing, and mortgage specialists are also in

demand.

17. A real-estate counselor Mr. Buwell said counsels clients on the best use of property.

18. But he continued counselors must have amassed years of experience.

19. Many people like the field Buwell said because they can work part time and work out

of their home office.

Using the nursery rhyme printed below, write two paragraphs. In the first paragraph show (1) how to quote three lines or less of poetry and (2) how to use ellipsis marks to show the omission of word(s) from a quotation. In the second paragraph, show (1) how to quote more than three lines of poetry and (2) how to insert editorial remarks into quoted material. For your editorial remark, you might want to indicate that St. Ives is an English town or that kits are kittens. (By the way, the answer to the riddle that the nursery rhyme poses is *not* 29.)

As I was going to St. Ives,
I met a man with seven wives.
Each wife had a sack,
Each sack had a cat,
Each cat had a kit.
Kits, cats, sacks, and wives—
How many were going to St. Ives?

(Paragraph 1) _____

_____

_____

_____

_____

_____

_____

(Paragraph 2) _____

_____

_____

_____

_____

39

ITALICS (27)

Word punctuation signals that a word has a special use or particular grammatical function. Italics, capitals, apostrophes, and hyphens are the punctuation marks used to signal special word uses and functions. For example, when you write a word with an apostrophe, you are signalling that the word is either a possessive form or a contraction because convention has led readers to recognize possessives and contractions by means of the apostrophe.

Italics are letters sloped to the right in print. In handwritten or typewritten manuscript, italics are indicated by underlining. This word punctuation is used for titles of books, newspapers, magazines and journals, and all works that are published separately—that is, not published as part of another work.

An item such as a short story, article, chapter, or poem that is published as part of a larger work is set off by quotation marks (see Section 38). For example, John Milton's lengthy poem about creation and the fall of Adam and Eve is punctuated *Paradise Lost* when it appears as a separate publication; it is punctuated "Paradise Lost" when it appears in the collection *John Milton: Complete Poems and Major Prose.*

Be sure to italicize the word *The* only if it is actually part of a specific title:

> *The New York Times*

BUT

> the *Reader's Digest*

The names of plays, movies, record albums, television or radio programs, and works of art, as well as the names of ships and aircraft, are italicized.

Hamlet	*Superman II*
Hill Street Blues	the *U.S.S. Nimitz*
Hard Day's Night	the *Concorde*

Italics are used to set off foreign words and expressions that have not yet been adopted into English. They are also used to indicate letters, words, and numbers used as words. Quotation marks are also used to set off words used in a special sense (Section 38), but if your subject requires you to refer to words as words frequently, italics are the more scholarly convention. Finally, italics can be used to give special stress to a word. However, don't overuse italics for stress or emphasis. Otherwise, your writing will seem shrill and sound immature.

He graduated *magna cum laude.*
I cannot distinguish your *n*'s from your *u*'s.
The word *empathy* does not mean the same as *sympathy.*
That was *her* suggestion, not mine.

EXERCISE 39, ITALICS   (27)

In the following sentences, indicate by underlining the words or expressions that should be italicized.

Example   The word <u>liberal</u>, as it is used in education, does not refer to politics.

1.   The Occupational Outlook Handbook projects future demand for careers.

2.   Time and Newsweek articles claim that the supply of humanities graduates exceeds demand.

3.   The word underemployment was created to describe their circumstances.

4.   If these students watch their p's and q's, they need not fear.

5.   A sine qua non of humanities study is writing and research.

6.   Exempli gratia, students of English read and write constantly.

7.   Despite despairing movies like Getting Straight and frightening articles in AAUP Bulletin, students continue to study the fascinating field.

8.   Sylvia Plath's novel The Bell Jar illustrates the disillusionment of the humanities student.

9.   However, as the author of What Color Is Your Parachute? says, these students have very marketable skills.

10.   The Prentice-Hall Workbook for Writers lists dozens of jobs for writers.

11.   If you simply know whether i goes before e, you have a skill employers will pay for.

12.   Realizing you have skills makes you feel as if you rolled a 4 and a 3.

13.   A familiarity with Chicago Manual of Style is worth thousands of dollars in publishing.

14.   There are hundreds of positions listed in Dictionary of Occupational Titles that require writing ability.

15.   Do you think a show like 60 Minutes just appears without someone writing it first?

16.   Anyone who has read and understood Paradise Lost or The Faerie Queene can work easily with technical prose.

17.   College English listed many nontraditional teaching jobs in one issue.

18.   Editors on Editing, Words Into Type, and The Complete Guide to Editorial Freelancing should be read by every English major.

19.   I think that Jobs for Writers, published by Writer's Digest Books, is even more interesting and useful.

20.   Aside From Teaching English, What in the World Can You Do? by Dorothy K. Bestor should be read by English majors early in their education.

Write sentences including the information called for in parentheses. Be sure to use correct word punctuation.

Example   (word used as word; letter used as word)

Is the e always capitalized in English?

21. (title of magazine and title of magazine article)

_____

22. (title of work of art and word punctuated for emphasis)

_____

23. (title of book and title of short story or poem)

_____

24. (title of movie, television program, or play)

_____

25. (foreign expression or word used as word)

_____

26. (title of record album)

_____

27. (name of ship or aircraft)

_____

28. (title of newspaper)

_____

29. (letter or number used as word)

_____

30. (word punctuated for emphasis)

_____

40

CAPITALS (28)

A century or more ago, writers commonly capitalized almost all nouns. Today conventions governing capitalization have changed so that we capitalize only proper nouns, their derivatives and abbreviations, and common nouns used as part of proper nouns. A proper noun is one that names a particular person, place, or thing rather than a general category: *Chrysler* versus *car*.

We also always capitalize the first word of a sentence or a line of poetry as well as the pronoun *I* and the interjection *O*.

The following guidelines illustrate uses of capitals for categories of proper nouns.

1. Specific persons, races, nationalities, languages, ethnic or religious groups.

Robert	African	Chicanos	Moslems
Liz G. Brown	Cuban	Quakers	Chinese

2. Specific places.

Miami	Iceland	Rockefeller Center	Saturn
Delaware	Lake Michigan	Nile River	U.S.S.R.

3. Specific organizations (including widely used abbreviations), historical events, and documents.

Knights of Columbus	Declaration of Independence	NAACP
World War II	Cleveland Symphony Orchestra	Gray Panthers

4. Days of the week, months, holidays.

Monday	Christmas	Ramadan
May	Passover	Memorial Day

5. Sacred religious terms.

the Virgin Mary	Allah	the Torah
the Saviour	the Creation	Mass

6. Titles of books, plays, magazines, newspapers, articles, and poems. Capitalize the first word and all other words except articles, conjunctions, and prepositions of fewer than five letters.

Mutiny on the Bounty	*Newsweek*	*The Wall Street Journal*
Fiddler on the Roof	*King Lear*	*Ms.*

7. Titles when they precede a proper noun.

President Reagan	Mr. John Doe	the Reverend Paul Mills
General Bradley	Dr. Hilda Vail	Treasurer Jean Ritchie

8. Common nouns used as part of a proper name.

Fifth Street	Yale University	First National Bank
Atlantic Ocean	Shedd Aquarium	Exxon Corporation

Avoid unnecessary capitalization. The following items are usually *not* capitalized:

1. Directions. *North, east, south,* and *west* are capitalized only when they occur at the beginning of a sentence or when they refer to specific geographical locations.

He drove south for ten miles.	the Middle East
He liked the Deep South.	the northern states

2. Seasons. *Fall, autumn, winter, spring,* and *summer* are not capitalized.

3. Family relationships. Capitalize nouns indicating family relationships only when they are used as names or titles or in combination with proper names.

I hoped to hear from Mother soon.
I have great regard for my mother.
My sister Harriett is a lawyer.
I received a letter from Uncle Carl.

4. Common nouns and adjectives used in place of proper nouns and adjectives.

	He graduated from high school.
BUT	He graduated from Cedar Falls High School.
	He traveled by car.
BUT	He traveled by Delta Air Lines.
	She enjoyed sociology and statistics.
BUT	She registered for Sociology 235 and Mathematics 201, Statistical Analysis.

Sometimes it is difficult to decide whether a word is a proper noun or a common noun. For example, if you write *The wedding was held at a Lutheran church,* should *church* be capitalized or not? In this case, no, it should not be capitalized. However, if you write *The wedding was held at Trinity Lutheran Church,* you need to capitalize *church.* In the first instance, the word *church* is a general term (common noun) rather than part of the name or "title" of a specific church (proper noun), as is the case in the second instance. It may help you to think of proper nouns as being like formal titles or given names.

One indicator to help you decide whether or not to capitalize is the article used with a word. If the article is *a* or *an,* the word is probably a common noun: *a board of directors.* Sometimes, but by no means always, the article *the* will indicate that a word is a proper noun: *the Board of Directors of General Motors.* Your best bet is to determine if a word belongs to a collective category or if it refers to a "titled" person, place, or thing.

A second issue is whether or not to capitalize nouns that refer to and are the same as proper nouns: for example, *The Mulberry City Council met Tuesday, and the council voted to deny the rezoning request.* When the complete title of a person, place, or thing is not used, ordinarily the repeated words are treated as common nouns (as in category 4 under "Unnecessary Capitalization" above). Sometimes, however, the shortened form of a proper noun will be capitalized to signify respect, as in *The Reverend Joseph West will deliver Sunday's sermon; the Reverend is a well-known clergyman.* Of course titles shortened to just proper names are always capitalized: *Visit Custom Upholstery Company for your upholstery needs because Custom guarantees satisfaction,* not *. . . because custom guarantees satisfaction.* The following sentences provide further illustrations of capitalization.

Having traveled by Delta Air Lines, he said the airline's staff was courteous and Delta flights are usually on time.
My favorite lake is Lake Louise.
The school board president attended a meeting of the National Association of Public School Boards.
Columbiana County is a county in eastern Ohio.

EXERCISE 40, CAPITALS   (28)

Rewrite the following sentences, correcting all errors in capitalization.

Example   He is a graduate of brown university.

He is a graduate of Brown University.

1.   He could not decide whether to major in french, spanish, or russian history.

   _____

2.   Historians who want to teach in high schools develop specialties in such areas as world history or asian, african, or latin american culture.

   _____

3.   Courses in chicano or indian studies are becoming common in high schools.

   _____

4.   Information on these jobs can be found at local school boards or at the united states employment service office closest to you.

   _____

5.   The american history association publishes the *employment information bulletin,* which lists available teaching jobs in colleges and universities.

   _____

6.   In fact, many historians are employed on wall street.

   _____

7.   Anyone who can research facts on the history of the south can research a business problem.

   _____

8.   All it takes is exchanging history texts for books like lorna daniell's *business reference sources.*

   _____

9.   The sunday *new york times* and tuesday's *wall street journal* carry ads for these sorts of jobs.

   _____

10.   The society of american archivists says historians hold many interesting positions in city museums, libraries, or archives.

   _____

11. One seminar in historical administration is held at williamsburg, virginia, every summer.

_____

12. Many internships, such as the ones at the institute of applied history in raleigh, north carolina, focus exclusively on historical administration.

_____

13. Other historians become archives technicians or archivists.

_____

14. Jack said he had worked with the manuscript collection of robert graves, the british poet.

_____

15. The horace walpole manuscripts are at yale, where several historians work in the archives and manuscripts collections.

_____

16. State, national, and local historical societies hire historians to edit the papers of historical figures like george washington, jane addams, henry laurens, or joseph henry.

_____

17. Local historical societies are particularly active in the northeast and in the south.

_____

18. The national historic preservation act of 1966 committed the federal government to the preservation of historic buildings and areas.

_____

19. As a result, agencies like the department of housing and urban development and many others hire historians to research the histories of local landmarks.

_____

20. In fact, as of july 1976, there were very few government agencies that were not planning to hire historians.

_____

41

APOSTROPHES AND HYPHENS   (29-30)

Apostrophes have three basic uses: (1) to show possession; (2) to indicate a contraction; and (3) to indicate the plural form of letters, numbers, and words used as words.

An apostrophe signals the possessive case of nouns and indefinite pronouns. The following guidelines illustrate its use in forming the possessive case.

1. Words not ending in *s* add an apostrophe and *s* to form the possessive.

    the man's suitcase   the women's suitcases

2. Singular words ending in *s* add an apostrophe and *s* unless the second *s* makes pronunciation difficult.

    James's bike   Euripides' plays

3. Plural words ending in *s* add only the apostrophe.

    the dogs' food   the babies' shoes   the Browns' mailbox

4. With compounds, only the last word is made possessive.

    my father-in-law's chair   someone else's locker

5. With nouns of joint possession, only the last noun is made possessive.

    George and John's bedroom

6. With nouns of individual possession, both nouns are made possessives.

    Beth's and Bart's swimsuits

Do not use an apostrophe with the possessive form of personal pronouns *his, hers, its, ours, your, theirs,* and *whose.*

An apostrophe indicates the omission of a letter or number.

    you are   you're
    cannot   can't
    it is   it's
    would not   wouldn't
    of the clock   o'clock
    class of 1978   class of '78

An apostrophe is also used to form the plurals of letters, numbers, and words used as words. Note that these are the *only* instances in which apostrophes are used in forming plurals. Apostrophes are *never* used to form the plurals of proper names or other nouns.

    Mind your *p*'s and *q*'s.
    The *'30*'s were called the Jazz Age.
    Don't put too many *and*'s in one sentence.

The **hyphen** has two different uses. It is used to indicate that a word is continued from one line to the next (see "Syllabication" in Section 27), and it is used to punctuate compound words. The following guidelines give the conventions for using hyphens in compound words.

1. To form compound words that are not accepted as single words. Since there is no general rule that can be applied to such compounds, the best way to determine whether a compound word is hyphenated is to consult the dictionary.

2. To join two or more words serving as a single adjective before a noun.

a well-liked person   an ill-fitting suit

Omit the hyphen when the first word is an adverb ending in *-ly*.

a rapidly fired pistol   a slowly sinking ship

Do not hyphenate adjectives that follow the verb as predicate adjectives.

	They were well-known actors.
BUT	The actors were well known.

3. To avoid an awkward union of letters such as *bell-like*.

4. To form compound numbers from twenty-one through ninety-nine and to designate spelled-out fractions.

twenty-two   three-fourths

5. In conjunction with prefixes *self-*, *all-*, and *ex-*, and the suffix *-elect*.

self-confidence	all-important	ex-President Carter
vice president-elect	Governor-elect Orr	ex-champion

EXERCISE 41-1, APOSTROPHES   (29)

In the blanks, write the singular possessive for the following nouns.

Example   duchess   *duchess's*

1. Jane   _____   2. Arkansas   _____

3. Ross   _____   4. John   _____

5. someone   _____   6. anyone   _____

7. Congress   _____   8. Lois   _____

9. Moses   _____   10. Sophocles   _____

In the appropriate blanks, write the singular possessives and the plural possessives for the following nouns.

		SINGULAR	PLURAL
Example	bus	*bus's*	*buses'*
1.	class	_____	_____
2.	dog	_____	_____
3.	money	_____	_____
4.	brother-in-law	_____	_____
5.	car	_____	_____
6.	waitress	_____	_____
7.	duck	_____	_____
8.	night	_____	_____
9.	sheep	_____	_____
10.	jazz	_____	_____
11.	secretary	_____	_____
12.	monkey	_____	_____
13.	pie	_____	_____

	SINGULAR	PLURAL
14. *wife*	_____	_____
15. *day*	_____	_____
16. *woman*	_____	_____
17. *city*	_____	_____
18. *record*	_____	_____
19. *Jones*	_____	_____
20. *comrade*	_____	_____
21. *church*	_____	_____
22. *wreck*	_____	_____
23. *model*	_____	_____
24. *heroine*	_____	_____
25. *baby*	_____	_____
26. *match*	_____	_____
27. *treasurer*	_____	_____
28. *chief*	_____	_____
29. *lady*	_____	_____
30. *man*	_____	_____

Form the correct contractions for the following words.

Example   *was not*   _____*wasn't*_____

1. *I will*	_____	2. *they are*	_____
3. *do not*	_____	4. *I am*	_____
5. *were not*	_____	6. *you are*	_____
7. *it is*	_____	8. *they will*	_____
9. *we have*	_____	10. *who is*	_____

EXERCISE 41-2, APOSTROPHES AND HYPHENS (29-30)

Insert apostrophes, *'s,* and hyphens where they are needed in the following sentences.

Example   My roommate's sister is a psychologist.

1. A well informed graduate should check the projected growth rate for jobs in his or her major.
2. Psychologys growth rate was 45 percent for the years between 1974 and 1985.
3. Lois brother is attending law school now after majoring in psychology.
4. Many medical schools admissions officers look for applicants with backgrounds in psychology.
5. Our schools counselor says psychology is a good background for any professional school.
6. Its not rare for ones internship to lead to a permanent job.
7. Is this really such a half baked idea?
8. Our mothers in laws views are not compatible.
9. Smith and Haskins Department Store personnel are, many of them, trained in psychology.
10. One of the best internships available is at Doctors [*plural*] Hospital.
11. Interns, graded for clinical work, may see scales of *0*s to *4*s or *A*s to *F*s.
12. St. Josephs Hospital has an innovative hospice program that offers a good internship.
13. The largest number of interns is placed at Veterans [*plural*] Hospital.
14. A psychology majors detailed knowledge of the minds workings is useful in sales.
15. In 1981, *U. S. News and World Report* called psychology the "in" profession of the 80s.
16. A masters degree in psychology opens up professional psychological positions.
17. Dont just say, "Id like to major in psychology."
18. Self employed psychologists earn very substantial incomes.
19. A clinical psychologists time is spent testing patients, scoring the tests, interviewing patients, and discussing the tests results with other professionals.
20. In mental health centers, psychologists time may be split between group therapy classes and conferences.
21. I really didn't think Id enjoy the conferences, but I did.
22. Many successful psychologists say a vague interest in helping people wasnt enough.

23. Psychology isnt only helping people; experimental psychology, for example, may not even involve human subjects.

24. In fact, the American Psychological Associations rules recognize twenty nine specialties.

25. A developmental psychologist studies childrens behavioral growth.

26. Industrial psychologists attempt to solve industrial problems and improve workers morale.

27. Engineering psychology is the field that redesigns industries machines and environments to better suit workers.

28. The colleges pride and joy is its well conceived and effectively administered psychology major program.

29. The long range planning you have done will pay off in the end.

30. Can I get a psychology degree while attending school part time?

42

PUNCTUATION REVIEW   (19-30)

Revise the following sentences, providing necessary end, internal, and word punctuation.

Example   Americans are some people claim the most mobile people on the Earth

Americans are, some people claim, the most mobile people on the Earth.

1. Americans change homes change jobs and even change their careers in ever larger numbers

_____

2. Americans move an average of thirteen times in a lifetime Americans switch jobs an average of ten times per lifetime

_____

3. The modern migration to the cities has stopped and people are returning to rural areas

_____

4. For 150 years or more people went to urban areas to find jobs

_____

5. Engineers salesmen and teachers are switching jobs in order to migrate to smaller towns which offer a less hectic mode of living

_____

6. I wonder whether mobility later retirement ages and the urge for change havent caused millions of americans to begin second careers

_____

7. Adele scheeles book skills for success explains the process of starting a second career

_____

8. Richard Bolles he wrote what color is your parachute gives lectures and seminars on career changes

_____

9. John Holland creator of the Holland theory of careers maintains this the most efficient way to predict vocational choice is simply to ask the person what he wants to be

_____

10. Most of the theories and books about career change even Hollands and Bolless are methods of helping people discover their own hopes

_____

11. Modern workers invented the word burnout to describe extreme disenchantment with ones job

_____

12. Nowadays according to some skeptics anyone who finds himself or herself leaving *i*s undotted and *t*s uncrossed claims burnout is at fault

_____

13. Dont you agree that either stress or boredom can certainly cause ones interest in a job to burn out

_____

14. Probably the best cure for burnout which can even lead to physical ailments is a change of job or scenery.

_____

15. If you find yourself sitting at your desk and fantasizing about becoming a lumberjack or opening a restaurant perhaps it is time to think about a second career

_____

16. Before you run off to farm twenty acres of organic turnips make some inquiries about the location youre considering

_____

17. Cant the chamber of commerce give you information about taxes utility costs and the local economy

_____

18. The books burnout and beyond burnout can help you distinguish between real psychological symptoms and mere boredom

_____

19. Self evaluation says one author is probably the most frustrating thing you can do

_____

20. The national institute for work and learning which is located at 1211 Connecticut Avenue Washington D C publishes a directory of career change seminars

_____

21. If you can arrange to do some work in the field youre considering try working part time at it for a while

_____

22. One very handy reference Places Rated Almanac rates cities by climate housing crime rates economic conditions and transportation systems

_____

23. This book claims that atlanta is the best city in america the authors claim its good points outweigh its bad points

_____

24. Local banks often provide newcomers kits wonderful sources of information about a city and its people

_____

25. Some of the most authoritative information sources are the following the census bureau the bureau of labor statistics and the commerce departments bureau of economic analysis

_____

26. Book of the states which is a reference work found in almost all libraries lists the tax rates of each state and county

_____

27. Above all visit a city or region before you move there

_____

28. Talk with people read local newspapers and walk through neighborhoods before making up your mind

_____

29. Things havent really changed a great deal daniel boone probably did a lot of planning before deciding to move to Kentucky

_____

30. Switching jobs may be an appealing idea but it can backfire if it isnt well planned

_____

Insert punctuation where it is needed in the following sentences. (Use a pen or pencil that writes in a color other than black.)

31. Many people particularly owners of businesses and people with families stayed on in

    Nome

32. Even today Nome is still struggling with the problems caused by its history as a "boom town"

33. The town which is located just south of the Arctic Circle is hoping to attract tourists who want to ski fish or hunt and city officials hope tourists will find Nome's history fascinating

34. Obviously modern cities with diversified economic bases can control these cycles in better fashion

35. The lesson you should learn from this is that moving simply to be located in a "boom" area is probably unwise

36. Unless you're among the first arrivals life in a "boom town" can be pretty miserable

37. And the cycle of "boom and bust" is still possible as the histories of some modern industries illustrates

38. A prudent well-prepared graduate should research the location of a company just as carefully as he or she researches the operation of the company

39. Many of the people served by these agencies are actually civilians the dependents of military personnel

40. To be a service club program recreation specialist you'll need a bachelor's degree major in recreation, physical education, music, art, or related areas

41. One interesting position is that of entertainment program recreation specialist a supervisor or director of base theatrical productions

42. I recommend this field it allows you to pursue your different interests

43. It takes only four years or even less to prepare yourself

44. It takes two characteristics to enjoy this kind of work one must enjoy working with people and enjoy creating programs where none existed before

45. The principle of a sensible basic wardrobe that evolves as pieces are added is now widely accepted even by designers

43

THE WRITING PROCESS   (31)

Sometimes when we have a writing assignment the words flow easily, and sometimes we spend hours before the blank sheets of paper, struggling to produce a few lines—filling the wastebasket with rejected efforts. All writers, including professionals, face dry spells; *Writer's Digest,* a magazine for free-lance writers, periodically features articles about how to overcome "writer's block."

Although the ultimate goal of every writer is to create a well-crafted, effective product—whether it be an essay, a poem, a newspaper article, or a memo to the boss—that product is the result of a process. The writing process is the method a writer uses to create his or her essay, poem, or memo. When writers talk about writer's block, they are talking about ways to get the process rolling so the words will flow successfully.

We all use some process, some mental system for producing writing. One method may be more successful for you than another. Many people find that they most easily become involved in a subject if they just begin to fill pages with ideas, everything they can think of concerning their subject. Then they go back and pick and choose, order and shape, revise and edit, until they are satisfied with the result. Other people do this sort of "brainstorming" mentally and do not put words on paper until they have a fairly clear notion of what the contents and structure of the finished piece will be. Some people edit their sentences as they write them—correcting and revising as they go. Other writers edit and revise only after they have completed a first draft.

There is no one "best" or "right" writing process. You should observe your own methods and use the ones that work best for you. If your own system doesn't seem to be working, try some tactics others have found successful. One student, for example, felt dissatisfied with the "stuffy tone that just isn't 'me'" in a job application letter she had written. At her teacher's suggestion, she visualized what the letter's recipient might be like. Although she had never met the personnel officer to whom she was writing, she discovered that when she thought about a real reader the tone of her letter became more forthright and better reflected her personality.

While you may find you work best with a different or modified version of the writing process described below, its steps outline a method that many writers use successfully. The following sections and exercises will enable you to try this method and see if it works for you.

PLANNING

1. Select a topic; then narrow it to fit the length of your writing assignment.

2. Make a list of ideas, assertions, facts, and examples that are related to your subject, and work this list into preliminary logical groupings.

3. Decide on the purpose of your piece of writing, and frame a specific thesis statement for that purpose.

4. Think carefully about the kind of reader you are writing to; the identity of the reader largely determines what you want to say and how you want to say it.

5. Decide on the pattern of organization and methods of development that will best serve your purpose and most effectively communicate your ideas to the reader.

6. Choose those items in your preliminary list that fit your purpose and support your thesis; add any new ones that are relevant. Then work these items into an outline.

7. Begin writing, and keep writing until you have completed a rough draft. Don't be overly concerned about wording, phrasing, grammar, or punctuation; at this stage pursue your thoughts instead of concentrating upon correctness.

8. Try to think of an illustration, an anecdote, or an example to use as an interesting introduction for your paper. Reread each paragraph to be sure it is clearly related to your thesis. Look at your ending paragraph: it should bring your essay to a *close* and not just *quit*.

9. Go over your first draft, checking it for correct spelling, punctuation, grammar, and effective sentences. Read it again for clarity, effective organization, and sound reasoning. Revise as necessary.

10. Give your paper a cooling-off period. Leave it for a while. When you reread it later, you may find rough spots that escaped your notice during the first writing and that you now want to rework or polish.

11. Prepare the final copy. Don't forget to create a title for your paper that indicates the topic and catches the reader's interest.

Practice: Brainstorming about topics   *Most people love a soapbox—a chance to stand up and speak their minds about a subject. A writing assignment is a ready-made soapbox: you have decided, or someone has asked you, to speak your mind. List at least three topics you'd like to pursue. Think about each one for a while. Then jot down some points that you think are especially important for each. Now imagine that you will be speaking from your soapbox to an audience. Compose an opening sentence for each of the topics, a sentence you could use to begin a speech.*

44

LIMITING TOPICS AND FORMING THESIS STATEMENTS (31a-d)

Settling on a subject about which to write is usually not so much a matter of "finding" a topic as "creating" one. The Practice in Section 43 gave you some experience with this type of activity. Whether you are assigned a subject or choose one on your own, selecting a general subject area often requires less thought than deciding just which aspect of the subject to use as your **topic**.

While you were brainstorming for the Practice, you probably "found" quite a few subjects that interested you and about which you had opinions. But when you listed points about those subjects and composed the opening sentences for the speeches, you also probably discovered that you needed to narrow your focus—limit the range of the subject. You were engaged in the process of creating the topic, defining its limits to make it interesting and effective for your audience. In other words, you were shaping the topic so that it was manageable.

The most manageable topics for short essays, such as those you write in English composition classes, are limited, specific topics. In order to do justice to a topic, you will need one that is specific rather than general. Obviously, if you try to tackle freedom of speech in a short essay, you will either run out of space and time (after all, whole books have been written about it), or your treatment of the subject will be extremely superficial and loaded with unsupported generalizations. On the other hand, the high-school administrators' censorship of your student newspaper is a topic that would enable you to discuss the principle of free speech in some detail, using concrete examples in a manageable context. You would be exploring general truths through specific applications and illustrations of them.

If you examine magazine articles by professional writers, you will see that they use the same method. For example, an author writing about good ethnic restaurants may focus on one aspect of the subject—outstanding Greek restaurants in Chicago.

In the process of limiting your topic, you are already planning what you want to say about it just by choosing which aspect you want to focus on. When you jot down a list of points and then choose the pertinent, important ones, your brainstorming produces further "invention," further creation and development of the topic. As you arrange your points, deleting some and adding others, you are deciding in what direction you want to go with your topic. You are working out your purpose and preparing to compose the thesis statement for your paper.

The **thesis statement** presents the controlling idea you will develop in the body of your paper. Often it sets forth not only the main idea but also the important points, or **aspects**, that make up the idea. During the process of developing a thesis statement, you are thinking your topic through, determining what is relevant and what is not. You are deciding exactly what assertion you want to make about your topic and what points, examples, or illustrations you will need to support that assertion.

Usually the thesis statement can be expressed in one sentence, the subject identifying the topic and the predicate making an assertion about the topic:

Subject
The golden years of retirement

Predicate
have become grim years of poverty for many senior citizens.

Mentioning the topic's major aspects will give you a good organizing statement for the development of the body of your paper and will also prepare your reader for what lies ahead:

> The golden years of retirement have become grim years of poverty for many senior citizens because their fixed incomes have left them defenseless against rising prices.

Just as a topic should be limited and specific, so should a thesis statement. If you are writing a 500-word essay on alcohol abuse, you know you can't say everything there is to be said about the subject, so you may decide to limit your discussion to alcohol abuse among teenagers or alcohol abuse among women. Even so, you can't say everything there is to be said about such a partially limited topic as alcohol abuse among women (causes, profile of abusers, physical and emotional effects on the drinker, effects on the family, various types of treatment and rehabilitation, recurring problems, life-long scars, etc.). So you won't want to compose a thesis that touches on all these points. Instead, you can focus in your thesis statement on one or two of them: for example, *Women who become alcoholics are often bored, lonely housewives who literally drink to "drown their sorrows."*

Notice how much more manageable this thesis statement is than *Lots of women are alcoholics* or even *Lots of women drink because they are unhappy.* A good thesis statement restricts a topic to something you can reasonably discuss in some depth, focuses that topic on several specific aspects, and indicates the plan you intend to use in the rest of your paper to make the case you set up in the thesis statement.

Practice A: Limiting subjects   *Which of the following topics are too broad and general as stated to be manageable in a 500-word essay? The answers are listed at the end of this section.*

1. Unemployment
2. Tips for buying your first home
3. The advantages of money-market funds for the small investor
4. College expenses
5. Presidential elections

Practice B: Restricting and focusing thesis statements   *Which of the following thesis statements are too vague and imprecise to be effective? The answers are listed at the end of this section.*

1. The nation's economy is in terrible shape.
2. Anyone can be a success.
3. In finding a job, whom you know may be as important as what you can do.
4. Some people don't know how to relax.
5. Career burnout can be cured by a change of scene or a change of job.

Answers to Practice A   1. too general   2. manageable
3. manageable   4. too general   5. too general

Answers to Practice B   1. too vague   2. too vague   3. manageable
4. too vague   5. manageable

EXERCISE 44-1, LIMITING TOPICS   (31a–d)

For each general subject below, list three examples—each one more specific than the
one that precedes it.

Examples   Food   Mammal

A. Dessert   A. Cat
B. Cake   B. Domestic cat
C. German chocolate cake   C. Siamese cat

1. Music   2. Sports

A. _____   A. _____

B. _____   B. _____

C. _____   C. _____

3. Energy   4. Family

A. _____   A. _____

B. _____   B. _____

C. _____   C. _____

For each general subject below, list four specific essay topics. Each topic should be
more specific than the one that precedes it.

Examples   Baseball   Money

A. College baseball   A. Investments
B. The positions on a baseball team   B. The stock market
C. How to pitch   C. Blue-chip stocks
D. How to throw a curve ball   D. Blue-chip stocks with the highest
                                                      return on investment

5. The space age   6. Reading

A. _____   A. _____

B. _____   B. _____

C. _____   C. _____

D. _____   D. _____

7. Popular fads

A. _____

B. _____

C. _____

D. _____

8. Education

A. _____

B. _____

C. _____

D. _____

9. Choice of a career

A. _____

B. _____

C. _____

D. _____

10. Pets

A. _____

B. _____

C. _____

D. _____

11. Neighborhoods

A. _____

B. _____

C. _____

D. _____

12. Football

A. _____

B. _____

C. _____

D. _____

13. Television

A. _____

B. _____

C. _____

D. _____

14. Politics

A. _____

B. _____

C. _____

D. _____

15. (Topic of your choice) _____

_____

A. _____

B. _____

C. _____

D. _____

16. (Topic of your choice) _____

_____

A. _____

B. _____

C. _____

D. _____

EXERCISE 44-2, DEVELOPING A THESIS STATEMENT   (31d)

At each number below, list a general subject about which you would like to write. You may wish to use some of the subjects you listed in the previous exercise. Brainstorm for a while, and then write down the specific topic you would explore in an essay. Brainstorm some more, and then list six aspects of the topic that you might discuss in your paper.

Example　　*General subject:*　Television
　　　　　　　Specific topic:　　Violence on television
　　　　　　　A. Develops a jaded attitude toward human suffering
　　　　　　　B. Makes heroes out of violent persons
　　　　　　　C. Gives impression violence is best way to settle disputes
　　　　　　　D. Has little intellectual value
　　　　　　　E. Degrades human beings
　　　　　　　F. Takes important programing time from more worthwhile topics

1. *General subject* _____

   Specific topic _____

   A. _____

   B. _____

   C. _____

   D. _____

   E. _____

   F. _____

2. *General subject* _____

   Specific topic _____

   A. _____

   B. _____

   C. _____

   D. _____

   E. _____

   F. _____

3. *General subject* _____

   Specific topic _____

   A. _____

   B. _____

   C. _____

   D. _____

   E. _____

   F. _____

4. *General subject* _____

   Specific topic _____

   A. _____

   B. _____

   C. _____

   D. _____

   E. _____

   F. _____

5. *General subject* _____

   Specific topic _____

   A. _____

   B. _____

   C. _____

   D. _____

   E. _____

   F. _____

For each of your five topics, now select three of the aspects that would be manageable in a 500-word essay. List them. Then compose a focused thesis statement for the essay you would write on each topic.

Example   *Specific topic:*   Violence on television
A. Develops a jaded attitude toward human suffering
B. Makes heroes out of violent persons
C. Degrades human beings

Thesis statement: Violence on television is bad because it engenders a jaded attitude toward human suffering, makes heroes out of violent persons, and degrades human beings.

Or

Television's violent programs degrade human beings; toughness is portrayed as heroic while human suffering is viewed with cynicism rather than sympathy.

1. *Specific topic* _____

   A. _____

   B. _____

   C. _____

   Thesis statement _____

   _____

   _____

   _____

2. *Specific topic* _____

   A. _____

   B. _____

   C. _____

   Thesis statement _____

   _____

   _____

   _____

3. *Specific topic* _____

   A. _____

   B. _____

   C. _____

   Thesis statement _____

   _____

   _____

   _____

   _____

4. *Specific topic* _____

    A. _____

    B. _____

    C. _____

    Thesis statement _____

    _____

    _____

    _____

    _____

5. *Specific topic* _____

    A. _____

    B. _____

    C. _____

    Thesis statement _____

    _____

    _____

    _____

    _____

45

OUTLINING   (31g)

Outlining comprises an important part of the planning for the writing of a paper. Once you have identified the aspects you want to discuss in the composition, you must consider the order in which to present them. The outline provides a visible arrangement of aspects and subaspects, showing the logical sequence and rank of major and minor points.

The two types of outlines generally preferred in composition classes are sentence outlines and topic outlines. In the **sentence outline**, all headings and subheadings must be sentences. In the **topic outline**, headings and subheadings are not sentences; frequently they are composed of a few words or of phrases. Each type of outline has advantages. The sentence outline usually requires the outliner to think the subject through very thoroughly and also provides training in constructing short, to-the-point sentences. The topic outline usually requires less time to develop.

Outlines can have several levels. The first level is the main headings, designated by Roman numerals: I, II, III, etc. Level two is designated by capital letters: *A, B, C,* etc. Level three uses arabic numbers: 1, 2, 3, etc. Fourth and fifth levels, when used, are indicated by small letters: *a, b, c,* etc., and numbers in parentheses: (1), (2), (3), etc.

One important thing to remember about an outline is that when a heading or subheading is divided, it is always divided into at least two parts.

NOT	I.	BUT	I.
	A.		A.
			B.

Of course, headings or subheadings may be divided into more than two parts. Insofar as possible, all headings and subheadings of the same level of importance should be written in parallel form, with the same grammatical structure. Thus, if I is a noun phrase, II and III should also be noun phrases. If *A* begins with a gerund, *B* and *C* should too.

Following is a sentence outline that could provide the basis for the introduction of a composition on finding a summer job.

Thesis statement in outline form

I. Students can choose among several ways to spend their time during summer vacation.
   A. They may take it easy.
      1. Loafing is a lot of fun.
      2. Doing nothing requires little effort.
   B. They may get summer jobs.
      1. Working includes many worthwhile experiences.
      2. Working enables them to make money.
      3. If they desire to work during the summer they must do the following.
         a. They must consult job sources.
         b. They must write letters of application for employment.
         c. They must make a good appearance at their job interviews.

Once you have completed the outline for the introduction of the paper, you should develop the outline for the body and conclusion. If you have developed the introduction to provide for a thesis statement, you can now take the aspects of your thesis and use them for the main headings of the body of the outline.

The first aspect of the thesis statement contained in the outline on finding a summer job will now be used for main heading II of the outline. This main heading will then be developed to three levels.

II. They must consult job sources.
    A. They can study the newspapers.
        1. The want ad sections list many job opportunities.
        2. They can acquaint themselves with firms through their advertising.
    B. They can utilize the college's employment service.
        1. Many employers advertise for help through the above service.
        2. They can advertise their services through this function.

Part II of the outline has now been developed to three levels. *A* pertains to studying the newspapers. Subheadings 1 and 2 under *A* offer advice concerning the study of newspapers. *B* concerns the college's employment service. Subheadings 1 and 2 under *B* provide information concerning this service. *A* and *B*, in turn, by discussing the newspapers and utilizing the college's employment service, pertain to the consulting of job sources mentioned in II.

Up to this point, the outline has continued to perform its basic functions.

1. It has provided details for development of this portion of the body of the composition.

2. Since each subheading relates to the subheading level above it, and subheadings in level II relate to the level-I main heading, the outline has continued to stick to the subject.

CRITERIA FOR TOPIC OUTLINES

In the topic outline there are no sentences. Instead, each heading and subheading must be followed by a noun or substantive or a phrase. You should avoid verbs in a topic outline since the resulting construction is often a sentence with an understood subject. To say *Follow the instructions carefully,* for example, is really to say *(You) follow the instructions carefully.* Also avoid constructions that are not sentences only because they lack verbs. For example, *Schools not as good as they used to be* is really only an incomplete sentence; all it needs to qualify as a sentence is the verb *are.*

The topic outline should of course follow the basic requirements of all outlines: each heading and subheading, when divided, should be broken down into at least two parts, and each level should relate to the level above it. In addition, keep the following points in mind:

1. Use no verbs.

2. Use no expressions that would be sentences if only a verb or subject were added.

3. Strive for phrases that will contain a noun (substantive) with modifiers, e.g., *Progress in testing* or *Testing progress.* Generally, a noun by itself may be insufficient. Enough should be said in the outline to provide a definite guide to the writer. The outline should indicate not only the aspect, but also the particular point to be discussed concerning that aspect. *Testing,* for example, provides much less guidance to the writer than does *Progress in testing.*

EXERCISE 45, OUTLINING (31g)

Below you will find part I of a sentence outline for a paper titled "What a Family Must Do If It Adopts a Pet." To the right of each entry of the outline, insert the appropriate letter or letters of items *A–D*, which describe the flaws you will find in the outline. Errors in the outline include the following:

- **A.** Subheading is not a sentence.
- **B.** Subheading is not broken into a minimum of two parts.
- **C.** Subheading does not relate to the subhead level above it.
- **D.** Subheading does not provide the basis for a thesis statement with three aspects.

I. Although owning a pet can have advantages, there are also responsibilities

    A. It brings a lot of pleasure

        1. Children can romp with it   ————

    B. Instilling of a sense of responsibility   ————

        1. It helps children to mature

        2. It need not cost much   ————

    C. If a family decides to get one

        1. It must pay veterinarian bills

        2. It must give it the proper food   ————

Complete the following sentence outline for the introduction of a paper titled "The Advantages of Going to College." Be sure that you write a complete sentence after each subheading.

I. High school students have two choices after graduation.

    A. They may go to work.

        1. _____

        2. _____

    B. They may go to college.

        1. _____

        2. _____

        3. If they go to college, they will profit in three ways.

            a. _____

            b. _____

            c. _____

Develop main headings III and IV of the outline for a paper about finding a summer job. Go to three levels, and make sure that each subheading is a full sentence. Also be sure that each subheading relates to the subheading or heading above it. The main headings, of course, relate to the other two aspects of the thesis statement. In developing III, you may wish to consider the parts of a letter of application for employment: the introductory covering statement and the resumé. You may also wish to consider what the letter will and will not do for the applicant.

III. Students must write letters of application for employment.

    A. _____

        1. _____

        2. _____

    B. _____

        1. _____

        2. _____

In the main heading IV, you may want to consider the impression the job interviewee's appearance makes on the employer and how important appearance may be to the employer's customers.

IV. They must make good appearances at job interviews.

    A. _____

        1. _____

        2. _____

    B. _____

        1. _____

        2. _____

Develop main heading V of the outline for the paper "Finding a Summer Job." Since this will be the conclusion of the essay, suitable development might include advice to students concerning the basis on which they would select their jobs. Be sure that each subheading is a sentence and that it relates to the outline level above it.

V. Students should consider two factors in selecting jobs.

    A. _____

        1. _____

        2. _____

B. _____

    1. _____

    2. _____

Portions of the outline for the paper "Finding A Summer Job" are reproduced below as a topic outline. Certain parts, however, are incorrect according to the criteria we have discussed throughout Section 45. Study each outline heading and subheading carefully. Then, to the right of each entry, either rewrite the entry correctly or insert *Correct*. (The sentence outline form of I and II below is given in Section 45.)

I. Option of student concerning summer activity

    A. Take it easy _____

        1. Fun of loafing _____

        2. Doing nothing little effort _____

    B. Getting a summer job _____

        1. Worthwhile experiences of working _____

        2. Make money _____

II. Methods of finding a job _____

    A. Newspapers _____

        1. Job opportunities in classified ad sections _____

        2. Advertising of firms _____

    B. Utilize college's employment service _____

        1. Employers _____

        2. Advertise student's own services _____

Change the following portion of a sentence outline to a topic outline, using the criteria discussed in Section 45.

II. One of the most important uses of a dictionary is looking up the meanings of words.

    A. An individual should understand the significance of the order in which meanings are given.

        1. Some dictionaries give the most common meanings first.

        2. Others give the definition with the centralized meaning first.

        3. Still others give definitions in chronological order, with the original meanings before the ones in current use.

B. The consulter should notice if the definition is labeled as a special or technical meaning.

    1. Some words have both a general and a special meaning.

    2. Some words are used only in a technical field.

II. _____

  A. _____

    1. _____

    2. _____

    3. _____

  B. _____

    1. _____

    2. _____

Using your own paper, choose one of the topics for which you composed a thesis statement in Exercise 44–2 and develop a three-level outline for it. You may develop either a sentence outline or a topic outline; your instructor may specify one or the other.

46

EFFECTIVE BEGINNINGS AND ENDINGS   (31h)

BEGINNINGS

Oddly enough, the best time to think about the beginning of your essay is usually after you have finished the first draft. Occasionally an interesting opening may come to mind as soon as you decide on a specific topic. If that happens, fine. Write it down so you won't forget it. But more frequently the process of writing the paper will clarify your purpose, and composing a beginning will be easier after your first draft is complete.

Journalists and other professional writers talk about creating a "lead" or a "hook" for their stories. They want an opening that will grab the readers' interest—get them "hooked" in the opening paragraph so they will want to read the whole article. You will want a strong, direct, compelling opening for your own paper, too.

An effective beginning attracts the reader's interest and introduces him or her to the topic. Although the beginning should not be too long in proportion to the rest of the paper (it is only the introduction, after all), it should be long enough to achieve some rapport with the reader and to establish a clear statement of purpose before you launch into the development of your topic's aspects. Other points to remember in beginning your paper include the following:

1. Try to get the reader's attention with a suitable anecdote, a justification of the subject, a startling statement, or a statement of the relevance of the subject to some local issue or happening.

2. Discuss briefly the general area or the subject matter, or supply background information as appropriate.

3. Indicate the purpose of the paper. A good way of doing this is to insert the thesis statement as the last sentence of the introduction.

4. Do not ramble. Make what is said in the introduction relevant either to the specific subject or to the background information.

5. Do not launch immediately into the principal topic of discussion without first providing some indication as to what the topic is going to be.

6. Do not comment upon the title without first introducing the idea in the title as a basis for discussion.

7. Do not insert material that has nothing to do with the topic.

Consider the following introduction written by a student in an English composition class:

> As we cruised down the moonlit country road, my ancient Volkswagen Beetle began to sputter. Throwing my date a worried glance, I steered to the berm, where the car finally died. "We're out of gas," I said. "Sure, sure," she replied in exasperation. "What a cheap, corny old trick. Now start this car and take me home." We really were out of gas; the fuel gauge on my VW hadn't worked in ten years, and since the car guzzled gas one minute and sipped it the next, I never knew for certain how much was in the tank. My date would not believe me. That night I learned the first of many lessons in how young women thoroughly accept stereotypes about male dating behavior.

The student's beginning paragraph accomplishes several things. First, it shows he has a sense of humor, inviting the readers to join the student as he laughs ruefully at himself and at human nature. The anecdotal opening engages the readers' interest and holds it by turning the tables on a stereotyped dating scene. Both male and female readers will identify with the

229

characters in the anecdote and enjoy the turn of events. And finally, the student author introduces his topic—one that is quite specific. His general subject is human behavior, but he has narrowed it to dating behavior. His thesis statement focuses the topic even more tightly: women's stereotypes of their dates.

In this fairly long introduction, the author has used each sentence purposefully to get his paper on the stereotypes of dating off to a good start. He might have begun his paper in a number of other equally successful ways, but the method he chose is effective.

ENDINGS

A well-crafted paper needs an effective ending as well as good introductory and body paragraphs. Nothing detracts more from an otherwise appealing paper than to have it end abruptly or trail off into a weak or meaningless conclusion. Two things to avoid are apologizing for any weaknesses in the paper or introducing another aspect of the topic at the last moment. The first type of ending will pique readers' impatience and make them wonder why you didn't get rid of weaknesses rather than apologizing for them. They will be left with a negative impression instead of a positive one. The second type of ending causes readers to feel cheated. No one likes to be left hanging at the end of an essay, wondering what you might have said if you had gone on to explore the topic's new aspect.

The ending of your paper should make the reader feel the discussion has been tied up, no loose ends, and rounded off in a satisfying way. A good ending can be compared to the bow tied on a birthday package or the icing on a cake—something good finished off with a flourish that makes the whole experience of reading your paper especially satisfying. Your reader should feel that without the conclusion the paper would have been incomplete. Some things you may do to achieve such a satisfactory ending include the following:

1. Restate briefly (not repeat word for word) the thesis statement of your paper.
2. Summarize briefly the major points of the paper.
3. Use a short anecdote or quotation that illustrates and supports your viewpoint.
4. Draw a conclusion from the discussion that shows the meaning of the facts and information you have presented.

The student who wrote the essay about dating behavior ended his paper by combining the second and fourth methods listed above:

Each of my youthful episodes contributes greatly to my understanding of female stereotypes about male dating behavior. I learned that running out of gas is always deliberate, that taking a girl to a fancy restaurant means you'll try to attack her later, and that you invite a homely girl to the prom *only* because ten other cute girls turned you down—*never* because you find her more interesting to talk to. I also learned another valuable lesson: as a stereotype, I'm a complete failure.

EXERCISE 46-1, EFFECTIVE BEGINNINGS   (31h)

Questions 1–10 give the titles and introductions of compositions. In the blanks, write the letters of the characteristics listed in items *A–F* that best describe each introduction.

A. No clear purpose
B. Too short
C. Rambles
D. Discusses topic without first indicating what the topic is
E. Comments upon the title without first introducing the title into the discussion
F. Satisfactory

Example   Careers in Medicine

For decades mothers have wanted their sons to grow up to be doctors. Doctors make high salaries. The American Dream, of course, holds that any boy can grow up to be President.   *B, C*

1. Women at the Top

Experts on organizational behavior cite several reasons for the lack of women at top executive levels in business. First, there are simply fewer women than men in management. Second, women are not easily accepted by the male-dominated manage-ment "club." Finally, most female managers are just beginning to learn to play promotion politics.   _____

2. Continuing Education

People who have college degrees are returning to the class-room five, ten, even twenty years after graduation. My Uncle Milton went back to school for a master's degree when he was 45 years old. We all thought he was crazy, but he got straight *A*'s.   _____

3. How to Pass Examinations Without Really Trying

The first thing to do is not to worry. Worrying detracts from your ability to think. Take it easy. Everything will come out all right. You can pass examinations if you take them in stride, use my patented system for answering objective-type tests, and write a lot on a question even though you may not say much.   _____

4. Starving Artists

It's not hard to understand why this is true. Most people spend their money on life's necessities: food, clothing, housing. Only a small minority buy works of art. Besides, if an artist charges anything comparable to the time he or she spends on a work, few people can afford the price.   _____

5. Highway Safety

       Last week, on Route 441, a truck and a passenger automobile collided. Four people were killed and two others were seriously injured. Two of the injured were small children. One of those killed was the truck driver, who had had twenty years of driving previously without an accident. The car was a total loss. That day it had been raining. Several other accidents occurred in the city that day.

                     _____

6. Flying the Friendly Skies

       Being a flight attendant is not as glamorous as you might think. Sure, you get to see the world—but from the inside of an airplane. The hours are long, especially on overseas flights; the passengers can be cranky and rude; and when you land, you're often too tired to go sightseeing.

                     _____

7. Women's Fashions

       Since I am not a woman, I don't know much about women's fashions. So writing a paper like this is hard for me. Besides, I could care less for the subject. There are other subjects I probably could write about. But I can't think of one right now. Anyhow, women's fashions are interesting as long as women are in them.

                     _____

8. Computer World

       Computers are revolutionizing the business world. The largest computer company, appropriately named International Business Machines Corporation (IBM), has sales of over $26 million.

                     _____

9. Status Symbols on the Job

       On Friday afternoon you leave your large, carpeted office with the nice view of the park. On Monday morning you discover you've been moved to an office with no windows and with linoleum on the floor. Is the boss trying to tell you something? In many companies, office location and furnishings are clear indications of status—who is on the way up, and who is on the way down or out.

                     _____

10. Keeping Fit

       This is particularly difficult to do if you don't have a daily exercise routine. Students, working women and men with high-pressure jobs, senior citizens, almost everybody has an excuse to put it off until tomorrow, but tomorrow may be too late.

                     _____

Below each of the following titles, write an introductory sentence or two using the specific technique for effective beginnings called for in parentheses. For the last item in this exercise, use one of the topics you developed in Section 44.

Example   Be Prepared—For Career Changes

(Repeat the title.) *Be prepared to change careers at some point in your life. That's what career counselors are telling students these days.*

(Paraphrase the title.) *Career counselors are advising students not to expect to work in one field for the rest of their lives. Instead, their education should prepare them to change to related fields if necessary.*

(Start with a statement of fact.) *The majority of working Americans have changed careers at least twice. As technology affects the job market, that figure is likely to grow.*

(Use a startling statement.) *Leslie Richards has a master's degree in political science, but today you'll find her tending bar. "I like bartending," she says. "I didn't like my government job."*

11.   If I Could Choose Any Job in the World

(Repeat the title.) _____

_____

_____

(Paraphrase the title.) _____

_____

_____

(Start with a statement of fact.) _____

_____

_____

(Use a startling statement or anecdote.) _____

_____

_____

12.   Why Video Games Are Popular

(Repeat the title.) _____

_____

_____

(Paraphrase the title.) _____

_____

_____

(Start with a statement of fact.) _____

_____

_____

(Use a startling statement or anecdote.) _____

_____

_____

13. (Title for a topic you developed in Section 44) _____

(Repeat the title.) _____

_____

_____

(Paraphrase the title.) _____

_____

_____

(Start with a statement of fact.) _____

_____

_____

(Use a startling statement or anecdote.) _____

_____

_____

EXERCISE 46-2, EFFECTIVE ENDINGS   (31h)

Using your own paper, develop thesis statements for the given composition titles. Then, for each of the approaches indicated in parentheses, write at least four sentences that would end the composition suitably.

Example   Be Prepared—For Career Change

(Thesis statement) The evidence shows that most people change careers several times, so college students would be wise to choose courses that give them some career flexibility.

(Restate thesis statement.) Many college students choose their majors with one career goal in mind and resent having to take courses that do not fit their short-term employment plans. A few years after graduation, they may find themselves out of work, a narrowly focused education having locked them into a dead-end career path.

(Summarize briefly major points of paper.) Although it's not easy to take a long-range view when one is primarily concerned about landing that first job after graduation, wise students consider the variety of career options their education will provide. They take courses that will give them a well-rounded, general education as well as those that train them for a specific job. They also choose extracurricular activities that offer a range of experiences. In short, they develop flexible skills that have several career applications.

(Use an anecdote or quotation.) *Chicago Tribune* columnist Dan Dorfman writes of "society's growing disenchantment with the so-called 'specialist' or 'professional'—not only in supply-demand factors, but in changing public attitudes." The point is, today's specialist may be on tomorrow's unemployment line, because technological, economic, or social change can make a profession overcrowded or obsolete. Career changes, increasingly, are not only possible but probable. The graduates with the most flexible career skills are the best prepared to meet them.

(Draw conclusion from paper.) Whether he or she is aware of it, today's college student faces the likelihood of an eventual career change. Consequently, educational institutions and their career counselors have an obligation. They must help students develop a long-range perspective; they must stress that, although training for the first job is important, an interdisciplinary education—featuring a working knowledge of different specialties—is more serviceable over the long haul.

1.   If I Could Choose Any Job in the World
     (Thesis statement)
     (Restate thesis statement.)
     (Briefly summarize major points of paper.)
     (Use supporting anecdote or quotation.)
     (Draw conclusion from paper.)

2. Why Video Games Are Popular
   (Thesis statement)
   (Restate thesis statement.)
   (Briefly summarize major points of paper.)
   (Use supporting anecdote or quotation.)
   (Draw conclusion from paper.)

3. Drunk Drivers
   (Thesis statement)
   (Restate thesis statement.)
   (Briefly summarize major points of paper.)
   (Use supporting anecdote or quotation.)
   (Draw conclusion from paper.)

4. Schools Fail to Educate Students—Whose Fault?
   (Thesis statement)
   (Restate thesis statement.)
   (Briefly summarize major points of paper.)
   (Use supporting anecdote or quotation.)
   (Draw conclusion from paper.)

5. (Title for the topic of your choice)
   (Thesis statement)
   (Restate thesis statement.)
   (Briefly summarize major points of paper.)
   (Use supporting anecdote or quotation.)
   (Draw conclusion from paper.)

47

PARAGRAPH UNITY   (32a-b)

Paragraphs are the building blocks of essays. As noted in the process outlined in Section 43, every paragraph should be related to the thesis of your essay. Each paragraph furthers your purpose, supports your thesis, and explains your thinking about the topic.

The aspects of your topic thus become the paragraphs of your paper. Sometimes an aspect can be handled in a single paragraph; sometimes more than one paragraph will be necessary because an aspect of your topic may contain subaspects that need explaining.

No matter how many paragraphs your finished essay contains, each one should be unified, coherent, and adequately developed. (The next several sections define and explain those abstract terms.) A good paragraph needs all three characteristics to be effective. A good essay needs them as well. In fact, you may find it helpful to think of a paragraph as a mini-essay.

A paragraph is **unified** if it has a clear, controlling idea and if all the sentences in the paragraph relate to that idea. Most paragraphs use a **topic sentence** to state the paragraph's controlling idea. The topic sentence in a paragraph functions in the same way as the thesis statement in an essay: both express a central idea. The topic sentence of a paragraph focuses on one of the aspects or subaspects of the topic encompassed by the thesis. For example, if your thesis statement mentions three aspects (let's say, stripping, sanding, and varnishing) of a topic (refinishing furniture), then your essay will probably have three body paragraphs with corresponding topic sentences: one on stripping furniture, one on sanding it, and one on varnishing it.

The topic sentence may be the first sentence of a paragraph, it may be the last sentence of a paragraph, or it may appear in slightly different form in both places—particularly if the paragraph is long, involved, and needs summing up at the end.

Some paragraphs have implied topic sentences; but even when the topic sentence is unstated, the reader should be able to tell from the paragraph's details that a central idea is controlling the discussion. If your reader cannot formulate a topic sentence from the paragraph's discussion, then your paragraph is not controlled or unified. A paragraph that lacks a clear focus and contains irrelevant statements will cause your reader to wonder where you are headed and what the information has to do with your topic.

Practice A: Identifying topic sentences   Underline the topic sentence in each of the following paragraphs. If a paragraph has an implied topic sentence, compose your version of what the topic sentence might be. The answers are listed at the end of this section.

[1] When a company and a labor union negotiate a contract, some of the negotiators are likely to have degrees in industrial relations. When an employee receives a performance review, industrial relations is being practiced. Personnel officers; wages, benefits, and payroll managers; employee development and training directors—all these people have probably studied industrial relations.

[2] You may have heard about corporations that give raises to employees who quit smoking or that build gyms for staff physical fitness programs. Losing valuable employees through illness or death is costly. Corporations are learning that spending money on their employees' physical fitness is good business sense.

Practice B: Identifying irrelevant statements   *Read the following topic sentences and the groups of sentences that accompany them. Circle the letters of the sentences in each group that are not closely related to that group's topic sentence. The answers are listed at the end of this section.*

1. The term *money* refers to two concepts: an abstract unit by which the value of goods, services, or obligations can be measured; and a concrete substance used to pay for them.

    A. The standard of value (money the abstract concept) is often, but not always, the same as the medium of exchange (money the physical substance).
    B. For example, in many ancient societies cows were the standard of value, but more portable items were the medium of exchange.
    C. Monetary institutions such as banks have usually developed along with the growth of a society's trade and industry.
    D. A tribesman might set his daughter's dowry at thirty cows.
    E. However, he might actually give her bridegroom ten cows plus the equivalent of the other twenty in cooking pots, furs, and chickens.
    F. Sometimes, vestiges of the ancient standard of value remain long after currency replaces commodities as the exchange medium.
    G. In both Latin and Anglo-Saxon, for instance, the word for cattle also denotes money.
    H. Paper money appeared about 300 years ago.

2. Whenever people lose confidence in their government's currency, they buy and hoard commodities with high intrinsic value, such as precious metals and gems.

    A. During the economic chaos in Europe before World War II, currency was devalued from one day to the next by inflation.
    B. One anecdote tells of a German collecting his week's pay in a wheelbarrow and then hurrying to the grocer's to buy bread before the mound of cash became worthless.
    C. Those who fled Hitler tried to smuggle out gold and jewelry because these were the only universally reliable mediums of exchange.
    D. As recently as 1979, when the U.S. dollar was dropping sharply against other currencies, people invested heavily in gold, silver, and diamonds.
    E. In 1980, a multimillionaire Texas family, the Hunts, nearly cornered the world silver market, controlling more than 6,200 tons of silver and silver futures—more than that owned by the U.S. government.
    F. The price of silver had risen from an average of $2.56 an ounce in 1973 to more than $50 in 1979—and then plummeted to $10.80 on March 27, 1980, a day known as "Silver Thursday."

Answers to Practice A   [1] Topic sentence is implied: one possibility is *A career in industrial relations involves working with the people who do the work.*
[2] *Corporations are learning that spending money on their employees' physical fitness is good business sense.*

Answers to Practice B   1. C, H   2. B, E, F

EXERCISE 47, PARAGRAPH UNITY   (32a-b)

Some sentences in the following paragraphs are irrelevant to the central ideas of the paragraphs. Write the letters of such irrelevant sentences in the blank to the right of each paragraph.

1. (A) The expression "mint condition" originally referred to coins that were in a "mint state": that is, unused, uncirculated, and in the same condition as when they came from the mint where they were stamped. (B) There are two mints manufacturing legal coinage in the United States, one in Philadelphia and one in Denver. (C) "Mint condition" has been borrowed from numismatics and in popular usage has come to mean something that is just like new or in its original condition.   _____

2. (A) One hundred years ago, youths dreamed of growing up to be railroad engineers. (B) Engineers were worthy of hero worship because they piloted the fastest form of transportation then in existence. (C) America's railroads are now in terrible shape. (D) Roadbeds have deteriorated, highways have siphoned off passengers and freight, and many railway companies have gone bankrupt. (E) The dream of being an engineer has been replaced today by the desire to be an airline pilot or even an astronaut. (F) Instead of barreling down the tracks, today's young speed demons want to soar among the stars.   _____

3. (A) We've been conditioned by movies and television shows to associate "loot" with gold coins. (B) The robbers jumped off the train, the outlaws held up the stage coach or Army pay wagon— and made off with the gold. (C) What has become of all the gold coins? (D) The Gold Reserve Act of 1934 stipulated that gold could not be used as a medium of domestic exchange. (E) It was also illegal for private citizens or firms to own gold bullion. (F) As people exchanged their gold coins for paper currency at banks, the coins were removed from circulation. (G) America's days of bags of gold had ended. (H) Other countries such as South Africa and Mexico have continued to mint gold coins, however,   _____

4. (A) If you borrow money to purchase a car or a home, you pay an interest charge for using the money. (B) The bank, on the other hand, pays interest to depositors. (C) Although charging interest is an ancient custom, it has not always been legal. (D) The Jews and the early Christian Church outlawed interest charges among their own groups. (D) Demanding interest for the use of money was called *usury,* appropriately enough. (F) Not until 1545 were interest charges legalized in Europe, when England removed the prohibition and set an upper limit on allowable rates.   _____

5. (A) Traveling in foreign countries presents some unexpected money problems. (B) It's not that traveling is expensive. (C) We expect that. (D) It's not that mentally converting foreign prices

into dollars so we know what things really cost takes some getting used to. (E) It's not even that at first we can't tell a pound from a franc—the money is all funny colors and designs. (F) It's that foreign currency comes in such funny sizes, and none of it fits our American-made billfolds properly. (G) I bought a gorgeous billfold in Florence, Italy, famous for its leather goods. _____

6. (A) Working for wages is a relatively recent phenomenon in human social history—dating from the Industrial Revolution (1750–1850). (B) The Industrial Revolution marked a shift from an agricultural and commercial society to an industrialized society that relied on machinery rather than tools. (C) Some historians object to the term *revolution* because it suggests a violent upheaval. (D) In reality the change was relatively gradual. (E) Whereas previously people had grown or made products which they themselves sold for cash or bartered for the goods they personally needed, the Industrial Revolution created a class of workers whose sole product was their labor. (F) The goods that resulted from their labor were sold by someone else, the factory owner who banked the profits and returned wages to the workers. _____

7. (A) College seniors enjoy a lot of prestige. (B) They are the oldest and most experienced class on campus, looking forward to the end of their labors—graduation. (C) Popular topics of conversation during a college student's senior year are job hunting, job offers, and starting salaries. (D) Word quickly spreads about who has been offered the highest salary and which companies are paying the most. (E) Rather than concentrate on salary alone, students should consider a company's total package of wages and benefits. (F) Benefits such as health and life insurance, retirement plans, and profit-sharing programs are as important in the long run as actual salary. (G) Students should also consider the cost of living in the area where a company is located. (H) Don't be impressed by a high salary; also check out how the benefits package compares to those offered by similar companies. _____

Using your own paper, write four topic sentences on subjects of your choice. Underneath each topic sentence, write four sentences related to that topic sentence. Be sure that every sentence you write directly concerns the subject matter introduced in your topic sentence.

48

PARAGRAPH COHERENCE (32c)

A paragraph is **coherent** if the sentences convey a smooth, logical flow of thought from one idea to the next. Each sentence should show an evident relationship to the one that precedes it and a clear connection to the one that follows it, as well as a bearing on the paragraph's controlling idea.

Whereas unity depends upon your selecting ideas that are relevant to the topic of your paragraph, coherence depends upon your ability to show how the ideas are relevant by presenting them in a smooth, orderly, well-knit arrangement. Smoothness in a paragraph is achieved partially by using transitional elements; these will be discussed more fully in Section 49. Orderliness can be achieved by using one of several organizational patterns for your sentences. The ones you choose for your paragraphs will depend upon your topic and purpose; each is a means for creating coherence in your writing.

Descriptions and examples of four common organizational patterns follow. Transitional links in the example paragraphs are italicized.

1. Time order (chronology) is the order in which events occur: one thing happening after another.

> My visit to Professor Crump's office for help with an astronomy problem *at first* seemed more like a social call than a tutorial. *After* I knocked and entered the room, he invited me to be seated in one of his overstuffed chairs. We spent *the next several* minutes of our conference discussing my work in other courses, and I *began* to realize he was trying to put me at ease. *Then* he offered me a cup of tea, which he poured into china cups. *Only when* I was settled comfortably with my tea cup *did he* spread his astronomical models on the desk and ask, *"Now,* which aspect of retrograde motion would you like me to explain?"

2. Space order is sentence arrangement according to physical layout, such as top to bottom, left to right, back to front, east to west, and so forth.

> The astronomy professor's office was unlike any other faculty office in the science building. Visitors noticed first the enormous antique desk *against the far wall. On the right* were heavy, glass-fronted bookcases. *On the left* were several overstuffed chairs. The *overhead* fluorescent lights had been turned off. *Instead,* Tiffany lamps cast a warm glow through their colorful glass shades. The Victorian decor was completed by the oriental rug *underfoot.*

3. Order of climax is order by increasing importance: minor details leading to the main point.

> *Sometimes* Professor Crump digressed from his class lectures on astronomy and *told anecdotes about his life. On various occasions he told about* helping to build one of the nation's first big reflecting telescopes, *about* his transcendental religious experience on a mountaintop in Kashmir, *about* a picnic lunch with an attractive stranger who turned out to be Mussolini's mistress. *Most of these stories* had little if anything to do with astronomy. We gradually realized, *however,* that for Dr. Crump the mysteries of the stars were just one aspect of life's rich, diverse mystery.

4. General to particular or particular to general order is a general statement followed by (1) supporting evidence and illustrations or (2) particular evidence and illustrations leading to a concluding generalization. When either of these arrangements is used, the generalization usually appears in the topic sentence—at the beginning of the paragraph in the first case, at the end of the paragraph in the second. The previous paragraph illustrating order of climax is also an example of particular to general order. The following paragraph shows general to particular order.

To the students on our small college campus, Professor Crump *was more than an elderly astronomer:* he *was a chunk of civilization.* At nearly eighty years of age, *he had seen* astronomy grow from its relative infancy; *he had worked* with many of the century's greatest scientists. *He had witnessed* two world wars, *taught* at five colleges and universities, *and led* a full—even exotic—life. *Yet he chose* to end his long career with us. We were flattered.

EXERCISE 48, PARAGRAPH COHERENCE   (32c)

In the blank following each set of sentences, write the numbers of each group in the order that develops a coherent paragraph.

Example

1. The working person also bears the brunt of constantly rising prices.
2. Most cruelly affected of all are the aged.
3. The prices go up and up—when inflation rages, a head of lettuce may or may not be fit food for a king.
4. Inflation is a very cruel taskmaster.
5. It exacts tribute from many different groups of people.
6. Even if salaries go up, prices usually go up even more.
7. His or her pay check buys less and less.
8. It affects consumers every time they go the market.
9. Even though they have tried to save for their retirement, few have been able to save enough.
10. But only a king can afford it.
11. The result is often a wretched existence—unable to work and with insufficient funds for food and medicine, they can only sit and rock their lives away.

4, 5, 8, 3, 10, 2, 9, 11, 1, 6, 7

A.

1. Jerking your head up again as a solemn voice breaks the silence, you hear the Grand Inquisitor say, "Let us begin."
2. Finally your eyes drop to the middle of the table.
3. The defense can only be compared to appearing before the Spanish Inquisition or going on trial for your life—your academic life.
4. Then you nervously glance at the members of your doctoral committee—the Inquisitors, both judges and jury—seated along both sides.
5. There, in front of each professor, is a copy of your dissertation—the incriminating evidence.
6. Raising your eyes, you see your major professor at the table's head.
7. After more than a year of research and writing, the final step before your Ph.D. is granted is the oral defense of your dissertation.
8. You enter the room and silently take your place at the foot of the long table.

_____

B.

1. While a doctoral student, a person also usually learns whether he or she is cut out to be a teacher.
2. With a few exceptions, college professors do not earn high salaries.
3. One must also be interested enough in a research topic to devote a full year to writing a scholarly dissertation totaling several hundred pages.
4. T.A.'s teach undergraduate classes in their department, supervised by a faculty member.

5. To earn the Ph.D. necessary to become a college professor, a person must be willing to devote at least three years to graduate study after receiving a bachelor's degree.
6. Professors in technical disciplines such as engineering or science could earn more money working in industry.
7. A career as a college professor is ideal for people who thrive on scholarship and research, enjoy teaching, and don't mind not getting rich.
8. However, they often prefer the mix of teaching and research, the flexibility and variety available in academia but rare in industry jobs.
9. Most doctoral students serve as teaching assistants, called T.A.'s.

C.

1. Soon I was giving a monologue, answering my own questions.
2. So the ones who had managed to look reasonably awake at the beginning of the period got groggier as the hour passed and the room got hotter.
3. Never assign a new chapter for the morning a term paper is due.
4. Although the students had been assigned a chapter to read, most of them had spent all their homework time on their term papers.
5. I knew the class was off to a bad start almost as soon as I walked to the lectern.
6. As a result, they didn't know the material, and class discussion became impossible.
7. From the experience I learned "Teaching Assistant Rule #6."
8. The room was overheated and stuffy.
9. To begin with, most of the students had obviously been up all night finishing their term papers because they looked as if they were half asleep.

Using your own paper, first list four different paragraph topics. You may want to choose some of the topics you developed in earlier exercises. Then write a coherent paragraph for each topic, using a different organizational pattern each time. The organizational patterns are *chronological order, spatial order, order of climax, general to particular order,* and *particular to general order.*

49

TRANSITIONS WITHIN PARAGRAPHS   (32d)

Sentence arrangement helps to achieve coherence in paragraphs; but to establish the relationships between ideas clearly, you will need to guide your reader smoothly from one thought to the next. Doing so involves the effective use of transitional elements. These are (1) a consistent point of view; (2) parallel grammatical structure; (3) repeated words and phrases, synonyms, or repeated ideas; and (4) transitional words and phrases.

   1. **Consistent point of view** is maintained if you avoid unnecessary shifts in person, verb tense, or number within a paragraph (see Section 21). The following paragraph shows how these types of unnecessary shifts can ruin continuity and confuse the reader.

> Many fanciful beliefs have surrounded the moon. People at one time or another believed the moon was a goddess, it is a man's face, or it was thought to be the cause of various diseases. You know, strange creatures even had been thought to live on the moon. Thanks to space exploration, we find the moon much less mysterious.

Notice how much smoother the revision is.

> People have believed many fanciful things about the moon. At one time or another they have believed the moon to be a goddess, a man's face, or the cause of various diseases. People have even thought strange creatures lived on the moon. Thanks to space exploration, the moon has become much less mysterious.

   2. **Parallel grammatical structure in successive sentences** emphasizes the relationship between them and the relationship between them and the relationship to the paragraph's main idea. The sentences in the general-to-particular paragraph in Section 48 use parallel structure to reinforce their relationship. The subject-verb arrangement of the clauses beginning *he had seen, he had worked, he had witnessed . . . taught . . . and led* echo the structure as they support with examples the controlling idea in the topic sentence *he was a chunk of civilization.* In the following paragraph, written by the college president after the death of the astronomy professor described in Section 48, the parallel grammatical structures are italicized.

> His gentle presence will be sorely missed from this campus. *It is clear that he loved* the college and its students deeply, and *it is a challenge to live* up to his high standards of character and academic excellence. *Clifford Crump believed in the life of the mind; he believed in the life of the spirit,* and his own life proved that the two can be one in daily practice.

   3. **Repeated key words or phrases, synonyms, or repeated ideas** indicate to the reader that relationships exist between thoughts in a paragraph. Something as simple as using a pronoun to refer to a clearly established antecedent or inserting a synonym can provide coherence for a paragraph. The preceding example paragraph not only uses parallel structure but also repeats words and phrases to cement relationships between ideas and to provide a smooth flow. The three crucial repetitions in that paragraph are *it is, believed in,* and *life of.* The pronouns *his* and *he,* referring to Professor Crump, remind the reader that the same individual is the subject throughout the paragraph. The following paragraph relies even more heavily on repetition to achieve coherence:

Star gazing on a winter night *is not necessarily a romantic pastime.* Even when *your* boyfriend is the instructor, *learning constellations for your* astronomy mid-term *is not necessarily a heart-warming experience. All you* can think about is *your cold* feet, *your cold* hands, *your cold* nose. *All you* want to do is *get someplace* warm, and *get there* as quickly as possible.

4. **Transitional words and phrases** that appear at or near the beginning of a sentence indicate a relationship between that sentence and the one preceding it. Coordinating conjunctions such as *and, but, or, nor, so,* and *yet* are often used in informal writing to provide bridges between sentences. However, you can use many other words and phrases to establish connections in more formal writing. A number of them are listed below.

ADDITION	again, also, and, and then, besides, equally important, finally, first, furthermore, in addition, last, likewise, moreover, next, second, third, too
CAUSE AND EFFECT	accordingly, as a result, because, consequently, hence, otherwise, since, so, then, therefore, thus
COMPARISON	by the same token, in a like manner, likewise, similarly
CONCESSION	after all, at the same time, even though, of course
CONTRAST	although, at the same time, but, by contrast, for all that, however, in spite of, nevertheless, on the contrary, on the other hand, still, yet
EXAMPLE OR ILLUSTRATION	for example, for instance, in fact, in other words, specifically, such as, that is, to illustrate
SUMMARY	in brief, in conclusion, in essence, in short, on the whole, to conclude, to sum up
TIME RELATIONS	after, afterwards, as long as, as soon as, at last, at that time, before, immediately, in the meantime, later, meanwhile, next, presently, soon, then, thereafter, thereupon, until, when, while

Use transitional elements appropriately. Remember what these words mean, and do not simply throw them into your sentences without regard for sense.

Be aware, too, that transitional words can become extremely tiresome if they are overused. If every sentence in a paragraph begins with one of these words, the paragraph can become very choppy, as the following example shows.

Many of the constellations were named by the Greeks. *However,* the Greeks were not the first people to name configurations of stars. *In fact,* five thousand years ago the Mesopotamians saw patterns or pictures in the stars and named them after animals and occupations. *Moreover,* today we still use many of the ancient names for constellations. *For example,* the constellation containing the Big Dipper is called Ursa Major, the Great Bear. *Furthermore,* we call the constellation that looked to some ancients like a bowman, Sagittarius, the Archer.

Learn to use a variety of means to show relationships between your ideas. Notice how much smoother the revision of the preceding example paragraph becomes when several types of transitions are used to replace some of the transitional words at the beginnings of sentences. Also notice how combining some of the sentences smooths the flow of ideas.

Although the Greeks named many of the constellations, they were not the first people to name configurations of stars. In fact, five thousand years ago the Mesopotamians saw patterns or pictures in the stars and named them for animals and occupations. Today we see the same heavenly patterns and call them by many of the same ancient names: Ursa Major, the Great Bear, the constellation containing the Big Dipper; Sagittarius, the Archer, the constellation that looks like a bowman.

EXERCISE 49, TRANSITIONS FOR UNITY AND COHERENCE   (32d)

Using your own paper, revise the following paragraphs, eliminating unnecessary shifts in point of view and providing transitional elements where they are needed. You may combine or rearrange sentences to achieve a smooth, coherent paragraph.

1. Vocational schools were once regarded as being all right for inferior types of people, but nobody with any real intelligence will have anything to do with it. Today, we look at the matter differently. When you consider the amount of money that is earned by plumbers and how much a good technician took home each week, it is not unusual that one considers vocational training quite seriously. Perhaps some snobbery is still involved; if so, and if you are a vocational school graduate, you can console yourself by crying on the way to the bank with your earnings.

2. Compared to some of the other sciences, astronomy is a rather small field. For instance, there were fewer astronomers than chemists or biologists. However, the field has a vast scope. It is considered to be the whole universe. You can define astronomy narrowly as the study of the motions and natures of celestial bodies. It can also be defined more generally by us as the investigation of matter and energy in the universe at large.

3. Students aspiring to be an astronomer take many physics courses. Astronomy is a branch of physics. Numerous math courses must be taken by them also. Astronomers' interest shifted from determining the positions and distance of the stars. Astronomers increasingly are studying the physical composition of the stars, the planets' make-up, and what interstellar space is made of. Astronomy students need several chemistry courses to have studied the molecules the universe is composed of.

4. Galileo constructed the first complete astronomical telescope in 1609. With it he had discovered the mountains on the moon. He discovered the satellites of Jupiter. Sun spots have been observed by him. Galileo knows the earth moves around the sun. The sun is believed to revolve around the Earth, according to the Church. They tried Galileo for heresy. His beliefs based on scientific observations were recanted by him. We hear that he whispered "Nevertheless, it does move" as he rises from his knees after the trial.

5. Carl Sagan is an astronomer. He has taught at Harvard and Cornell University. NASA was advised about its unmanned space missions by him. The book *Cosmos* was written by Sagan, and he acted as host-narrator for the popular public television series developed from his book by him. If one tunes in the *Johnny Carson Show,* you may have seen Carl Sagan as a guest on the program. He was called by *Time* magazine "America's most effective salesman of science." Sagan's excitement about the universe is catching. When he talks about the "billions and billions of stars," you couldn't help but be interested in it. He is probably the most eloquent spokesman for astronomy we have.

Using your own paper, write paragraphs at least four sentences long that illustrate the use of the transitional elements called for in items 6 through 9. Underline and label the transitional elements you use.

Example   comparison, contrast, concession, example, summary

A sentence outline and a topic outline are alike in some respects. The sentence
comparison
outline uses headings and subheadings. The topic outline proceeds similarly in this
comparison   _example_
respect. Likewise, both outlines, if they are properly developed, will be unified; that
                                                          comparison
is, all subheadings will relate to the subheadings or headings above them. In turn, the

main headings will pertain to the subject of the paper. The two papers differ,
contrast
on the other hand, in that whereas the sentence outline contains only sentences, the
                    concession   _summary_
topic outline has none. Of course, both outlines are good. In essence, the one should

be used which best fits the needs of the occasion.

6. comparison, contrast, examples, parallel structure

7. cause and effect, addition, summary, synonyms

8. time relations, concession, contrast, summary

9. word repetition, addition, examples

50

PARAGRAPH DEVELOPMENT   (32e-g)

A paragraph is adequately **developed** if it has enough evidence, examples, supporting facts, details, and reasons for your reader to understand your topic sentence fully and be persuaded of its validity. Just as all the paragraphs in your essay should explain and support your thesis statement, so the sentences in your paragraphs should clarify and support the topic sentences. The most frequently used methods of paragraph development are (1) details, examples, and illustrations; (2) comparison and contrast; (3) definition; (4) cause and effect; and (5) analysis and classification.

1. **Details, examples, and illustrations** are the most common type of support for a paragraph's controlling idea. In fact, most other methods of development also rely on details and examples. Details are a catalog of particulars, usually presented without much explanation. Examples, on the other hand, require some explanation to show their relevance to the paragraph's main topic. Development by illustration is the same as development by example, except that instead of using several examples to support the main point, you use one example that you explain at considerable length. The first paragraph below is developed with details. It makes use of chronological arrangement to ensure the coherence of these details. The second paragraph is developed with examples.

PARAGRAPH DEVELOPED WITH DETAILS

Getting ready to write a composition is quite an ordeal. First, you have to find a quiet place where you can concentrate. Then you have to make sure you have a good pen, plenty of paper, a dictionary, a handbook, and plenty of hot coffee. When you are finally settled and ready to go, you have to think next of a subject, construct a thesis statement, and make up an outline with the right number of headings and subheadings. If you are still with it after having done all the above, then you write a rough draft. The next to the last step is to revise the composition, making sure it is coherent, unified, properly developed with good sentences and paragraphs, and that there are no errors in spelling, mechanics, punctuation, and diction. The last step is to endorse it, say a short prayer, and collapse on your bed. As you do, you hope there will be no nightmares in which English instructors will be chasing you with gigantic red pens and waving papers you have written that have more red marks on them than anything else.

PARAGRAPH DEVELOPED WITH EXAMPLES

One can meet all kinds of drivers on the road. First, there is Obnoxious Oscar. Oscar careens down the street with the throttle wide open, poisoning the atmosphere with noxious smoke, waking up everyone within miles with his noisy muffler, and honking insistently at anyone who happens to be driving ahead of him. Second, there is Cautious Chauncey. Chauncey putters along at only ten miles per hour. He slows down to two miles per hour at each driveway and displays massive indifference to the immense traffic jam behind him. Third, there is Slippery Sam. Sam writhes in and out of traffic like an eel among coral. Nothing ever seems to happen to him, but such is not true of the other drivers who have been around him. Most of them are basket cases, with thoroughly jangled nerves and with hips that have been hopelessly dislocated by jamming down on the brakes in trying to avoid him.

2. **Comparison and contrast** are natural methods of development for many topics. Comparison stresses similarities between items. Contrast explains their differences. Sometimes you will develop an entire paragraph using just one method or just the other; sometimes you will both compare and contrast in the same paragraph. The example paragraph in Exercise 49 shows the use of both comparison and contrast in the same paragraph. Notice how the transitional words provide the reader with clear connections between ideas. The following paragraph principally uses contrast to develop its controlling idea.

Except for the fact that dogs and cats are both four-legged, furry mammals, they are distinctly different types of pets. Dogs are very loyal and subservient to their masters. Cats, on the other hand, never totally commit their allegiance to anyone, maintaining their independence. Cats are relatively self-sufficient and can be left alone if their owners go away for the weekend. All they need is a supply of food and fresh water and a clean litter box. Dogs, however, wolf all their food immediately and have to be taken out every few hours. Woe to owners whose dogs get lonely while they are gone; upon returning they will find chewed shoes, hats, gloves, and furniture.

3. **Definition** is a useful method of development for clarifying terms or concepts the reader may not know or understand in just the way you want them understood. Sometimes you need not go into much detail as you define. In this case, you will be employing an informal definition, which can involve as little as a word or a phrase.

The eosin (dye) was smeared all over the page.
The kibitzer (an onlooker who offers advice) infuriated the card players.

At other times, though, you may choose or need to be more detailed or explicit when you define. Then you may employ a **formal definition**, which consists of a term to be defined; a genus (class), which is a general category in which the term can logically be included; and a differentia, which is a statement of the way the term differs from other members of the genus. The following is a formal definition:

TERM TO BE DEFINED	GENUS (CLASS)	DIFFERENTIA
A straw boss is	a person	who gives orders or oversees work but who has no power, authority, or executive status with which to support his or her orders.

Often a formal definition will be expanded into an **extended definition**. The extended definition may use examples, comparison and contrast, and any of the other forms of development to explain its subject more fully.

PARAGRAPH CONTAINING AN EXTENDED DEFINITION
BEGINNING WITH A FORMAL DEFINITION

A door is a movable structure contained within a framework that separates two areas by covering an opening and whose principal purpose is to facilitate entrances and exits. There are all kinds of doors. There are hanging doors, swinging doors, overhead doors, trap doors, and sliding doors. As a matter of fact, even strings of beads or sheets of canvas or leather have been used as doors. Doors come in all sizes and shapes. In addition to being made of beads or canvas, they more customarily are made of wood, steel, aluminum, or glass. However we describe them, we have to conclude that they are pretty handy devices. Without them, our living wouldn't be nearly as comfortable or secure as it is.

4. **Development by cause and effect** works in one of two ways. You can list the effect, condition, or result first and then discuss the causes or reasons why the effect has come about. Or you can reverse the process, first investigating the causes or reasons and then discussing what effects, conditions, or results they have produced. Like comparisons and contrasts, causes and effects may be handled in the same paragraph, or you may want to divide them among several paragraphs—one or more on causes, one or more on effects—depending on the nature and complexity of your topic. The following paragraphs first detail effects and then explore the causes of those effects.

> My mother could not understand why her left arm was swollen, itching, and covered with a red rash. When the rash turned to blisters that broke and suppurated, and when the itching kept her awake at night, she went to the doctor. His diagnosis was poison ivy.
>
> She protested that she had not come in contact with any poison ivy plants, although the salve the doctor gave her healed the blisters. A few days later my father mentioned that the highway department had sprayed the poison ivy along our road. The mystery of the rash was solved. While driving with her arm out the car window, my mother had come in contact with the oily fumes of the dying poison ivy plants.

5. **Analysis and classification** are methods of development that take things apart and put them together again. When you **analyze** something, you break it down into its various parts and look at the characteristics of those parts and at how they fit together to comprise the whole. For example, if you analyze the time you spend doing homework, you are likely to find you spend so many minutes on getting your books and cup of coffee; so many minutes on daydreaming, petting the dog, and rereading the assignment; and so many minutes actually studying productively.

When you **classify**, you put items into groups according to their common characteristics. Suppose you want to classify fruit. First you have to establish a basis for classification: natural fruits. Once you have established this basis, you must be sure that the classifications are mutually exclusive, that the items being classified are comparable, and that you do not shift the basis of classification (an error known as **cross-classification**). These points are illustrated following:

BASIS OF CLASSIFICATION: FRUITS IN THEIR NATURAL STATE

1	2	3	4	5
citrus fruit	oranges	oranges	oranges	oranges
noncitrus fruit	apples	apples	winesaps	apples
	grapefruit	grapefruit	grapefruit	grapefruit
	pears	winesaps	pears	potatoes
	peaches	peaches	peaches	peaches

In list 1 are broad groupings of fruit. In 2 are listed various species of fruit. Both 1 and 2 classify fruit in accordance with the stated basis of classification. In 3, however, both apples and winesaps are listed. This classification is not **mutually exclusive**; that is, it lists a subcategory as a separate aspect of discussion. If the subcategory is to be discussed, it must be discussed under the category of which it is a member. In 4, by contrast, winesaps, a subcategory of apples, are listed as being comparable to the categories oranges, grapefruit, pears, and peaches. Hence, the classification is not **comparable** because the subcategory is classified at the same level as the main category. Finally, list 5 departs altogether from the basis of classification, which was fruits, by listing potatoes, which are, of course, vegetables. The result is a **cross-classification**.

We can communicate in three basic ways. Each way has its advantages. One way is by speaking. When we speak we have a chance to judge our audience's reactions. If they don't understand, we can reword as necessary to make our points. We can also invite additional questions and clarify additional aspects for our listeners. Another way of communicating is by writing. When we write, we have more time. We can think our subject through thoroughly. We can modify our development and polish our phraseology until we get it the way we want it. The third way of communicating is nonverbal. Such actions as a look, a nod of the head, or a shake of the hand constitute communication of this type. Nonverbal communication can be quite effective in a very noisy atmosphere or when we don't want to dignify a response with actual words.

The above paragraph establishes as the basis for classification ways of communicating. Its classification is mutually exclusive since it analyzes subaspects of speaking, writing, and nonverbal communication only under the aspects to which they pertain. The aspects in its classification are comparable, and no cross-classification occurs since speaking, writing, and nonverbal communication are all methods of communication.

How much paragraph development is enough? That is a hard question to answer. Only your readers know for sure. If readers are not given enough examples or explanations to understand or accept your topic sentence, your paragraph is not sufficiently developed and, hence, one or more of the aspects of your thesis will be weakened.

Put yourself in the reader's position. If you were seeing the essay for the first time, would you find enough information in the body paragraphs to follow the author's ideas and understand the essay's generalizations and conclusions?

EXERCISE 50, PARAGRAPH DEVELOPMENT   (32e–g)

Read the following paragraphs and decide if they are sufficiently developed with supporting evidence. If a paragraph is sufficiently developed, write *Yes* in the upper blank at the right; if it is not, write *No*. Then decide which principal method of development is being used (details, examples, illustration, comparison, contrast, definition, cause and effect, analysis, classification), and write the method in the lower blank.

Example   Plants are a lot like children.   _____*No*_____

Both thrive on being spoiled and fussed over.   _____*comparison*_____

1. For some people a satisfying career results not from going to college but from dropping out of college. A friend of mine left school after her sophomore year because she felt uncertain about her goals. She took a secretarial job where she met the fellow who cared for the plants in the large office building. From him she got the idea she has since developed into a career. Businesses, doctors, restaurants, and even wealthy home owners hire her to decorate their interiors with plants. She chooses the greenery, pays a "house call" each week to keep it healthy, and replaces plants that die or become unsightly. My friend calls her business "*Leave* It to Me"— a business that resulted from leaving school.   _____   _____

2. Although many plants are easy to grow, some wilt and die unless they get special treatment. If you don't provide just the right environment, plants that looked great at the florist's will turn to brown, withered garbage because they are too delicate to survive in your home.   _____   _____

3. Want to impress a date? Give her an orchid corsage. Women find these irregularly shaped tropical flowers extremely appealing.   _____   _____

4. There are two methods of doing yardwork. Both lead to complaints from the neighbors. The *laissez faire* method is based on noninterference—a sort of "live and let live" philosophy that requires mowing and trimming only when it is no longer possible for the mail carrier to get to the front door. Neighbors hate this method, claiming the looks of your jungle lowers their property values. The manicurist's method, on the other hand, requires mowing so often that your grass never seems to grow at all. Neighbors won't even speak to a manicurist. After all, nobody likes a fanatic.   _____   _____

5. Plant science can be divided into three areas of study. Botanists study plants in their wild state, as they occur in nature. Horticulturists study plants under cultivation: fruits, vegetables, flowers, and ornamental plants. Horticulture generally refers to small-scale gardening, whereas agriculture, the third area, refers to the study of field crops grown on a large scale.

    _____

    _____

6. Plant science has contributed greatly to human well-being. It has improved food crops, helping to feed the world's people. It has discovered new uses for plants, such as in pharmaceuticals and pollution control.

    _____

    _____

Choose a topic, and then, using your own paper, write a paragraph developed by the method called for in each of items 7 through 12. Be sure to write a topic heading above each paragraph.

7. Choose a topic and use details about the topic to develop a paragraph of at least four sentences.

8. Choose a topic and use examples and explanatory remarks concerning those examples to develop a paragraph of at least four sentences.

9. Choose a topic and develop a paragraph of at least four sentences. Start the paragraph with a formal definition and then extend the definition, using examples, comparison and contrast, and any other forms of development you find suitable.

10. Choose a topic and develop a paragraph of at least four sentences in which you explain an effect or result in terms of its causes.

11. Choose a topic and write a paragraph containing at least four sentences using comparison and contrast as the method of development. Be sure that you have at least one comparison and at least one contrast in the paragraph.

12. Choose a topic and then develop it in a paragraph of at least four sentences using classification and analysis. Be sure to indicate your basis of classification. Also be sure that the aspects in your classification are mutually exclusive and comparable and do not result in cross-classification.

51

CONSISTENCY OF PARAGRAPH TONE   (32h)

A paragraph is **consistent** if its tone does not change unexpectedly for no apparent reason. The tone of your writing should be appropriate—both for your assumed audience and for your purpose and subject matter. Readers are unlikely to find your ideas and point of view credible if the language is sarcastic in one sentence, light and humorous in the next, and solemn in the next. They will not trust you if the tone keeps shifting, because tone is an indication of attitude.

That is not to say that an essay may not shift among lighter moments and more serious ones; good writing often does that deliberately, to further the purpose and achieve desired effects. But unnecessary changes in tone will disconcert the reader, an experience you have probably had yourself. Imagine reading a paragraph that has a fairly serious tone when suddenly the author seems to find the subject very funny. You may become uncomfortable, even rather embarrassed, and begin to wonder if you've somehow overlooked the punch line or missed the point.

Tone is a cue to readers about the attitude you are taking toward the subject—and the attitude you want them to take. It is also a cue about your attitude toward the readers. If the level or type of vocabulary is inappropriate and inconsistent, not only will readers be confused and unsettled, they are likely to become irritated or even insulted.

The type and level of vocabulary used in a paragraph give it its tone. Notice how the tone of the following two paragraphs differs, although the subject is the same in both.

> Last night I had a blind date with one of the most attractive but least popular women in the class. She has a very superior attitude and makes men feel that they are not good enough for her. In view of her attitude toward the opposite sex, few men date her twice.

> Last night I was set up with one of our class's real losers. She's a knock-out as far as looks go, but as for personality—a drag for sure. Talk about stuck up! She made it plain that on a scale of 1 to 10 I was a −2. No wonder none of the guys are beating down her door.

The tone in each paragraph is consistent. In the first paragraph it is fairly formal, impersonal, and unemotional. The tone in the second paragraph is very informal. The use of slang emphasizes the writer's intensely personal feelings. The word choice conveys a sarcastic, somewhat angry attitude.

The tone of the second paragraph would be appropriate for a letter written to one of the author's close friends. The tone of the first paragraph is appropriate for a broader, more general audience. Imagine how inappropriate the second paragraph would be for that audience. Furthermore, imagine how inappropriate a mixture of the two tones would be.

> Last night I had a blind date with a real knock-out as far as looks go, but she is one of the least popular women in the class. A real drag for sure, she has a very superior attitude and makes men feel like a −2. In view of her attitude toward the opposite sex, none of the guys are beating down her door for dates.

Tone is one way of telling the reader how you want the meaning of a paragraph to be understood. If the tone is inconsistent, readers may dismiss your writing as amateurish and uncontrolled.

EXERCISE 51, CONSISTENCY OF PARAGRAPH TONE (32h)

Using your own paper, revise the following paragraphs so that they reflect a consistent tone appropriate for a thoughtful, college-level audience.

1. Writing a research paper is an intellectual challenge—one that requires a great deal of application and a great deal of patience. One of the first things a researcher has to do is locate reference junk that will impress the prof. It's best to use highbrow periodicals, the types that are read only by grinds. You also should use books that sound like they were put together by jerks who never come out of the tombs into the sunlight. Be sure to draw upon several sources and when you copy anything, only put quotes around it once in awhile. Otherwise, they'll get the idea you can't put in your own lingo.

2. Ask a student enrolled in an MBA program what kind of job he or she wants after graduation, and you're likely to be told "one in consulting." Consulting jobs are hot stuff with megabuck salaries. Clients bring their tough business problems to consulting firms where staff members are assigned to find the flies in the ointment and propose solutions. A consultant's job tends to have more variety than some other types of business careers that can be the pits as far as routine goes.

3. According to surveys by professional pollsters, for admirability and trustworthiness the public ranks politicians at the bottom of the scale, along with used-car salesmen. For sure! In my opinion, politicians are a bunch of deceitful, money-grabbing bums. I wouldn't trust them any further than I can throw my Aunt Martha, and she weighs 300 pounds. Most politicians are beholden to cronies and special-interest groups; consequently, they vote the way the people who financed their campaigns want them to. Or else they're slipperier than greased pigs, eschewing promises and party platform planks whenever it suits them. If it means getting elected, politicians will change directions faster than a jack rabbit being chased by a cougar.

4. Everyone knows that police officers undergo special training, often attending a police academy. Most folks, however, aren't aware that today's fuzz includes a number of college graduates. Kids who want to go into law enforcement may major in criminal justice at college. No, they don't bone up on finger-printing and other cloak-and-dagger stuff. That Dick Tracy jazz is still the prerogative of the police academies. Instead, criminal justice types hit the books in courses such as sociology, law, technical writing, psychology, and computer science.

5. The pill pusher behind the counter at your corner drug store has a pretty fancy education. A registered pharmacist not only has a college education but often has had the benefit of five, rather than four years, in an institution of higher learning. Pharmacy students get hit with pre-med courses including extra-heavy-duty doses of chemistry. They also complete an internship and have to ace a state licensing exam.

52

WRITING PERSUASIVELY   (33d-e)

To be effective, writing must not only be unified, coherent, developed, and consistent, it must also be persuasive. An essay with a clear, manageable thesis that is sufficiently supported with well-organized, well-developed paragraphs will not be successful unless the reasoning used in the paragraphs is logical and fair.

That means the generalizations presented in the thesis statement, topic sentences, and conclusions should not be so broad or overstated that they cannot be supported adequately by evidence. Judgments should be fair and soundly based in facts, not emotions or prejudices. The reasoning used to draw conclusions about the topic and to show the truth of a point of view should be logical, not filled with fallacies and errors. If you want to convince your readers, your writing must be credible. Credibility is built on supportable generalizations, fair judgments, and sound reasoning.

An unqualified **generalization** asserts that what is sometimes true is always true.

I know two members of the varsity football team and they are very poor students.

It's too bad that football players are so stupid.

In this example, a sweeping statement has been made based upon very limited evidence. Checking the scholastic records of all members of the team, however, very likely would have shown that on an overall basis, football players make about the same grades as other students. Some may be poor students, but others are good students and the majority, like the majority of all students, are probably average in their studies.

The point is, of course, that generalizations should be based upon a scrutiny of representative samples of actual, verifiable evidence. If, for example, the scholastic records of an entire football team were examined and it was determined that the scholastic average of these players was below average, it could be stated with authority—in this particular instance, at that particular school—that football players were below-average performers in the classroom. But to go further and state that all football players are below average would be making a generalization that had not been substantiated.

Unless you are certain about the absolute truth of a generalization and certain your readers are aware of its truth, you will need to qualify the generalization to conform to the evidence. For example, the assertion about football players would have been more accurate and acceptable if the author had written, "It's too bad some football players are so stupid." If the reader can think of exceptions to the "rule" asserted in your generalization, then the generalization is "hasty." It is too broad, and making it weakens the credibility of your argument.

Fair judgments, like generalizations, must be based on facts. Making a judgment on what you want to believe is rarely as good as making a judgment on what you know. You should be particularly careful to avoid prejudice. Prejudiced statements can be not only those based on your own prejudice but also those that appeal to the prejudice of others. Another tactic you should avoid is making your argument against an individual instead of against the issue; this type of argument is known as *argumentum ad hominem*, "argument to the man."

For example, one politician may say of an opponent, "Candidate Robbins will not represent working people's interests in the legislature. She inherited all her money. What could she know about the problems of average, working people?" This argument attacks Robbins personally because she has inherited wealth. It does not deal with the issue of her abilities as a state legislator. Robbins certainly does not necessarily have to be poor or even middle class to understand her constituents' problems or to speak on their behalf.

If a judgment cannot be supported by worthwhile evidence, no amount of name calling or appealing to readers' personal biases will make it legitimate. Even if your prejudices are shared by readers, you are still responsible for presenting a fair and truthful point of view. Besides, thoughtful and questioning readers—unlikely to be fooled by prejudicial judgments derived from sketchy, loaded, or manipulated evidence—will respond negatively to arguments so constructed.

Various forms of unsound reasoning are known as **logical fallacies**. Two of the more common types of fallacious reasoning are broadly categorized as fallacies of oversimplification and fallacies of distortion. Two fallacies have already been mentioned: hasty, broad generalization, a fallacy of oversimplification; and argument to the man, a fallacy of distortion. Other fallacies in these two categories include the following:

FALLACIES OF OVERSIMPLIFICATION

1. *Post hoc, ergo propter hoc* ("after this, therefore because of this") is an inappropriate assumption that a cause-and-effect relationship exists.

> I knew when that black cat crossed my path last week I would have some bad luck. Sure enough, today I broke my leg. [It's very doubtful the cat was a contributing cause.]

2. *False analogy* occurs when the arguer assumes that because two things are alike in some respects, they are alike in all respects.

> Children are like fragile spring flowers. To be properly raised, both need lots of tender, loving care and plenty of protection from life's cold winds. [Children and flowers do benefit from loving care, but as many parents will testify, children are also resilient and suffer if they are overprotected and kept from learning to deal with life's disappointments.]

3. *Either/or* (also known as *"all or nothing"*) *fallacy* is a statement that assumes only two alternatives when more than two are involved. This fallacy is sometimes called a "false dilemma."

> I know she isn't a Republican so she must be a Democrat. [The woman may be an Independent, a Communist, a Libertarian, have no political party affiliation, and so on.]

FALLACIES OF DISTORTION

4. *Argumentum ad verecundiam* (transfer fallacy) is an attempt to transfer characteristics, knowledge, or authority from one area of expertise to an unrelated area. This fallacy is commonly used in political campaigns and consumer advertisements such as endorsements by celebrities.

> Indianapolis 500-winner Ralph Racer says Super-slick Oil is best. I'd better get some for my car. [There aren't many similarities between a race car and the family station wagon; Ralph's testimony may be less "expert" than it is being made to seem.]

5. *Argumentum ad populum* ("argument to the people") is an appeal to readers' emotions and biases, usually playing on beliefs that are widely held to be sacred (such as motherhood or patriotism) or on deeply ingrained distrust and fear (such as threats of Communist invasion or nuclear war). A related fallacy is known as "bandwagon"; it appeals to people's instincts to "join the crowd."

> Every right-thinking citizen believes the federal government interferes too much in Americans' lives—except for Nicholas, but then he's an admitted socialist. [The "glitter" words *right-thinking citizen* and the "scare" word *socialist* play upon the crowd's desire to belong to an in-group.]

6. *Non sequitur* ("it does not follow") is a wrong inference instead of a logically sound conclusion, usually a leap in logic that omits proof.

> He is the person the class voted to be most successful. He is bound to be a company president. [Success has many definitions, and it's a long way to the executive suite.]

7. *Begging the question* is an assumption of the truth of a statement when, in fact, the truth has to be proven.

> Since they're rich, they must have done something illegal to get all that money. [Wealth is assumed to be evil or at least the result of evil doings. The writer assumes but does not prove that wealth cannot be acquired honestly. The fact is, many fortunes are built on honest labor and sound, legal investments.]

8. *Red herring* is a false "scent" or "trail," an attempt to distract the reader from the real issue needing proof by changing the subject to something else. A red herring often introduces an emotional subject intended to divert the reader's attention.

> I didn't deserve a D on the French test. Besides, the instructor doesn't like me. [Personal dislike, whether true or not, is beside the point. The issue is the quality of the student's work.]

Practice: Identifying unqualified generalizations   *Some of the following statements contain qualifying words that make them acceptable generalizations. Other statements do not contain qualifiers, are too sweeping, and thus are unacceptable generalizations. Underline the qualifying words in the acceptable generalizations. Note as unacceptable those generalizations that are unqualified and too sweeping. The answers are listed at the end of the section.*

[1] Anybody who gets straight A's must cheat. [2] People in the military are very dogmatic and can't think for themselves. [3] Some Mexicans are hot-headed and love to argue. [3] Beautiful women don't make good wives. [5] Swedes are big, blonde, and dumb. [6] Because of the Southerners' record of slavery and racial prejudice, Blacks occasionally cannot get a square deal in parts of the South. [7] Orientals sometimes have trouble learning English because the linguistic systems of Indo-European languages and Oriental languages are so different. [8] Environmentalists will oppose his nomination for Secretary of the Interior. He voted against environmental issues when he was in Congress. [9] A person who has taken three writing courses will generally write better than the person who has taken none. [10] Almost everyone enjoys sports, but a few people become fanatical sports fans.

Answers to the Practice   [1] unacceptable [*Anybody* is too sweeping and all-inclusive; many students who get all A's do not cheat.]   [2] unacceptable [*People* is all-inclusive, suggesting that *all those* who are in the military are dogmatic.]   [3] Some   [4] unacceptable [*Beautiful women* is too sweeping; many beautiful women are good wives.]   [5] unacceptable [*Swedes* is all-inclusive; not all Swedes are big, blonde, and dumb.]   [6] occasionally; parts   [7] sometimes   [8] unacceptable [*Environmentalists* is all-inclusive; some environmentalists probably will approve the nomination. The second sentence needs no qualification because it is a matter of record.]   [9] generally   [10] Almost; a few

EXERCISE 52-1, GENERALIZATIONS AND FAIRNESS   (33d)

For each of the following statements, insert an *X* in the blank at the right if the statement is a faulty generalization; if the statement is not faulty, write *OK*.

Examples	Women make poor business managers; they're too emotional.	X
	Some high school students are not college material.	OK

1. All politicians are dishonest. _____

2. Jones is a well-liked instructor. In student evaluations, over 90 percent of his students give him the highest possible rating. _____

3. When the barometer drops sharply, it indicates that rain or some kind of inclement weather is probable. _____

4. College graduates are more intelligent than anyone else. _____

5. If you go out with wet hair, you are bound to catch a cold. _____

6. There's no doubt about it: Latin people are very warmhearted and outgoing, whereas Swedish people are very reserved. _____

7. Fat people don't care about their looks or they would lose weight. _____

8. We sold twice as many Lee jeans in our store as all other brands combined. Our customers obviously prefer Lees. _____

9. Sales in district A have dropped. We need a new district manager. _____

10. Statistics show that over 50,000 people die and over 2 million others are injured in automobile accidents every year in the U.S.A. You take your life in your hands every time you get into a car. _____

11. Less than half the people in the 18–21 age group voted last year. Obviously, young people don't care about their country. _____

12. O'Malley flunked biology, chemistry, anatomy, and physiology. I think she should give up trying to be a doctor. _____

13. It never snows in Miami. _____

14. Since Americans are law-abiding citizens, they obey the 55-mile-per-hour speed limit. _____

15. He voted against the school bond issue. I wonder why he is against children. _____

16. Hemingway is regarded as one of the great writers of this century. Everyone who reads him likes him. _____

17. On our campus, engineering students take only one semester of the English composition sequence. Obviously, they are good writers and don't need the second writing course. _____

18. You can't play tackle in professional football unless you weigh over two hundred pounds. _____

19. All of Professor Simpkin's students get A's and B's. This proves he is a good teacher. _____

20. Every time I go to the doctor, he finds something wrong with me. _____
Doctors are certainly out after the money.
21. Capital punishment involves the destruction of a human being. _____
Consequently, everyone who favors it is a murderer at heart.
22. College entrance scores have gone down considerably over the _____
past ten years. This proves that young people are not as smart as
they used to be.
23. Grades are bad because they give some students an inferiority _____
complex. Consequently, we should do away with grades.
24. We know we have a good coach because our team has won the _____
championship six years in a row.
25. Prices at the grocery keep going up. Farmers must be making a _____
nice profit.

For each of the following statements, insert an *X* in the blank to the right if the
statement is unfair, unethical, prejudiced, or based on apparent wishful thinking
rather than on a straightforward examination of the evidence. If the statement is
correct, write *OK*.

Example   My neighbor Jack says Ann Jones hates   ___X___
children; no wonder she's a lousy teacher.

26. They made their money in the liquor business so they are _____
obviously an immoral lot.
27. I know that they have a much better record than we do, but our _____
team has spirit and will win.
28. Hudson County would vote for the devil himself if he were on _____
the Democratic ticket.
29. My son says he saw the minister's daughter shoplifting at the _____
discount store. He must have been mistaken.
30. He has been convicted twice for graft. I can't see voting for him _____
for county treasurer.
31. There must be something wrong with their merchandise since _____
their prices are so low.
32. College professors are smart in the classroom, but they don't have _____
enough common sense to walk across the street.
33. Teenagers pay more for insurance because statistics show that a _____
greater percentage of that age group is involved in accidents than
are other groups.

EXERCISE 52-2, UNSOUND REASONING: FALLACIES   (33d–e)

For each of the following statements, write an *X* in the blank to the right if the statement contains any of the fallacies discussed in Section 52. If the statement is logical, write *OK*.

Example   When you have insomnia, you can either   *X*
toss and turn or take a sleeping pill.

1. All twentieth-century wars the United States has been involved   _____
   in were started under Democratic administrations. So if you want
   war, vote Democratic.
2. If *The New York Times* says so, it's probably true.   _____

3. Senator Millstrom says the Russians will never attack us, so let's   _____
   do away with our ICBM's.
4. They pull their pants on one leg at a time just as we do, so they   _____
   can't be any better than we are.
5. The poor are not industrious. If they were industrious, they   _____
   wouldn't be poor.
6. I'm sure she isn't Catholic, so she must be Protestant.   _____

7. I have had trouble with botany, so I'll probably have trouble   _____
   with zoology.
8. Since he was a Heisman Trophy winner, his chances of being a   _____
   starter for the Cowboys are good.
9. Professor Stillwell kicked the demonstrators out of his class. He   _____
   certainly doesn't believe in free speech.
10. Joe worked twenty hours a week this term and flunked out. It   _____
    just goes to prove you can't go to school and work at the same
    time.
11. She is a very inconsistent person because she does one thing one   _____
    time and just the opposite the next.
12. Flu shots work only about three-fourths of the time. But it's still   _____
    a good idea to take them if a flu epidemic is suspected.
13. They won the national championship last year and have most of   _____
    their personnel back. So they're bound to win it again this year.
14. Twenty movie stars have endorsed this brand of cosmetics. If   _____
    it's good enough for them, it's good enough for you.
15. American auto workers have sabotaged several cars on   _____
    automobile production lines. You're better off buying a foreign
    automobile.
16. The rain came because the Indians staged their rain dance.   _____

17. Since he received nothing but A's in accounting, he should be a   _____
    good accountant.
18. To become a successful person, one must be successful in what   _____
    he or she attempts.
19. Buying stocks in our company is a good investment. We are going   _____
    to expand our market and the value of your shares will skyrocket.

20. Professor Jones is one of the top psychologists in the country; so when she says that nuclear power is dangerous, we should listen to her. _____

21. Cleenzo must be the best detergent or it wouldn't be the leading brand. _____

22. I said you're too young to drive 400 miles to your grandmother's by yourself. Since I'm your parent, I know what's best. _____

23. Television programs that portray homosexuality and extramarital affairs are a threat to American family values. _____

24. A prison can be a lot like a pressure cooker. If the prisoners' anger and frustration reach the boiling point and find no safe release, the lid can blow off. _____

25. After Marcia dyed her hair, she had many more dates. It is true that blondes have more fun. _____

53

EFFECTIVE SENTENCES:
COORDINATION AND SUBORDINATION (34)

Sections 6-8 on phrases, clauses, and sentence types introduced some ideas we now need to review. As you discovered in those earlier sections, phrases enable a writer to elaborate, amplify, and qualify the information provided in the core of the sentence—in the simple subject and simple predicate. Clauses enable a writer to combine several related ideas into one sentence. Using coordination and subordination, a writer can express related thoughts in one sentence, instead of having to write a separate sentence for each thought. By using different types of sentence patterns, a writer can achieve greater sentence variety and emphasis.

In the next four sections, we will explore in detail these techniques that will give you more control over your writing and thus your ability to express your meaning in interesting and effective ways.

COORDINATION

The simplest kind of coordination involves joining words, phrases, or clauses with the coordinating conjunctions *and, but, or, nor, for, so,* and *yet.* Coordination establishes relationships of approximately equal rank or importance between ideas. Coordination also allows you to condense and compress information. Notice how the information in the following series of sentences is compressed and smoothed when it is combined into one sentence using coordinating conjunctions:

> Switzerland is a tiny country. It has few natural resources. It has become prosperous as an international banking center.
> Switzerland is a tiny country *and* has few natural resources, *but* it has become prosperous as an international banking center. [Two independent clauses coordinated by the conjunction *but,* showing contrast; verbs within the first clause coordinated by the conjunction *and.*]

You have probably also noticed the coordinated sentence makes more sense than the three separate sentences—because the relationships among ideas have been clearly expressed by the conjunctions, rather than left for the reader to figure out.

In addition to the coordinating conjunctions previously mentioned, parts of sentences can be joined by correlative conjunctions—coordinating conjunctions that work in pairs—such as *both . . . and, either . . . or, neither . . . nor, not . . . but, not only . . . but also.* For example: *Not only the stability of Swiss politics but also the stability of Swiss currency attracts foreign depositors.*

Conjunctive adverbs such as *however, nevertheless, therefore,* and *furthermore* do not connect words, phrases, and clauses but, when used with a semicolon, link whole sentences: *Swiss currency is backed by huge gold reserves; consequently, Swiss banks are a very safe place for one's money.*

SUBORDINATION

Another effective method of combining and relating ideas is subordination. Coordination will not provide the focus you need if, for example, two ideas are not of equal importance or one depends on the other for its meaning. Consider the following pair of sentences:

| IDEAS COORDINATED | Swiss bank account numbers are secret, *and* a depositor's identity can be hidden. |
| IDEAS SUBORDINATED | *Because* Swiss bank account numbers are secret, a depositor's identity can be hidden. |

In the first sentence the two facts are given equal importance and rank by the coordinating conjunction *and.* The second sentence, however, expresses a more specific cause-and-effect relationship that establishes the dependence of one fact upon the other: identities can be hidden *because* account numbers are secret.

If you combine too many ideas—or illogically combine ideas—with coordinating conjunctions, your writing will reflect what is known as "primer style," parts of sentences monotonously and unemphatically connected by *and* or *but: Zurich is Switzerland's largest city, and banks line its main street, and the train station is at one end, but Lake Zurich is at the other.*

Another form of primer style is successive, short, choppy sentences: *The main street is called Bahnhofstrasse. Bahnhof means "train station." Strasse means "street." The train station is on Bahnhofstrasse.*

Subordinating details, qualifications, and ideas of lesser importance indicate your focus to the reader. Subordinating conjunctions include *although, because, if, when, since, before, unless,* and *after,* as well as the relative pronouns *who, which,* and *that* (see Section 7 for a more complete list): *The main street is called Bahnhofstrasse, which means "train station street," because the train station is on it.*

Remember that because a subordinate clause is of lesser importance, the information in it should not contain your main idea. The main idea belongs in the main clause. You do not want to mislead your reader by illogically burying the most important idea in a dependent clause.

| ILLOGICAL SUBORDINATION OF MAIN IDEA | Swiss bankers guard so much "treasure" because they are called "gnomes." |
| LOGICAL SUBORDINATION OF QUALIFYING IDEA | Swiss bankers are called "gnomes" because they guard so much "treasure." |

In many cases, of course, only you know for sure which idea is your primary focus and which is a modifier. The following examples show how subordination can affect meaning by changing the focus in the same collection of information:

Switzerland is famous for its chocolate and fine watches although it is well known for banking. [Stresses chocolate and watches in main clause.]

Switzerland is well known for banking although it is famous for its chocolate and fine watches. [Stresses banking in the main clause.]

APPOSITIVES, PARTICIPIAL PHRASES, AND ABSOLUTE PHRASES

Besides subordinate clauses, three other types of constructions can be used to subordinate ideas and economically add details to core sentences.

An **appositive** is a word or phrase that renames or further identifies another word, usually a noun or pronoun. In the sentence *A commercial bank demand deposit, a checking account, is a necessity in today's world,* the words *a checking account* are the appositive renaming *deposit.* An appositive can often be substituted for a subordinate clause or even several subordinate clauses or sentences, thus providing a more streamlined way of supplying details. Notice how the following examples proceed from separate ideas in separate primer-style sentences, to sentences combined using clauses, to sentences combined using an appositive.

PRIMER-STYLE SEPARATE SENTENCES	A commercial bank demand deposit is a checking account. A checking account has become a necessity in today's world.
SENTENCES COMBINED WITH A CLAUSE	A commercial bank demand deposit is a checking account, *which has become a necessity in today's world.*
SENTENCES COMBINED WITH AN APPOSITIVE	A commercial bank demand deposit, *a checking account,* has become a necessity in today's world.

A **participle** is a verb form ending in *-ing* (present participle: *moving, eating, sleeping*), ending in *-ed* or *-en,* or having another irregular form (past participle: *moved, eaten, slept*). Participles, together with their objects and modifiers forming participial phrases, can function as adjectives. They offer another alternative to subordinate clauses for combining ideas in sentences, as the following examples show.

SEPARATE SENTENCES	Checks account for about 90 percent of the payments made in America. People prefer checks. Checks are safer and more efficient than cash for paying bills.
SENTENCES COMBINED WITH CLAUSES	People prefer checks, *which account for about 90 percent of the payments made in America, because they are safer and more efficient for paying bills.*
SENTENCES COMBINED WITH PARTICIPIAL PHRASES	People prefer checks, *accounting for about 90 percent of the payments made in America, finding them safer and more efficient for paying bills.*
	Finding them safer and more efficient for paying bills, people prefer checks, *accounting for about 90 percent of the payments made in America.*

Participles are fairly flexible in their placement, as the previous examples show. However, be careful not to create misplaced or dangling modifiers when you use participles to combine ideas (see Sections 22–23).

An **absolute phrase** is an especially compressed modifier that, because it modifies the whole sentence rather than any single word, can be placed effectively at many locations in a sentence. An absolute phrase consists of a subject (usually a noun or pronoun), a participle, and any modifiers of the participle. Almost any sentence containing a form of the verb *be* followed by a present or past participle can be transformed into an absolute phrase by omitting the *be* form of the verb. Absolute phrases can also be formed by changing a main verb into its *-ing* form.

SENTENCE	The check had been stolen, so I stopped payment on it.
ABSOLUTE	*The check stolen,* I stopped payment on it.
SENTENCE	The amount was large, and I phoned the bank immediately.
ABSOLUTE	*The amount being large,* I phoned the bank immediately.

Practice: Identifying subordinated modifiers   *Underline the appositives, participial phrases, and absolute phrases in the following sentences. The answers are listed at the end of this section.*

267

[1] Our society, sometimes called a cashless society, is rapidly becoming a plastic society. [2] Carrying less and less cash, people increasingly charge purchases on credit cards. [3] Too many Americans find themselves seriously in debt, their purchases having exceeded their ability to pay for them. [4] The bills due, some people carry part of their charges over to the next month, thus incurring a hefty finance charge. [5] Their personal finances hopelessly a mess, these people, the "plastic addicts," finally declare bankruptcy in extreme cases.

Answers to the Practice   [1] sometimes called a cashless society [participial phrase; appositive]   [2] Carrying less and less cash [participial phrase]   [3] their purchases having exceeded their ability to pay for them [absolute phrase]
[4] The bills due [absolute phrase] ; thus incurring a hefty finance charge [participial phrase]   [5] Their personal finances hopelessly a mess [absolute phrase] ; the "plastic addicts" [appositive]

EXERCISE 53-1, COORDINATION AND SUBORDINATION   (34a–b)

Revise the following sentences using coordinating conjunctions, subordinating conjunctions, and relative pronouns to combine ideas and eliminate primer style.

Example   Banking is a huge business. American banks employ over 300,000 bank officers. There are even more bank employees.

Banking is a huge business, which in America employs over 300,000 bank officers and even more other employees.

1.   A loan officer makes decisions on loan applications. A trust officer manages property. Trust officers also manage money or real estate. They plan taxes and investments.

_____

2.   Operations officers manage the day-to-day procedures at the bank. They make sure the operations are efficient and orderly.

_____

3.   Customer relations officers help solve customers' problems. They help plan advertising campaigns. Some customer relations officers even represent the bank in its dealings with other banks. They plan special offers to new customers.

_____

4.   Branch managers oversee the operations of a branch office. They have full responsibility for the branch office. These positions are sought after. They offer very good experience for a bank officer moving up into still higher positions.

_____

5.   There are other positions available in banking. Banks employ secretaries, guards, and public relations officers. Large banks have personnel departments and transportation divisions.

_____

6.   Many bank officers have degrees in business administration or accounting. Some majored in economics. Many have very specific training. They majored in banking.

_____

7.   Banks in large cities often have special training programs. These programs train liberal arts or other majors. The training deals specifically with bank operations.

_____

8.   The American Institute of Banking gives training to bank employees, and its courses are taught during the workday at the bank, and employees can earn certification in more specialized fields by taking these courses.

_____

9. Good bank officers must be assertive, and they must be able to analyze details, and they must inspire confidence, but they must be interested in working with money.

_____

10. Small banks in small towns usually pay less than big city banks. Officers in small banks usually start as tellers. They work their way up.

_____

11. Bank officers in large banks are promoted from investment departments. They are promoted from operations departments. High-ranking positions are seldom filled from personnel departments or public relations.

_____

12. You must get the relevant college training. You must get the relevant experience. You have to have the right first job to move up into higher positions at large banks.

_____

13. Bank officers once were considered staid. Or at least they were considered cautious. Today bankers make exciting deals. They deal in gigantic sums. Some of their deals may even be considered risky.

_____

14. The current trend in banking is toward all-electronic transfers of funds. This will make check writing obsolete. Paper work will disappear.

_____

15. This trend is gaining momentum. Even the smallest banks are using computers to track their accounts. Banking will become a major employer of computer-science graduates.

_____

16. Bankers say their work isn't all numbers. They help people with their problems, and people trust bankers, and tell them so.

_____

17. A loan officer may decide on loan applications from many different kinds of businesses. This requires a lot of research. Every day he or she may be learning about a new product or service.

_____

18. Medieval goldsmiths were the first bankers. They sold gold to the wealthy. Customers then left the gold with the goldsmith for safety.

_____

EXERCISE 53-2, PARTICIPLES, APPOSITIVES, AND ABSOLUTES (34d)

Combine the following sentences, expressing what you believe to be the most important idea in the main clause and using participial phrases, appositives, or absolute phrases to subordinate other ideas. Be sure to avoid dangling or misplaced modifiers in your revisions.

Example   The field of finance offers career possibilities for all kinds of graduates. Finance is an industry that is absolutely essential to economic growth.

Offering career possibilities for all kinds of graduates, finance is an industry that is absolutely essential to economic growth.

1. The center of financial activity in America is Wall Street. The finance industry makes money available to government and industry.

    _____

2. Data processing by computer has allowed instant transfer and communications. Now the finance industry has spread offices and branches coast to coast.

    _____

3. A stockbroker buys and sells securities for a client. Brokers take commissions on each transaction.

    _____

4. Brokers are sometimes called "account executives." They are basically salespeople. They quote prices and handle orders.

    _____

5. Stockbrokers must know the quality of various investments. They also must understand customer psychology.

    _____

6. Many brokers specialize in selling certain kinds of stocks. Others specialize in selling bonds or mutual funds. They recognize that the securities market is very complex.

    _____

7. Brokers make commissions that are based on the size of the customer's purchase. Block traders purchase large "blocks" of shares for individuals or institutions.

    _____

8. Financial analysis is a very challenging line of work. Analysts study companies in order to judge the value of the companies' stock.

    _____

9. Financial analysts travel widely. They specialize in a particular kind of industry. Some examples of the industries they study include oil, metals, automobiles, or retail.

    _____

10. Financial analysts study a company's financial statements and study its products. They make trips to factories to inspect the factories and interview managers.

    _____

11. Investment counselors are paid a fee by their clients. Their clients hire counselors to advise them about purchasing or selling stocks and bonds.

    _____

12. A portfolio manager also is paid by a client. The difference between a counselor and a manager is that a manager buys and sells securities for the client.

    _____

13. Managers and counselors once were as conservative as bankers. Now the field is highly competitive, and managers and counselors have become very aggressive.

    _____

14. Most brokers and managers are college graduates. Their degrees are not always in business-related fields. Economics and prelaw majors are the majors of the majority of trainees.

    _____

15. Earnings for securities salespeople are very good. The amount of commission earned is related directly to the size and number of transactions a broker initiates.

    _____

16. The largest firms have their own training programs. Smaller brokerage houses depend on hiring graduates of schools that specialize in securities sales training.

    _____

17. (Write your own sentence using coordinating conjunctions and subordinating conjunctions.)

    _____

18. (Write your own sentence using a participial phrase.)

    _____

19. (Write your own sentence using an appositive.)

    _____

20. (Write your own sentence using an absolute phrase.)

    _____

54

PARALLELISM   (35)

Section 48 on paragraph coherence introduced the concept of parallel sentence structure. If successive parts of a sentence, or successive sentences, use the same grammatical construction, they are parallel. Parallel constructions emphasize coordinate relationships, stressing equal importance or rank by means of the repeated grammatical patterns.

You can create parallel structures in just about any part of a sentence by using coordination.

SUBJECTS	*The poor, the ill, and the aged* are assisted by social service agencies.
VERBS	Social workers *interview and counsel* people applying for aid.
DIRECT OBJECTS	Case workers explore *an applicant's needs, financial situation, and eligibility.*
INFINITIVE PHRASES	They have *to check and recheck* the eligibility regulations.
PARTICIPLES MODIFYING NOUNS	*Determining eligibility and detecting fraud* are part of a case worker's job.
ADJECTIVE COMPLEMENTS	Welfare fraud is *illegal but less common* than popularly believed.
NOUN COMPLEMENTS/ PREPOSITIONAL PHRASES	Case workers are *the watchdogs of social service as well as the distributors of aid.*

The equal emphasis stressed by parallel form provides you with yet another tool for indicating and reinforcing meaning in your sentences. Rather than having to say "this is ranked the same as that," you can indicate the ranking through sentence structure. Consequently, parallel structures are particularly useful for combining sentences, as the following examples show.

SUCCESSIVE SENTENCES	A career in social work can be rewarding. It can also be depressing.
SENTENCES COMBINED USING PARALLELISM	A career in social work can be both rewarding and depressing.

Because parallel structures are formed with coordinators—either coordinating conjunctions (*and, but, or, nor,* etc.) or correlative conjunctions (*either, or; neither, nor; not only, but also; both, and; whether, or*)—you must be careful to avoid faulty parallelism, which would destroy the sameness of structure and thus the equality of emphasis on each side of the coordinator. If you use a noun phrase on one side of the conjunction, for example, be sure to use a noun phrase on the other side as well. If you use *and who, and which,* or *and that* in the second half of a parallel structure, you must be sure to introduce the same type of structure in the first half, too.

FAULTY	One famous social reformer was Helen Sanger, a public health nurse and who was the founder of the birth-control movement in the early 1900's.
CORRECT	One famous social reformer was Helen Sanger, who was a public health nurse and who was the founder of the birth-control movement in the early 1900's.

CORRECT	One famous social reformer was Helen Sanger, a public health nurse and the founder of the birth-control movement in the early 1900's.
FAULTY	She was either cursed or she was praised for her work. [The conjunction *either* coordinates a verb phrase; *or* coordinates an independent clause. Consequently, the parallelism is faulty.]
CORRECT	Either she was cursed or she was praised for her work. [Two parallel clauses.]
FAULTY	The idea of birth control not only outraged the clergy but the public in general. [Verb *outraged* is not properly parallel with *public.*]
CORRECT	The idea of birth control outraged not only the clergy but the public in general. [Nouns *clergy* and *public* are parallel.]

EXERCISE 54, PARALLELISM   (35)

Revise the following sentences to express coordinate ideas in correct parallel form.

Example   Before studying social work, consider volunteering for a local social
agency and to observe social workers on the job.

*Before studying social work, consider volunteering for a local
social agency and observing social workers on the job.*

1.   Volunteers who are interested and can work hard are always welcome.

   _____

2.   Contact the volunteer supervisor of any particular agency, or some communities have
central placement offices where you should appply.

   _____

3.   You should work to understand the field and try to test your own interest in the field.

   _____

4.   Don't take a volunteer job to impress your professors, but you should be testing
yourself.

   _____

5.   A bachelor's degree is required for most jobs in social work, but many jobs make a
master's degree essential.

   _____

6.   Social work students have traditionally concentrated on three methods: case work,
group work, or working with a whole community all at once.

   _____

7.   In case work, a student learns how to help individuals meet their personal needs and
their needs caused by society's demands.

   _____

8.   Group work teaches a student how people in groups can solve mutual problems or
recreational activities can be done together.

   _____

9.   Sociology is a group of theories about the ways people are affected by their families,
their schools, and whatever work it is that they do.

   _____

10. Sociologists work at research that develops these theories, whereas the work of applying the theory in real situations is left up to social workers.

_____

11. Besides a knowledge of this theory, social workers must be aware and have consideration for the feelings of their clients.

_____

12. They must use theoretical ideas critically and be objective and honestly form their own judgments.

_____

13. Much of a social worker's time is spent in counseling sessions or in hours of interviews.

_____

14. Social workers must listen to other people's ideas without becoming angry and uneasiness must be concealed.

_____

15. Nine states currently require a license to practice a social work job, and licensing procedures are being considered by other states.

_____

On a sheet of your own paper, revise the following paragraph, using parallel constructions to combine ideas and eliminating any faulty parallelism.

Social workers work in a variety of settings. They plan activities for children or adults, and they conduct these activities in settlement houses or in hospitals and clinics. Some of this work is performed in correctional institutions. Some social workers, called family service workers, work with families to help them take advantage of agencies and services they might need. Foster care or financial aid are some of the services a social worker arranges. Medical or psychiatric care is also available. And, of course, vocational or educational guidance may also be called for. In addition to programs for the troubled, the deprived, or the disabled, social workers may help design programs for workers, or for people serving in the armed forces, or even populations overseas. The range of activities and the places in which social workers ply their trade are widely varied.

55

EMPHASIS　(36)

As you learned in Section 53 on coordination and subordination, the structure of a sentence plays a key role in focusing a reader's attention on the ideas you want to emphasize. If the most important idea appears in the main clause and information of lesser importance is subordinated, the reader receives valuable signals about the emphasis you intend. Parallel arrangements of information also provide emphasis, as Section 54 explained. Emphatic positioning, use of loose, periodic, and balanced sentences, and appropriate use of active and passive voice verbs also help you achieve emphasis in your writing.

One of the hazards of combining sentences, as you did for the exercises in Section 53, for example, is that emphasis can disappear as you join phrases and clauses together. While sentence combining helps to establish relationships between ideas and reduces unnecessary repetition, if you put too many ideas in a sentence that is not constructed with a clear emphasis, readers won't know where to focus their attention. First, don't be tempted to pile too much information into a single sentence. Second, be sure to structure your sentences for emphasis.

UNFOCUSED SENTENCE CONTAINING TOO MUCH DETAIL	The car with the broken axle and the smashed front end had turned over in the ditch after being hit by the train, but the tow truck began to right the wrecked vehicle because miraculously no one was injured.
SENTENCE REVISED FOR EMPHASIS	After being hit by the train, the car turned over in the ditch, its axle broken and its front end smashed. Miraculously, no one was injured, so the tow truck began to right the wrecked vehicle.

EMPHATIC POSITIONS WITHIN SENTENCES

The most emphatic place in a sentence is the ending. The next most emphatic place is the beginning. The middle of the sentence receives the least amount of emphasis. A good writer achieves forcefulness by inserting the strongest points either at the end or at the beginning of sentences.

WEAK	Most politicians can be trusted, in my opinion.
STRONGER	In my opinion, most politicians can be trusted.
	Most politicians, in my opinion, can be trusted.
WEAK	We will have a picnic if it does not rain.
STRONGER	If it does not rain, we will have a picnic.

Naturally, you are the one who must decide which information merits emphasis. In the first example above, the writer has decided in one case that *In my opinion* should be stressed. In the second case, *in my opinion* becomes the least important information in the sentence and so is inserted parenthetically in the middle. The point is that you should not inadvertently structure a sentence to destroy the emphasis you intend.

LOOSE, PERIODIC, AND BALANCED SENTENCES

A **loose sentence** is a sentence that concerns itself with its main idea first and its subordinate details later. The **periodic sentence** has an exactly opposite arrangement: its subordinate details come first and its main idea comes last. Thus, the periodic sentence often achieves an effect of drama and suspense. Although it provides forcefulness and a sense of climax, the periodic sentence must be used judiciously since its overuse may result in a loss of the very effect you want to achieve.

A **balanced sentence** is a compound sentence in which the independent clauses are exactly, or very nearly, parallel in all elements. Balanced sentences are useful for showing contrasts.

LOOSE	The skillful politician must be a consummate sales-person with a thoughtful answer for every question and a plausible solution for every problem.
PERIODIC	With a thoughtful answer for every question and a plausible solution for every problem, the skillful politician must be a consummate salesperson.
BALANCED	Politicians are sometimes in government, but they are always in sales.

ACTIVE AND PASSIVE VOICE

The **active voice** places emphasis upon the performer of the action, whereas the **passive voice** places emphasis upon that which receives the action. For the most part, you should utilize the active voice since the effect is more forceful. The passive voice results in a slower movement of context and in impersonal writing. Use it only if you wish to place emphasis upon the recipient of an action rather than to emphasize the action itself. In some instances, the performer of the action may not be known. In this case the passive voice is often used. (See Section 13 for more discussion of active and passive voice.)

ACTIVE	John broke the news to her at midnight.
PASSIVE	The news was broken to her by John at midnight.
PASSIVE	He was murdered between ten and eleven o'clock last night.
ACTIVE	Someone murdered him between ten and eleven o'clock last night.

In the second example above, the passive voice is probably preferable since the important aspect is the murder. With active voice and the emphasis that "someone did it," self-evident information gets the emphasis.

EXERCISE 55-1, EMPHASIS   (36a-d)

Revise the following sentences to achieve greater emphasis. Decide which elements are
more important and which are less important, and position the sentence elements to
reflect your choices.

Example   A sales career can be either a dead end or a great opportunity,
depending on how well a salesperson performs.

*Depending on how well a salesperson performs, a sales
career can be either a dead end or a great opportunity.*

1. Salespeople and careers in sales have somehow gained a bad image in America, despite
the fact that so much of the American economy depends on sales.

    _____

2. It seems to me that no new invention, without salespeople, could ever be brought to
consumers.

    _____

3. Very few consumers actually spend any of their time looking for new products to use,
you know.

    _____

4. Popular stories and jokes have portrayed salespeople as dishonest, probably unfairly.

    _____

5. In a recent survey of consumers, salespeople were rated very low in terms of honesty
in the public's opinion.

    _____

6. How many consumers go out to buy something like insurance, however?

    _____

7. People forget that there are many products that aren't even sold in stores, in fact.

    _____

8. As a matter of fact, many wholesale industries depend entirely on salespeople who
sell their products to other businesses or industries before they are made available to
consumers.

    _____

Revise the following sentences, making them periodic.

Example   You can be a good salesperson if you are outgoing and energetic.

If you are outgoing and energetic, you can be a good salesperson.

9. A salesperson needs a positive attitude, among other qualities such as poise and self-confidence.

_____

10. You must not be easily discouraged, because not every call means a sale.

_____

11. A salesperson must derive satisfaction from talking and being with people.

_____

12. A sales career can be demanding: frequent travel, long days, irregular hours.

_____

13. Advertising is a new type of sales, more technologically advanced.

_____

14. Person-to-person is still how most selling is done, because a person still has to complete a sales transaction.

_____

15. Salespersons outnumber advertising workers by 40 to 1, showing how important personal selling still is.

_____

16. You might make a good salesperson if you are alert to changes in speech and body language that express a customer's feelings.

_____

Using your own paper, write a paragraph containing at least two loose sentences, two periodic sentences, and one balanced sentence. Label your sentences according to type.

EXERCISE 55-2, ACTIVE AND PASSIVE VOICE   (36c)

Where appropriate, revise the following sentences using the active voice. If you believe that the passive voice is preferable in a sentence, write *Correct* in the blank.

Example   A lucrative career in sales has been enjoyed by many women.

many women have enjoyed a lucrative career in sales.

1. Sales occupations are categorized by the Department of Labor into six broad groups.

   _____

2. An important role is played by wholesale trade salespeople.

   _____

3. The retail goods consumers buy are sold to retail outlets by wholesale salespeople.

   _____

4. Products made by dozens of manufacturers may be handled by these workers.

   _____

5. The strengths and weaknesses of each product must be known by the salesperson.

   _____

6. A store's stock inventory may be checked by a wholesale salesperson.

   _____

7. Sometimes, new items are ordered directly by the salesperson.

   _____

8. These services are appreciated by retailers.

   _____

9. Time loss and aggravation are prevented by the salesperson who represents many manufacturers.

   _____

10. Manufacturers' representatives, who are independent business people, are paid a commission by the manufacturers for each sale.

    _____

12. Expenses are paid by the "reps" themselves.

    _____

13. One product, a group of similar products, or a wide variety of products are sold by these reps.

_____

14. People who sell only the products of one manufacturer are classified by the Department of Labor as manufacturers' sales workers.

_____

15. Their products are sold to businesses and institutions.

_____

16. Very technical products, such as computers and medical equipment, are sold by sales engineers.

_____

17. Technical problems that the customer experiences are solved by sales engineers.

_____

18. Sometimes a sales engineer is assigned to one account by his or her manufacturer, since these products are so complex.

_____

19. In a survey of New York sales executives, English and speech were ranked first as preferable backgrounds for salespeople.

_____

20. Proper speech techniques are obviously needed by a salesperson in a presentation.

_____

21. English was recommended by the executives because as a salesperson's career advances, writing becomes more important.

_____

22. Insurance is sold by a class of salespeople the Department of Labor classifies as agents.

_____

23. No limits are placed on a salesperson's commission.

_____

24. Sales is one of the few fields in which greater initiative and productivity are rewarded by higher income.

_____

25. In fact, higher salaries are earned by salespeople than are earned by the top executives in many companies.

_____

56

VARIETY (37)

Throughout the previous three sections of this text, we have been considering various ways to achieve effective expression in sentences. Coordination and subordination, parallelism, emphatic positioning of sentence elements, a mixture of loose, periodic, and balanced sentences, and proper use of active and passive voice are all means for adding variety to your writing.

While you may feel satisfied if you can simply put your ideas into grammatically correct sentences, your ideas will lose much of their impact if they are always presented in the same types of sentence constructions. If you rely too heavily on short, simple sentences, always use subject-verb-object sentence patterns, or begin every complex sentence with a subordinate clause, your writing may become monotonous and predictable. Consequently, the reader can be lulled, almost hypnotized, by the unvarying sentence style and may pay less attention to the meaning. Learn to vary the length, type, and pattern of your sentences to fit your meaning, to establish emphasis, and to keep your reader's attention engaged.

SENTENCE LENGTHS AND PATTERNS

Section 55 discussed the advantages and disadvantages of combining a series of short sentences into a larger sentence that relates ideas. The best writing uses a mixture of short sentences and long ones. Readers appreciate having related ideas combined into compound and complex sentences, because then they do not have to work at and guess about connections between thoughts. On the other hand, if you wish to establish a point dramatically, a short sentence will emphatically break the rhythm of a paragraph and draw the reader's attention. Compare the two following paragraphs, and notice how sentence variety helps to achieve emphasis in the second one.

> We could hear the wind howling above us. We huddled in the storm shelter. The tornado roared through the neighborhood like a freight train. It was quiet suddenly, so we climbed the stairs carefully. Our knees were shaking. Father opened the door, and our house was gone.
>
> We could hear the wind howling above us as we huddled in the storm shelter. Sounding like a freight train, the tornado roared through the neighborhood. Suddenly it was quiet. Our knees shaking, carefully we climbed the stairs, and Father opened the door. Our house was gone.

The second paragraph gains much of its dramatic effect from careful sentence construction. The writer has combined sentences in the first part of the paragraph, piling details together to reinforce the sense of chaos associated with the storm. The use of the participial phrase *Sounding like a freight train* and the absolute phrase *Our knees shaking* varies the subject-verb-object arrangement established in the first sentence. The free adverbial modifiers (ones that can be moved to several positions in the sentence) *suddenly* and *carefully* have been located near the front of their sentences for contrast and emphasis. A short sentence has been used to draw the attention to the contrast between the storm's noise and the ominous silence after it had passed. Finally, to emphasize the shock, the writer has used a short, blunt statement to say the house had been destroyed. As a result, the reader can participate in the feelings the writer experienced during the incident—from fear to shock— partially because of the varied sentence lengths and patterns.

Varying the beginnings of sentences often achieves effective expression. Note the revisions of the following sentence:

Little trouble developed in the beginning, and the manager looked forward to a harmonious future.

BEGINNING WITH A PREPOSITIONAL PHRASE	In the beginning, little trouble developed, and the manager looked forward to a harmonious future.
BEGINNING WITH AN ABSOLUTE PHRASE	Little trouble having developed in the beginning, the manager looked forward to a harmonious future.
BEGINNING WITH A PARTICIPIAL PHRASE	Having little trouble in the beginning, the manager looked forward to a harmonious future.
BEGINNING WITH AN EXPLETIVE	There was little trouble in the beginning, and the manager looked forward to a harmonious future.
BEGINNING WITH A SUBORDINATE CLAUSE	Because little trouble developed in the beginning, the manager looked forward to a harmonious future.
BEGINNING WITH A COORDINATING CONJUNCTION	But little trouble developed in the beginning, and the manager looked forward to a harmonious future.

Varying the position of free modifiers (those that can be moved from one place to another in sentences) can also be effective. Adverbs, adverb phrases and clauses, and some participial phrases and absolute phrases can be moved, giving you a choice of effects. Note, for example, the following sentences:

Struggling for a foothold, the mountain climber clung to the cliff.
The mountain climber, *struggling for a foothold,* clung to the cliff.
The mountain climber clung, *struggling for a foothold,* to the cliff.

The basic sentence pattern in English is subject-verb-object. We have already seen that opening a sentence with modifiers changes the effect of this pattern. **Inverting the pattern** can also provide variety, but you will want to use this pattern judiciously because it often strikes readers as somewhat abnormal. You can invert the subject and object; or you can open with a modifier, inverting the subject and verb.

These delays we would not tolerate. [Object-subject-verb]
Next to the newsstand on the corner stood the police officer. [Modifier-verb-subject]

Various types of sentences, too, can be used to create effects. Although you most often write declarative statements, an occasional question, command, or exclamation may better achieve the effect you desire. Notice how the changes, from question to command to statement to exclamation to statement, in the following paragraph lend variety and emphasis to the message.

Is it true that Americans eat one out of three meals away from home? Believe it. Studies show people increasingly rely on restaurants, cafeterias at school or work, or other food services for their meals. Home cooking—forget it! Market researches predict in ten years the meals eaten out will average one in two.

EXERCISE 56-1, CHANGING SENTENCE PATTERNS AND TYPES FOR VARIETY (37)

Revise each of the following sentences to begin with the listed types of constructions. Invent details as necessary to create these constructions.

Example   Many schools offer degrees in hotel management.

(prepositional phrase) *In the United States, many schools offer degrees in hotel management.*

(absolute) *The degree demanded by a growing industry, many schools offer degrees in hotel management.*

1. Restaurant and hotel managers find themselves in one of the most competitive businesses in modern America.

    A. (prepositional phrase) _____

    B. (participial phrase) _____

    C. (expletive) _____

    D. (subordinate clause) _____

    E. (coordinating conjunction) _____

2. There is always room for a new or unique idea.

    A. (subordinate clause) _____

    B. (expletive) _____

    C. (prepositional phrase) _____

    D. (absolute) _____

    E. (participial phrase) _____

3. Original ideas have made fortunes for many people.

    A. (subordinate clause) _____

    B. (participial phrase) _____

    C. (absolute) _____

    D. (expletive) _____

4. Most Americans are familiar with the hotel and restaurant industry.

   A. (prepositional phrase) _____

   B. (participial phrase) _____

   C. (absolute) _____

   D. (subordinate clause) _____

5. Training in hotel management is also valuable at country clubs and other private clubs.

   A. (subordinate clause) _____

   B. (absolute) _____

   C. (prepositional phrase) _____

   D. (coordinating conjunction) _____

Revise each of the following sentences as indicated.

Example   The profits shot upward.

(Invert subject and verb.) *Upward shot the profits.* _____

6. Americans, working and traveling more each year, eat more meals out than any other people.

   (Reposition participial phrase.) _____

   _____

7. The amount of money spent in restaurants seems enormous.

   (Invert subject and verb.) _____

   _____

EXERCISE 56-2, SENTENCE COMBINING FOR VARIETY
AND COHERENCE   (37)

On your own paper, use the techniques we have reviewed in this unit on effective sentences to revise the following paragraph. Strive for sentence variety and emphasis while achieving paragraph coherence. Your revision should contain at least one example of each of the following:

1. Short sentences combined into a complex sentence (subordinating conjunction)
2. Short sentences combined into a compound sentence (coordinating conjunction)
3. Parallel construction
4. Absolute phrase
5. Participial phrase
6. Inverted order—verb preceding subject
7. Appositive
8. Verbs in both the active and passive voices
9. Question or command
10. Effective subordination

At the turn of the century, there were few restaurants in America. Large cities might have several. A small town generally had one restaurant. Usually a hotel might serve food to its guests. Americans traveled less than they travel today. Almost all meals were eaten at home. People who worked away from home took their lunches from home with them to work. The automobile expanded distances from home. It expanded distances from home to school. It expanded the possible commuting distance from home to work. Disposable incomes are larger. More women work outside the home. This includes wives and mothers. Even by the middle of the century, only a few pennies of each food dollar were spent away from home. Now, almost half of each food dollar is spent away from home. Almost $90 billion is spent each year for eating away from home. There are over one-half million retail food outlets in America. We eat at restaurants. We eat at factory or office cafeterias and at institutions like schools and colleges. There are lunch counters at drugstores. Airplanes serve meals. There's even food available from pushcarts. Experts say the industry will continue to grow. Opportunities are abundant for owners or managers of food service firms.

Revise each of the following sentences as indicated.

1. Dean wants his own restaurant very badly.

   (Reposition free adverbial modifier.) _____

   _____

2. In classic European restaurants the service is performed by males only.

    (Reposition prepositional phrase.) _____

    _____

3. Dean worked diligently, his family having promised to help him.

    (Invert subject and verb.) _____

    _____

    (Reposition absolute.) _____

    _____

    (Reposition free adverbial modifier.) _____

    _____

4. Dean finally graduated with honors; he obtained a loan easily from his family; soon he was able to open his restaurant in Detroit.

    (Reposition free adverbial modifiers.) _____

    _____

    (Invert subject and verb.) _____

    _____

    (Reposition prepositional phrases.) _____

    _____

    (Create parallel constructions.) _____

    _____

57

THE DICTIONARY   (38)

Most people use a dictionary mainly for checking spelling and meaning, but a good dictionary can aid a writer in many other ways. A dictionary also records a word's pronunciation, origin (etymology), part of speech, principal parts and plurals or other forms, and frequently its synonyms, antonyms, and level of usage. Often, a dictionary also includes lists of abbreviations; spelling, capitalization, and punctuation rules; biographical and geographical information; vocabularies of rhymes and given names; and a list of U.S. colleges and universities.

Rather than just using your dictionary in the usual way—to look up spelling and meaning—familiarize yourself with the whole volume. Begin by reading the **front matter**. Read the user's guide or explanatory notes, which will tell you what each part of a dictionary entry means and what special information it contains.

Then read the pronunciation guide and the explanation of the abbreviations your dictionary uses. The purpose of the various type faces, labels, abbreviations, symbols, and other conventions found in a dictionary's entry is to achieve compactness and comprehensiveness. Unless you understand their meaning and use, you will miss a great deal of the information from various parts of dictionary entries, so you will need to have read the front matter in your dictionary before you can answer them correctly.

The **back matter** can provide a wealth of information you probably never even knew your dictionary contained. Look it over so that you will know where to find rules for capitalization, for instance, the next time you need them.

Contrary to popular belief, dictionaries do not "define" words. Rather, they record meanings of actual usage, past and present. Some dictionaries record the general, most current meaning first. Others, such as *Webster's Collegiate Dictionary,* list a word's meanings in historical order, the oldest meaning first. Check the front matter in your dictionary to see which type of order it uses.

Language constantly changes. Over time, meanings that once were current may be superseded by newer ones that have achieved wide usage and acceptance. New words enter a language, and other words disappear. For example, thirty years ago you would not have been able to find the word *astronaut* in any dictionary. Dictionaries are periodically revised to take such changes into account. Although you do not need to replace your dictionary every time a new edition is published, you will probably find that by the time you reach middle age the dictionary you used in high school or college will no longer suit your needs. The dictionary is a writer's best resource; be sure you have one that serves as a good working partner.

Name _____ Date _____ Score _____

EXERCISE 57, THE DICTIONARY   (38)

A. In the blanks, identify the language from which each word was borrowed; give only the earliest given source. Since the term *borrowing* refers to languages other than English, the answers *Middle English (ME)*, *Old English (OE)*, and *Anglo-Saxon (AS)* will not be correct.

1.	ampullaceous	_____	2.	aphorism	_____	3.	asseverate	_____
4.	beriberi	_____	5.	bodhisattva	_____	6.	centrifugal	_____
7.	coaptation	_____	8.	decoupage	_____	9.	equity	_____
10.	flocculent	_____	11.	gynandrous	_____	12.	intermezzo	_____
13.	oligarchy	_____	14.	reptile	_____	15.	satrap	_____

B. In the blanks, indicate the original or etymological meaning of each word; that is, give the meaning within the brackets in the dictionary, not the meaning in the definition of the word itself. For example, the etymological meaning of the word *animism* is "soul."

1.	austere	_____	2.	author	_____	3.	bonus	_____
4.	camera	_____	5.	clammy	_____	6.	glaze	_____
7.	herald	_____	8.	marital	_____	9.	picaresque	_____
10.	preach	_____	11.	raddle	_____	12.	sentient	_____
13.	swindler	_____	14.	tribute	_____	15.	volatile	_____

C. All the following words are derived from the name of a person or a place. In the blank after each word, indicate the name of the person or place from which that word is derived.

1.	bayonet	_____	2.	bedlam	_____
3.	bowdlerize	_____	4.	Caesarean section	_____
5.	canter	_____	6.	derringer	_____
7.	malapropism	_____	8.	quisling	_____
9.	shrapnel	_____	10.	tantalize	_____

D. After referring to the user's guide in your dictionary, describe how it indicates the plural form of nouns.

_____

_____

_____

_____

_____

E. Consult your dictionary and in the blanks list all the plural forms it gives for the following nouns.

1. alumna _____

2. amplitude _____

3. apparatus _____

4. bureaucracy _____

5. deer _____

6. dwarf _____

7. index _____

8. locus _____

9. ox _____

10. phenomenon _____

F. After referring to the user's guide in your dictionary, explain how it indicates the principal parts of verbs.

_____

_____

_____

_____

G. Consult your dictionary and in the blanks list all the past tenses and past participles it gives for the following verbs.

1. begin _____

2. depart _____

3. dive _____

4. forget _____

5. lead _____

6. lose _____

7. rise _____

8. thrive _____

9. throw _____

10. write _____

58

VOCABULARY (39)

Just as a variety of sentence patterns or methods of paragraph development can make your writing more interesting for a reader, so a varied and appropriate use of language can improve your writing. Your choice of vocabulary can be extremely important to many aspects of your writing. Not only do you want to use the most accurate and expressive words to convey your meaning, but as you learned in Section 48, vocabulary choices can improve coherence within paragraphs. Synonyms, for example, can help your reader see the connections between ideas as well as add variety to sentences.

On the other hand, you must be careful when you select synonyms. Many words are loosely synonymous, but each word has its own connotations or shades of meaning. If you consult a thesaurus, synonym dictionary, or the synonym entries in your desk dictionary, also be sure to look up the meaning of the synonym in the dictionary. You want to be certain that the connotations of the word fit the context in which you intend to use it. As Section 51 pointed out, some words may be inappropriate to the tone of your paragraph, even though they are synonymous.

A word's etymology can help you decide if it is an appropriate synonym. Suppose you are looking for an alternative to the word *famous* to describe the research on pickles at Dill University. You have narrowed the synonyms down to *reputed* and *renowned*, words you found listed under *famous* in the thesaurus. The dictionary defines *repute* to mean "to assign a reputation to." Its origin is a Latin word that loosely means "to be considered." *Renowned* means "being widely honored and acclaimed." Its origin is an Old French word that means "to name again." Although the shades of meaning are subtle, you may decide that *reputed* has less positive connotations and that its etymology suggests subjective opinion, whereas *renowned* seems more forceful and carries connotations that more exactly fit your sentence's meaning.

The previous example illustrates another important point about vocabulary. Thousands of words we use regularly have been borrowed or adapted from other languages. *Renowned* can be traced to the Old French word *renomer*. As the etymology indicates, the root form of the word means "name" and the prefix *re-* means "again": hence the word's meaning, "to name again."

If you study common prefixes and suffixes (attachments added to a word's beginning or ending) as well as learn to recognize common word roots, you will be able to increase your vocabulary considerably. Just by knowing the meaning of a word's parts, you can often decipher its approximate meaning even if you have never seen the word before. The following list of prefixes, suffixes, and combining forms taken from the *Prentice-Hall Handbook for Writers,* Eighth Edition, will help you increase your vocabulary.

PREFIXES

PREFIX	MEANING	EXAMPLE
ab-	away from	absent
ad-*	to *or* for	adverb
com-*	with	combine
de-	down, away from, *or* undoing	degrade, depart, dehumanize
dis-*	separation *or* reversal	disparate, disappoint
ex-*	out of *or* former	extend, ex-president
in-*	in *or* on	input

PREFIX	MEANING	EXAMPLE
in-*	not	inhuman
mis-	wrong	mistake
non-	not	non-Christian
ob-*	against	obtuse
pre-	before	prevent
pro-	for or forward	proceed
re-	back or again	repeat
sub-*	under	subcommittee
trans-	across	transcribe
un-	not	unclean

*The spelling of these prefixes varies, usually to make pronunciation easier. *Ad* becomes *ac* in *accuse*, *ag* in *aggregate*, *at* in *attack*. Similarly, the final consonant in the other prefixes is assimilated by the initial letter of the root word: *colleague* (*com* + *league*); *illicit* (*in* + *licit*); *offend* (*ob* + *fend*); *succeed* (*sub* + *ceed*).

SUFFIXES

Noun suffixes denoting *act of, state of, quality of*

SUFFIX	EXAMPLE	MEANING
-dom	freedom	*state of* being free
-hood	manhood	*state of* being a man
-ness	dimness	*state of* being dim
-ice	cowardice	*quality of* being a coward
-ation	flirtation	*act of* flirting
-ion	intercession	*act of* interceding
-sion	scansion	*act of* scanning
-tion	corruption	*state of* being corrupt
-ment	argument	*act of* arguing
-ship	friendship	*state of* being friends
-ance	continuance	*act of* continuing
-ence	precedence	*act of* preceding
-ancy	flippancy	*state of* being flippant
-ency	currency	*state of* being current
-ism	baptism	*act of* baptizing
-ery	bravery	*quality of* being brave

Noun suffixes denoting *doer, one who*

SUFFIX	EXAMPLE	MEANING
-eer (general)	auctioneer	*one who* auctions
-ess (female)	abbess	*a woman who* heads an abbey
-st	fascist	*one who* believes in fascism
-or	debtor	*one who* is in debt
-er	worker	*one who* works

Verb suffixes denoting *to make* or *to perform the act of*

SUFFIX	EXAMPLE	MEANING
-ate	perpetuate	*to make* perpetual
-en	soften	*to make* soft
-fy	dignify	*to make* dignified
-ize, ise	sterilize	*to make* sterile

294

Adjectival suffixes

SUFFIX	MEANING	EXAMPLE
-ful	full of	hateful
-ish	resembling	foolish
-ate	having	affectionate
-ic, ical	resembling	angelic
-ive	having	prospective
-ous	full of	zealous
-ulent	full of	fraudulent
-less	without	fatherless
-able, ible	capable of	peaceable
-ed	having	spirited
-ly	resembling	womanly
-like	resembling	childlike

COMBINING FORMS (appearing generally, but not always, as prefixes)

COMBINING FORM	MEANING	EXAMPLE
anthrop, anthropo	human	phil*anthrop*y, *anthropo*logy
arch	rule	*arch*duke, mon*arch*
auto	self	*auto*mobile
bene	well	*bene*ficial
eu	well	*eu*logy
graph	writing	*graph*ic, biog*raph*y
log, logue	word, speech	mono*logue*
magni	great	*magni*ficent
mal	bad	*mal*ady
mono	one	*mono*tone
multi	many	*multi*plication
neo	new	*neo*classic
omni	all	*omni*bus
pan, pant	all	*pan*hellenic
phil	loving	*phil*osophy
phono	sound	*phono*graph
poly	many	*poly*gamy
pseudo	false	*pseudo*nym
semi	half	*semi*formal
trans	across	*trans*continental

Practice A: Prefixes   Add the appropriate prefix to each of the following words to indicate a negative meaning. The answers are listed at the end of this section.

[1] agreeable   [2] accurate   [3] solved   [4] soluble

[5] discoverable   [6] capacity   [7] reformed   [8] appear

[9] believer   [10] distinct

Practice B: Suffixes   Add the appropriate suffix to each of the following words to indicate act of, state of, or quality of. Check the spelling of the new words since the addition of a suffix may change the spelling of the word. The answers are listed at the end of this section.

[1] deprive   [2] militant   [3] coward   [4] proceed   [5] slave

[6] fragment   [7] settle   [8] manly   [9] steward   [10] bore

Answers to Practice A   [1] dis   [2] in-   [3] un-   [4] dis *or* in-   [5] un-   [6] in-   [7] un-   [8] dis-   [9] un-   [10] in-

Answers to Practice B   [1] -tion (deprivation)   [2] -cy (militancy)   [3] -ice (cowardice)   [4] -sion (procession)   [5] -ery (slavery)   [6] -ation (fragmentation)   [7] -ment (settlement)   [8] -ness (manliness)   [9] -ship (stewardship)   [10] -dom (boredom)

EXERCISE 58-1, PREFIXES, SUFFIXES, AND COMBINING FORMS   (39)

Add the appropriate prefix to each of the roots below to form a word that will fit in the sentence to its right.

Example   *humanize*   Do factories *dehumanize* workers?

1. *-struct*   The supervisors may try to _____ our plans.

2. *-standard*   The work performed was _____ tonight.

3. *-integrate*   I was afraid the boat would _____ in the storm.

4. *-embark*   I was ready to _____ before the boat even docked.

5. *-seemly*   It was a very _____ act on the supervisor's part.

6. *-traced*   They _____ their steps but found nothing.

7. *-solved*   The judge _____ them from any guilt.

8. *-communicative*   The prisoner was _____ during his lawyer's questioning.

9. *-destination*   Presbyterians believe in _____ .

10. *-application*   It was a clear case of _____ of funds.

11. *-tended*   They _____ the hand of friendship.

12. *-descript*   The building was utterly _____ .

13. *-semble*   Don't _____ ! How do you really feel?

14. *-approval*   The stockholders indicated their _____ at the meeting.

15. *-jointed*   The presentation of his plan seemed _____ to me.

16. *-durately*   The manager _____ refuses to lower the rent.

17. *-entities*   Too many of them regard renters as _____ .

18. *-stain*   I intend to _____ from voting.

19. *-tract*   The tabloid had to _____ its rumor-filled article.

20. *-licit*   The utility company's latest rate hike is _____ .

Form verbs and adjectives by adding suffixes to the following nouns. Adjust spelling as necessary.

		VERB	ADJECTIVE
Example	beauty	*beautify*	*beautiful*
21.	peace		
22.	perpetuity		
23.	justice		
24.	glory		
25.	apology		
26.	analysis		
27.	satisfaction		
28.	character		
29.	tyranny		
30.	deputy		

Write two words constructed from each of the following combining forms.

Example	eu	*euphemism*	*euphoria*
31.	auto		
32.	bene		
33.	graph		
34.	mal		
35.	mono		
36.	omni		
37.	phil		
38.	phono		
39.	pseudo		
40.	trans		

On your own paper, write a sentence for each word of the pairs you constructed in items 31 through 40.

Example *"Let go" is a euphemism for "fired."*

Imagine my euphoria at getting the job!

EXERCISE 58-2, WORD MEANING   (39)

Circle the number of the word closest in meaning to the italicized word in each given phrase.

Example   to *plagiarize* a paper   (1) memorize   (2) edit   (3) praise
                              (4) steal by copying

1. A *myopic* point of view   (1) farsighted   (2) nearsighted   (3) clear   (4) neutral
2. A *pandemic* failing   (1) universal   (2) uncommon   (3) new   (4) old
3. An *acrimonious* disposition   (1) gentle   (2) benign   (3) bitter   (4) dull
4. An *exigent* matter   (1) common   (2) urgent   (3) unusual   (4) usual
5. An *inadvertent* act   (1) unbelieving   (2) unnecessary   (3) unintentional   (4) typical
6. A *subtle* argument   (1) quiet   (2) false   (3) ingenious   (4) inebriated
7. A *heterogeneous* group   (1) similar   (2) dissimilar   (3) identical   (4) expansive
8. An *obsequious* person   (1) assertive   (2) nonassertive   (3) fawning   (4) conscientious
9. A *concomitant* event   (1) similar   (2) unlikely   (3) accompanying   (4) noteworthy
10. A full measure of *rapport*   (1) dissonance   (2) agreement   (3) applause   (4) adulation
11. An *obnoxious* personality   (1) poisonous   (2) pleasing   (3) annoying   (4) amusing
12. A *lugubrious* look   (1) happy   (2) bland   (3) angry   (4) gloomy
13. A *flippant* act   (1) gay   (2) deceiving   (3) discourteous   (4) unthinking
14. A few *cryptic* words   (1) mysterious   (2) short   (3) contemptuous   (4) angry
15. A state of *dishabille*   (1) careful attire   (2) careless attire   (3) formality   (4) care
16. A manifestation of *masochism*   (1) pleasure from pain   (2) agony from pain
   (3) vindictiveness   (4) pleasure
17. His *senescent* years   (1) early   (2) middle   (3) aging   (4) aged
18. An *extirpated* race   (1) extinct   (2) comely   (3) ancient   (4) noteworthy
19. A *portentous* act   (1) timely   (2) important   (3) ominous   (4) noteworthy
20. An *insouciant* look   (1) gloomy   (2) harmful   (3) carefree   (4) ignorant
21. *Agrarian* surroundings   (1) urban   (2) slum   (3) agricultural   (4) polluted
22. An *ingenious* solution   (1) inept   (2) joyous   (3) very clever   (4) natural
23. A Democratic *apostate*   (1) a loyal member   (2) an angry member
   (3) a disloyal member   (4) a dejected member
24. A *dastardly* person   (1) of unknown birth   (2) unhappy   (3) dazed   (4) cowardly
25. A *facetious* remark   (1) droll   (2) contentious   (3) unthinking   (4) sagacious
26. An *ingenuous* youth   (1) clever   (2) sophisticated   (3) naive   (4) illiterate
27. His *garish* apparel   (1) gaudy   (2) dowdy   (3) opulent   (4) tawdry

28. An *enigmatic* reply   (1) mysterious   (2) short   (3) puzzling   (4) unclear

29. An unwelcome *schism*   (1) visitor   (2) division   (3) alliance   (4) dalliance

30. A shameless *demagogue*   (1) agitator   (2) politician   (3) lawyer   (4) speaker

31. An *eerie* event   (1) normal   (2) turbulent   (3) uncanny   (4) clownish

32. A master of *hyperbole*   (1) art   (2) exaggeration   (3) persuasion   (4) comedy

33. A *suave* person   (1) swarthy   (2) sinister   (3) polished   (4) artless

34. A *traumatic* experience   (1) shocking   (2) youthful   (3) unkind   (4) urbane

35. A *vitiated* condition   (1) disheveled   (2) spiteful   (3) emaciated   (4) perverted

36. An *arraigned* person   (1) notorious   (2) convicted   (3) accused   (4) acquitted

37. A noteworthy *epoch*   (1) long poem   (2) period of time   (3) novel   (4) song

38. A *noisome* act   (1) loud   (2) disgusting   (3) rambunctious   (4) talented

39. An *illicit* act   (1) sexual   (2) diplomatic   (3) illegal   (4) commendable

40. A *marital* argument   (1) warlike   (2) odd   (3) quiet   (4) between spouses

41. A disliked *canon*   (1) artillery   (2) song   (3) law   (4) priest

42. A *climatic* event   (1) episodic   (2) atmospheric   (3) notorious   (4) famous

43. A *pedantic* professor   (1) useful   (2) narrow-minded   (3) outgoing   (4) humble

44. A *blasphemous* act   (1) irreligious   (2) commendable   (3) treacherous   (4) humorous

45. A *sanguine* outlook   (1) colorful   (2) bloodthirsty   (3) gloomy   (4) favorable

46. A *pejorative* word   (1) helpful   (2) unselfish   (3) disparaging   (4) colorful

47. A *glib* reply   (1) facile   (2) reasonable   (3) reassuring   (4) angry

48. A *depraved* act   (1) notorious   (2) sinister   (3) immoral   (4) religious

49. A *parsimonious* person   (1) generous   (2) affable   (3) small   (4) stingy

50. A *lachrymose* disposition   (1) benign   (2) sad   (3) sunny   (4) insensitive

51. An *impassionate* attitude   (1) merciful   (2) tempestuous   (3) sedate   (4) imploring

52. *Imprecations* rained down   (1) missiles   (2) curses   (3) debris   (4) judgments

53. The *pellucid* waters   (1) murky   (2) dim   (3) transparent   (4) stormy

54. A *precocious* child   (1) spoiled   (2) bright   (3) dull   (4) deformed

55. A person of considerable *acumen*   (1) height   (2) weight   (3) prominence   (4) intellect

56. An *impecunious* person   (1) flamboyant   (2) immoral   (3) poor   (4) respectable

57. The *profligate* youth   (1) happy-go-lucky   (2) serious   (3) devoted   (4) wasteful

58. A *vortex* of emotions   (1) mixture   (2) absence   (3) whirlpool   (4) center

59. A pagan *amulet*   (1) bracelet   (2) egg preparation   (3) idol   (4) good luck token

60. An *ambrosial* odor   (1) fragrant   (2) smoky   (3) putrid   (4) musty

59

EXACTNESS   (40)

If a reader is to understand what you mean, your word choice needs to be exact. Selecting correct words and appropriate synonyms, avoiding invented words and improprieties, and using concrete and specific words are ways to achieve exactness in your writing.

The previous section on vocabulary briefly discussed synonyms. Synonyms are words that mean essentially, but not exactly, the same thing. Desk dictionaries discriminate between word meanings by means of **synonymies**. These explanatory passages, labeled either *Synonyms* or *Syn.*, usually follow the definition of a main entry word. The synonymy lists a group of synonyms for the main entry and explains the difference in meaning between the words listed. The following synonymy for the word *anger* is taken from *Webster's New World Dictionary of the American Language,* Second College Edition.

> **Syn.** *anger* is broadly applicable to feelings of resentful or vengeful displeasure; *indignation* implies righteous anger aroused by what seems unjust, mean, or insulting; *rage* suggests a violent outburst of anger in which self-control is lost; *fury* implies a frenzied rage that borders on madness; *ire,* chiefly a literary word, suggests a show of great anger in acts, words, looks, etc.; *wrath* implies deep indignation expressing itself in a desire to punish or get revenge.

When you consult a dictionary to locate the synonymy for a group of words, you may not always select the entry that contains the synonymy. In such a case, the dictionary will refer to the word where the synonymy occurs. In the above case, for example, had you first looked up the word *indignation,* you would have found the notation *Syn. see Anger.*

In being exact it is also important not to confuse words. Some words give trouble because of similarities in spelling or pronunciation or similarities in both respects. One such group of words is **homonyms**, words that are identical in spelling and pronunciation but that have different meanings (*butter*—a spread; *butter*—a goat in action). Another group of words, called **homographs**, are identical in spelling but have different pronunciations and meanings (*wind*—one of nature's forces; *wind*—to coil the spring of). A third group of words, called **homophones**, are pronounced the same but spelled differently and have different meanings (*red*—a color; *read*—the past tense of the verb *read*). Still a fourth group can be called **approximate homonyms**, that is, words that are pronounced or spelled approximately the same but have different meanings (*elicit,* to bring out; *illicit,* unlawful).

The best course of action when using words of these types is to look them up in the dictionary and learn their correct spellings and meanings.

Readers usually find words used in very unexpected ways to be troublesome because they do not fit convention and their meaning is therefore likely to be unclear. Invented words and improprieties should be used with great care and only when you are sure their meaning will be clear.

Invented words can be grouped into three categories. One group is **neologisms**: either new words or, more commonly, old words with new meanings or usages. For example, the noun *shot* originally referred to bullets or pellets for firearms. Since the invention of the camera, *shot* can also mean a photograph or single cinematic view. Another group is **coined words**: deliberately invented creations that often achieve some degree of general use. *Smog* (smoke + fog), *motel* (motor + hotel), and *flak* (antiaircraft gunfire) are examples. The third group is **noncewords**, words made up to fit special situations and generally not used more than once, as in *She committed final-examicide because she didn't study for the chemistry test.*

Usually you should avoid invented words. When in doubt about whether a word is invented, consult the dictionary. If the dictionary does not list it or labels it a substandard word, do not use the word in formal writing. In some instances in some contexts, your instructor may permit you to invent words yourself. Before doing so, however, you should determine his or her attitude toward such words.

Improprieties are legitimate words wrongly used: *The exits are signed clearly.* Sometimes you may wonder whether a word used as one part of speech can be used as another part of speech. English is fairly free in shifting words from one part of speech to another, a process called **functional shift.** For example, the noun *fire* is used as an adjective in *fire engine* and as a verb in *fire the cannon.* However, convention dictates whether a word shifts or not. Unless a shift has generally been accepted, you would be wise to avoid it. Otherwise, the reader may find your usage inappropriate and confusing. If you are in doubt, consult the dictionary to ensure that the shift you want to use is not an impropriety.

Writing that captures the reader's interest and most effectively conveys the author's exact meaning usually relies on a high proportion of concrete and specific words to give it life and clarity. **Concrete words** name things we can perceive with our senses, things we can see, hear, touch, taste, and smell. **Abstract words**, on the other hand, name qualities, ideas, and concepts. *Honesty* is an abstraction. To say someone turned in a lost wallet at the campus police station is to show concretely what honesty means. **Specific words** refer to the individual members of a class or group. **General words** refer to all the members of a class or group. *Clothing* is general, but *shoes, shirts,* and *skirts* are specific. Using concrete and specific words in conjunction with abstract and general terms provides definition for your ideas and helps your reader to understand exactly what you mean.

EXERCISE 59-1, SYNONYMS (40a)

In your dictionary, look up the synonymy that applies to each of the following groups of words. Write sentences in which you use and differentiate in meaning, according to the synonymy, each of the words in the group. You may change tense or part of speech in making up your sentences. The synonymies in this exercise are based on the *New World Dictionary of the American Language,* Second College Edition. If you are using a different dictionary, it may be necessary to look up some word meanings under the base entries for those words.

Example

anger *Her father stirred Jane's anger by refusing her the car.*

indignation *My indignation was great at their mean trick.*

rage *I raged like an unreasoning animal at their treachery.*

fury *She was so furious she slammed the door in my face.*

1. authorize _____

    commission _____

    accredit _____

2. wave _____

    ripple _____

    roller _____

    breaker _____

    billow _____

3. fast _____

    rapid _____

    swift _____

    fleet _____

    hasty _____

4. seethe _____

    boil _____

    simmer _____

    stew _____

5. *deliberate* _____

   think _____

   reason _____

   cogitate _____

   reflect _____

   speculate _____

6. *adversary* _____

   antagonist _____

   opponent _____

   enemy _____

   foe _____

7. *patience* _____

   endurance _____

   fortitude _____

   forbearance _____

   stoicism _____

8. *famous* _____

   renowned _____

   celebrated _____

   notorious _____

9. *declare* _____

   announce _____

   proclaim _____

EXERCISE 59-2, SIMILAR WORDS, INVENTED WORDS, IMPROPRIETIES
(40b–d)

Construct sentences in which each of the following words is used correctly. In the case of verbs, tense may be changed.

Example   *allude* *I alluded to his difficulties in my report.*

                elude *I was able to elude detection.*

1. *cannon* _____

   canon _____

2. *access* _____

   excess _____

3. *corps* _____

   corpse _____

4. *your* _____

   you're _____

5. *principle* _____

   principal _____

6. *censure* _____

   censor _____

7. *accept* _____

   except _____

8. *affect* _____

   effect _____

9. *humane* _____

   human _____

10. *capital* _____

    capitol _____

In the blanks, insert correct words for those italicized words that are substandard, invented words, or improprieties. Write *Correct* if the italicized word is correct.

Example He *opinioned* that his friend was wrong. *believed*

It was a press *blurb* of great interest. *Correct*

11. Your boss has very *conservativistic* ideas. _____

12. They *implied* that I was uncouth. _____

13. I like my dates to be *affectionish.* _____

14. The accountant is honest and *noncorruptible.* _____

15. My decision is *immutable.* _____

16. You are the most *unagreeable* person I know. _____

17. *Reforestation* will be a costly process. _____

18. Our team *steamrollered* them 40 to 0. _____

19. I'll *learn* you to repair this copier. _____

20. The assignment is simply *incomprehensive.* _____

21. We will *middle-aisle* it next week. _____

22. I am as *headstrongish* as I can be. _____

23. That child is a real *progeny* on a computer. _____

24. The stockmarket was very *bearish* during May. _____

25. We *instigated* new accounting procedures last week. _____

26. It was indeed a *ceremonial* occasion. _____

27. The guard had a *placatory* effect on the nervous customers. _____

28. We will have to *research* the matter further. _____

29. Leslie went into a state of *hystericism.* _____

30. The recession has *impacted* particularly severely on small businesses. _____

EXERCISE 59-3, SPECIFIC AND CONCRETE WORDS   (40f)

Revise the following sentences, replacing nouns, verbs, and adjectives with more specific concrete words where appropriate. Invent details as needed.

Examples   The man was cooking some food.

The chef was grating cheese for an eggplant casserole.

Antiques are popular.

Antique wicker chairs are a popular status symbol in offices now.

1.   Somebody is at the door.

_____

2.   They won the contract.

_____

3.   He died last night.

_____

4.   She read a book.

_____

5.   It was a nice day.

_____

6.   There is a fight going on.

_____

7.   We have a pretty good chance.

_____

8.   Delays make me nervous.

_____

9.   The furniture is old.

_____

10.   There is a crowd outside.

_____

11. We have a tree in the office.

_____

12. It is a nice plant.

_____

13. She is sick.

_____

14. I ate my meal.

_____

15. He went to jail for it.

_____

16. They voted the wrong way.

_____

17. That automobile must be expensive.

_____

18. Perseverance pays off.

_____

19. The play was a hit.

_____

20. There was a run on the bank.

_____

21. The noise attracted their attention.

_____ _ ___

22. Sloppiness often annoys people.

_____

60

IDIOMS   (40e)

An **idiom** is an expression peculiar to a given language; that is, it does not follow the normal pattern of the language, or it has a total meaning different from the one suggested by its separate words. In the previous sentence, the phrase *different from* is idiomatic: it does not follow the normal pattern of English. The expression *to lose one's head* exemplifies the second type of idiom: literally, the words indicate decapitation, but native speakers of English know the expression is not meant literally. To lose one's head is to become irrational or excessively emotional.

For any writer, the most troublesome idioms are those requiring a particular preposition after a given verb or adjective. The following list will help you know which idiomatic construction to use for a given meaning.

absolved by, from	I was *absolved by* the dean *from* all blame.
accede to	He *acceded to* his children's wishes.
accompany by, with	I was *accompanied by* George. The terms were *accompanied with* a plea for immediate peace.
acquitted of	They were *acquitted of* the crime.
adapted to, from	This machine can be *adapted to* farm work. The design was *adapted from* an Indian invention.
admit to, of	I *admitted to* the prank. The plan will *admit of* no alternative.
agree to, with, in	They *agreed to* the plan but *disagreed with* us. They *agreed* only *in* principle.
angry with, at	They are *angry with* me and *angry at* the treatment they received.
capable of	She is *capable of* great kindness.
charge for, with	He expected to be *charged for* his purchase, but he didn't expect to be *charged with* stealing something.
compare to, with	She *compared* the roundness of the earth *to* that of a baseball. She *compared* the economy of the Ford *with* that of the Plymouth.
concur with, in	I *concur with* you *in* your desire to use the revised edition.
confide in, to	*Confide in* me. You *confided to* me that you had stolen the car.
conform to, with **conformity with**	The specifications *conformed to* (or *with*) my original plans. You must act in *conformity with* our demands.
connected by, with	The rooms are *connected by* a corridor. I am officially *connected with* this university.
contend for, with	Because he needed to *contend for* his principles, he found himself *contending with* his parents.
differ about, from, with	We *differ about* our taste in clothes. My clothes *differ from* yours. We *differ with* one another.
different from*	Our grading system is *different from* yours.

*Different than is colloquially idiomatic when the object of the prepositional phrase is a clause:

This town looks *different from* what I had remembered. [Formal]
This town looks *different than* I had remembered it. [Colloquial]

enter into, on, upon	She *entered into* a new agreement and thereby *entered on* (or *upon**) a new career.
free from, of	He was *freed from* cultural assumptions by his education. He is *free of* prejudice.
identical with	Your reasons are *identical with* hers.
join in, to, with	He *joined in* the fun *with* the others. He *joined* the wire cables *to* each other.
live at, in, on	He *lives at* 14 Neil Avenue *in* a Dutch Colonial house. He *lives on* Neil Avenue.
necessity for, of	There was no *necessity* (*need*) *for* you to lose your temper.
need for, of	There was no *necessity* (*need*) *of* your losing your temper.
object to	I *object to* the statement in the third paragraph.
oblivious of	When he held a seance he was *oblivious of* the passing of time.
overcome by, with	I was *overcome by* the heat. I was *overcome with* grief.
parallel between, to, with	There is a *parallel between* your attitude and hers. This line is *parallel to* (or *with*) that one.
preferable to	A leisurely walk is *preferable to* violent exercise.
reason about, with	Why not *reason with* them *about* the matter?
reward by, for, with	They were *rewarded by* their employer *with* a raise *for* their work.
variance with	This conclusion is at *variance with* your facts.
vary from, in, with	The houses *vary from* one another *in* size. People's taste *vary with* their personalities.
wait for, on	They *waited for* someone to *wait on* them.
worthy of	That candidate is not *worthy of* your trust.

*In many phrases, *on* and *upon* are interchangeable: *depend on* or *depend upon; enter on* or *enter upon.*

EXERCISE 60, IDIOMS   (40e)

Refer to Section 60, as necessary, to complete this exercise. In each blank, write the preposition that forms the correct idiomatic construction.

Example   He was absolved ___*from*___ all guilt.

1. You must conform _____ the group if you are going to get along.

2. She is capable _____ getting the job done.

3. Mr. Brown lives _____ 1112 Ash Street.

4. He is a man who has been oblivious _____ changes in the world.

5. Unemployment is preferable _____ work under those conditions.

6. We disagree _____ many things,

7. but we agree _____ each other in others.

8. They are simply not worthy _____ your trust.

9. His lawyer was angry _____ him.

10. The necessity _____ your going is in doubt.

11. The two candidates vary _____ each other in appearance.

12. You and I differ greatly _____ our views.

13. She was overcome _____ the fact that she had succeeded.

14. The two sites were identical _____ each other.

15. The patient confided _____ the doctor all her troubles.

16. He acceded _____ the demands of the stockholders.

17. The report must conform _____ the company's style sheets.

18. Never have there been two people whose beliefs varied _____ one

    another so much.

19. I was angry _____ the way I was received.

20. They decided to enter _____ a new career.

In the following list, some expressions are idiomatically correct and some are not. In performing the exercise, refer either to Section 60 or to your dictionary, as necessary. Cross out the incorrect preposition and write the correct preposition to the right of each expression. If the expression is correct, write *Correct*.

Example	He acceded to the request.	*Correct*
	They always concurred ~~to~~ each other.	*with*

21. a recommendation to improvement   _____

22. different than we thought   _____

23. furnishing supplies for cattle ranchers   _____

24. If you need money, get it off the comptroller.   _____

25. not suitable to one of such eminence   _____

26. My quotation was of Adam Smith.   _____

27. a great confidence with me   _____

28. oblivious to everything around him   _____

29. a need to reappraise   _____

30. as different to each other as day and night   _____

31. embarrassed at my mistake   _____

32. ashamed at my bad mistake   _____

33. overcome with the assignment   _____

34. the authority vested to me   _____

35. in regard of her wishes   _____

36. the only one objecting from the resolution   _____

37. vary in several respects   _____

38. free of the chains that had bound them   _____

39. to refrain of further interference   _____

40. antithetical with our beliefs   _____

61

DIRECTNESS   (41)

Your writing will be more effective if it is direct—if you use only those words that contribute to your meaning. Words and phrases that contribute nothing to meaning cause your readers to work hard at plowing through the language, but for no real payoff. Eventually readers become tired, bored, impatient, and unwilling to continue. The following guidelines will help you to remove wordiness from your writing.

1. Eliminate words and phrases that do not contribute to meaning. Expressions such as *type of, in the case of, in the field of, aspect, factor, situation, I think, in my opinion* can often be cut from sentences. Expletives such as *there is, there are,* and *it is* can frequently be replaced by the true subject of the sentence to improve directness.

POOR	The best type of football team has the best quality of blockers.
IMPROVED	The best football team has the best blockers.
POOR	Pat majored in the field of engineering.
IMPROVED	Pat majored in engineering.
POOR	Another aspect of the situation that needs study, in my opinion, is the company's falling productivity.
IMPROVED	We should study the company's falling productivity.
POOR	There were four classes meeting on the third floor.
IMPROVED	Four classes were meeting on the third floor.

2. Prefer the active voice to the passive voice. Section 55 explained that active voice verbs make a sentence more lively and direct. They also use fewer words because active voice sentences require neither the helping verb used in a passive verb construction nor the prepositional phrase that identifies the agent of the action. Compare the following pair of sentences, and notice how much more economical and direct is the active voice sentence:

PASSIVE	The procedure was demonstrated by the lab technician.
ACTIVE	The lab technician demonstrated the procedure.

3. Reduce clauses to phrases and phrases to single words when possible. Section 53 shows how economical and effective participles, appositives, and absolutes can be. These constructions frequently result from reducing whole clauses to phrase modifiers, as when *The train, which ran on time, pulled into the station* is rewritten *The train, running on time, pulled into the station.* Phrases and clauses can sometimes be reduced to one-word modifiers for further directness.

WORDY	The slipper, which was made of glass, fit the foot of Cinderella.
REVISED	The glass slipper fit Cinderella's foot. [The clause *which was made of glass* has been reduced to the single adjective *glass;* the prepositional phrase *of Cinderella* has been reduced to the single possessive noun *Cinderella's.*]

4. Avoid ineffective repetition and redundancy. Unintentional repetition, unlike repetition intended to create emphasis and coherence, often adds unnecessary—even silly sounding—words to a sentence.

AWKWARD REPETITION	Improved communications improved the staff's ability to satisfy top management's expectations.
REVISED	Improved communications better enabled the staff to satisfy top management's expectations.

Redundant words say the same thing twice: for example, *visible to the eyes*. Note the following list of commonly used redundancies and their revisions.

REDUNDANT	DIRECT
advance forward	advance
continue on	continue
refer back	refer
combine together	combine
close proximity	close
circle around	circle
small in size	small
few in number	few
disappear from view	disappear
throughout the whole	throughout
basic fundamentals	fundamentals
important essentials	essentials

EXERCISE 61, WORDINESS, REDUNDANCY, AND AWKWARD REPETITION
(41a–d)

Revise the following sentences to eliminate unnecessary words and phrases and awkward repetition.

Example   This extremely tardy lateness was due to the fact that his car had a flat tire.

A flat tire made him late.

I think the issues are well formulated, it seems to me.

I think the issues are well formulated.

1. It is a tried and true product for cleaning and dirt loosening.

   _____

2. You spend a majority of the hours of your time doing much of nothing.

   _____

3. He likes plays and stage performances that have action and movement.

   _____

4. I shopped around and looked in various stores before I made my purchase.

   _____

5. Some things of the nature of debt and unpaid bills are causing us problems.

   _____

6. The ad we broadcast over the airways gave news and details of the sweepstakes.

   _____

7. The next move he made at the meeting of conferring was to indicate an action in the negative.

   _____

8. The off and on blinking of the computer was distracting and attention destroying.

   _____

9. She departed in haste and with very rapid movements.

   _____

10. At 2 P.M. in the afternoon we will gather and assemble for the meeting.

   _____

11. He parked his car in a space in the parking lot.

_____

12. On the other hand, the fact it is smoking probably means it is using oil, however.

_____

13. Certainly, the fact that he will leave is a virtual certainty.

_____

14. Returns from the ninth precinct helped return her to office.

_____

15. The location of the printer's office is located on Sixth Street.

_____

16. They circled in a circle and finally encircled the fire.

_____

17. I saw with my own eyes and heard with my own ears what happened.

_____

18. I refuse to pass judgment on the judge who judged the case.

_____

19. The doctor prescribed a very expensive prescription.

_____

20. The heart attack victim's face was white in color.

_____

21. They met in a meeting which lasted for a two-hour period of time.

_____

22. The management students are studying the works of Drucker and Korda.

_____

23. They happily exchanged greetings on what was a very happy occasion.

_____

24. Over the course of time my opponent of course will find that he is wrong.

_____

62

APPROPRIATENESS (42)

The appropriateness of your word choice directly affects the way readers respond to your writing. As Section 51 points out, inappropriate words will confuse readers and ultimately may irritate them. The words you choose set the tone of your writing; they tell readers the attitude you are taking toward your subject and toward them as well.

What constitutes appropriate language? That depends to some extent on your topic, your purpose, and your audience. A letter to a close friend will have a much more informal style than, and probably contain several slang expressions that would not be appropriate in, a research report written for a college psychology class. The research report would undoubtedly contain some social-science jargon understood by people in psychology but possibly unfamiliar to the general public.

Although appropriateness is a somewhat relative matter, several guidelines do apply to all but the most informal writing.

1. Avoid **slang expressions** and **nonstandard English** unless you are recording actual conversation that uses them. While slang is colorful and often lively, it is usually understood by a relatively small group of people. Furthermore, slang expressions quickly lose vigor. Today's slang may be meaningless to most readers in a year or two. Nonstandard English is normally associated with provincialism and lack of education; you should avoid it in your writing.

SLANG	That prof hit us with a really heavy number.
REVISION	That professor gave us a very difficult assignment.
NONSTANDARD ENGLISH	They wasn't on time, so let's don't wait for them.
REVISION	They weren't on time, so let's not wait for them.

2. Replace **trite expressions** and **stereotyped** or **hackneyed phrases** with new or original expressions. Supply fresh figurative language instead of relying on tired clichés worn thin by constant use. But be careful not to "mix" metaphors or use figures of speech that are illogical, inept, or ludicrous.

When we read expressions such as "white as the driven snow" or "hot as the noonday sun," our reaction is likely to be "If I've heard it once, I've heard it a thousand times." As the last sentence indicates, we are apt to respond to a cliché with another cliché! Similes (comparisons introduced by the words *like, as, as if, as when*) that we have heard "a thousand times" obviously no longer stir our imaginations. Similarly, tired metaphors (implied comparisons: for example, *she riveted him to the wall with her piercing gaze*) will not convince your readers that you have anything insightful to say about your topic. Illogical figures of speech not only fail to inform, they can be so absurd that readers may miss your point entirely or find your writing silly.

ILLOGICAL FIGURE OF SPEECH	His eyes, flashing like pools of flame, drowned me in their fire.
REVISION	His eyes, flashing like flames, seared me.

3. Avoid **jargon** when writing for a general audience, and replace **artificial diction** with more straightforward words. Like slang, jargon is a vocabulary well known only to those in a particular group or discipline. Computer programmers, for example, are quite familiar with terms such as *byte* and *baud-rate;* general readers are not. Unless you are writing for a special audience, use jargon sparingly and define terms you think your readers might not know.

Artificial diction, on the other hand, never adds anything desirable to writing. Choose simple, direct words instead of elaborate, pompous-sounding ones. The person who writes *Males of advanced years fail to maintain their recollective faculties* gains nothing. The one who writes *Old men forget* makes an effective point.

EXERCISE 62, SLANG, NONSTANDARD ENGLISH, TRITE EXPRESSIONS, FIGURATIVE LANGUAGE, AND ARTIFICIAL DICTION   (42)

Revise the following sentences to rid them of slang or nonstandard expressions.

Example   I ain't jive'n you, man. That turkey won't turn over.

I'm serious. The car won't start.

1.   The situation was really fouled up.

   _____

2.   He is a real ding-a-ling from Square Corners.

   _____

3.   She got the mumps off her brother.

   _____

4.   He didn't ought to have done nothing like that.

   _____

5.   The dog is nowhere around at the present time.

   _____

6.   You have to show a little gumption if you expect to get anywhere.

   _____

7.   Scarcely none of us wanted to go.

   _____

8.   She must don't have the class a broad should have.

   _____

9.   The mechanic shouldn't of put in those plugs on account of they aren't needed.

   _____

10.   The small fry are in poppin' out their eyeballs at the boob tube.

   _____

Revise the following sentences to eliminate all trite expressions, but be sure to preserve the ideas suggested by them.

Example   We have to take the bitter along with the sweet.

We should make the most of what happens.

11. Father Time denied him the good things of life.

12. We must buckle down and hit the line hard.

13. They kept their noses to the grindstone all the time.

14. You must rise to the occasion and bring home the bacon.

15. Keep the home fires burning because I'll be back tonight.

16. She is as pretty as a picture and as smart as a whip.

17. I think we should strike while the iron is hot.

18. His Achilles' heel is that he goes to pieces in an emergency.

19. He cashed in his chips and went to meet his Maker.

20. He was the rock of Gibraltar on defense.

21. He is a model of decorum and a pillar of society.

22. She is always as cool as a cucumber when the going gets rough.

Revise the following sentences using figures of speech that are apt and logical.

Example   In the cold light of day, our love slipped through our fingers like a greased pig.

In the chill wind of daily life, our love withered like a flower after the frost

23.   They should stiffen their backbones and apply muscle to the situation.

_____

24.   He played with him as a cat does a mouse in downing him with one quick blow.

_____

25.   The quest for knowledge snowballs, feeding the flames of desire.

_____

26.   We can no longer fleece the goose that laid the golden egg.

_____

27.   She is like a fish out of water as she runs madly to and fro.

_____

28.   He skimmed over the lesson by leaps and bounds.

_____

29.   He swept her off her feet and sold her the soap.

_____

30.   The sun rose like a raging ball of fire and shed its mellow beams upon us.

_____

31.   He hoped to break him like an anvil breaks a hammer.

_____

32.   He welcomed the young woman he wanted to marry like a cougar stalking its prey.

_____

33.   She had to bear a crown of thorns in not being accepted into law school.

_____

Revise the following sentences to correct artificial diction and any other inappropriate wording.

Example   Perceiving his visage occasioned affright in yours truly.

His face frightened me.

34.   She escalated her endeavors to amass resources for the purchase of the automotive vehicle.

35.   The female siblings verbalized falsehoods.

36.   The magnitude of the red rubber sphere dwarfed the little kid who transported it down the beach.

37.   Make haste and shut the window against the precipitation.

38.   We must commence the athletic contest without tarrying any further.

39.   Leave us depart so we can arrive at our destination on time.

40.   When he got done with his assignment, his friends and he decided to hoist a few at the nearest institute of inebriation.

41.   In the respect that it is not relevant to our needs, we deplore it.

42.   The early settlers were people who settled in new regions because they opined they offered good opportunities for livelihood.

43.   We can improve the performance of the engine as a whole by improving the efficiency of the carburetion system.

44.   The astronauts were in a relaxation mode after ingesting nutrients.

45.   Her boss considered her response to the inquiry inappropriate, and so her employment was terminated.

63

SPELLING   (44)

Many people, especially bad spellers, secretly believe good spellers are born, not made. There seem to be more exceptions than rules in spelling. Apart from correct pronunciation (which aids correct spelling), careful proofreading, and distinguishing between words that are similar in sound but different in meaning and spelling (such as *altar* and *alter*), the dictionary is your best resource. Learning spelling rules will also aid your spelling. Although there are exceptions to them, the following rules from the *Prentice-Hall Handbook for Writers*, Eighth Edition, provide general guidelines for correct spelling.

1. Avoid secondary and British spellings.

AMERICAN	BRITISH
encyclopedia	encyclopaedia
fetus	foetus
inquiry	enquiry
color	colour
center	centre
mold	mould
traveled	travelled
judgment	judgement

2. Distinguish between *ie* and *ei*: Write *i* before *e* except after *c* or when sounded like *a*, as in *neighbor* and *weigh*.

thief	conceive	sleigh
believe	ceiling	eight

3. Drop the final *e* before a suffix beginning with a vowel but not before a suffix beginning with a consonant.

hope	+ ing	= hoping		hope	+ ful	= hopeful
please	+ ure	= pleasure		sure	+ ly	= surely
slide	+ ing	= sliding		retire	+ ment	= retirement

4. A final *y* is usually changed to *i* before a suffix, unless the suffix begins with *i*.

defy	+ ance	= defiance		cry	+ ing	= crying
lively	+ hood	= livelihood		rely	+ ing	= relying

5. A final single consonant is doubled before a suffix beginning with a vowel when a single vowel precedes the consonant *and* the consonant ends an accented syllable or a one-syllable word. Unless *both* these conditions exist, the final consonant is not doubled.

stop	+ ing	= stopping		stoop	+ ing	= stooping
admit	+ ed	= admitted		benefit	+ ed	= benefited

6. Nouns ending in a sound that can be smoothly united with -*s* usually form their plurals by adding -*s*. Verbs ending in a sound that can be smoothly united with -*s* form their third person singular by adding -*s*.

SINGULAR	PLURAL	VERBS	
picture	pictures	blacken	blackens
radio	radios	criticize	criticizes

7. Nouns ending in a sound that cannot be smoothly united with -s form their plurals by adding -es. Verbs ending in a sound that cannot be smoothly united with -s form their third person singular by adding -es.

SINGULAR	PLURAL	VERBS	
porch	porches	tax	taxes
bush	bushes	finish	finishes

8. Nouns ending in y preceded by a consonant form their plurals by changing y to i and adding -es. Verbs ending in y preceded by a consonant form their third person singular in the same way.

SINGULAR	PLURAL	VERBS	
pity	pities	deny	denies
nursery	nurseries	fly	flies

9. Nouns ending in y preceded by a, e, o, or u form their plurals by adding -s only. Verbs ending in y preceded by a, e, o, or u form their third person singular in the same way.

SINGULAR	PLURAL	VERBS	
day	days	buy	buys
key	keys	employ	employs

10. The spelling of plural nouns borrowed from French, Greek, or Latin frequently retains the plural of the original language although some of these nouns have been anglicized.

SINGULAR	PLURAL (foreign)	PLURAL (anglicized)
analysis	analyses	
crisis	crises	
appendix	appendices	appendixes
radius	radii	radiuses

EXERCISE 63-1, SPELLING   (44)

Some of the following words reflect preferred spellings. Others reflect British or secondary spellings. Write the preferred spelling of each word in the blank to its right.

Example   *colour* _____*Color*_____

1.	*empanel*	_____	2.	*encyclopedia*	_____
3.	*odour*	_____	4.	*recognize*	_____
5.	*cheque*	_____	6.	*mediaeval*	_____
7.	*defense*	_____	8.	*enquiry*	_____
9.	*labour*	_____	10.	*theatre*	_____
11.	*judgment*	_____	12.	*connexion*	_____
13.	*councillor*	_____	14.	*programme*	_____
15.	*fibre*	_____	16.	*clamor*	_____
17.	*plough*	_____	18.	*fonetic*	_____
19.	*insure*	_____	20.	*reflexion*	_____

Draw a line through misspelled words in the following phrases and write them correctly in the blanks at the right. Where no word is misspelled, write *Correct* in the blank.

Example   a ~~tempermental~~ child   *temperamental*

21. accidently knocking over the vase   _____

22. a grievous error indeed   _____

23. a psychiatric convention   _____

24. the principle manufacturer   _____

25. a course in medieval history   _____

26. a cursury examination of the room   _____

27. a member of Parliment   _____

28. an iminent day of reckoning   _____

29. bachellor buttons and daisies   _____

30. the lonelyest person in town   _____

31. talking practicly all the time _____

32. a festive picinicing crowd _____

33. a good one, compartively speaking _____

34. a most contemptable act _____

35. a broken egg yolk _____

36. good for a sophmore _____

37. elected by acclommation _____

38. some defective auxilary equipment _____

39. some sort of foreign dialect _____

40. a most strenous voyage _____

41. playing a leading roll in student government _____

42. the principle reason for our defeat _____

43. not knowing weather to go or not _____

44. the rustling of the reads in the stream _____

45. a very important convasing of the area _____

46. unhappy over a loosing season _____

47. wondering who's bag it was _____

48. needing capitol to start our business _____

49. hating there existence very much _____

50. loving to hold fourth on your views _____

51. They decided to go their seperate ways. _____

52. The restaurant equipment was most desirable. _____

53. He disipated his financial resources. _____

54. Hasn't this ever occured to you? _____

EXERCISE 63-2, SPELLING   (44)

Fill in each blank with the appropriate choice, either *ie* or *ei*. Don't guess. Use your dictionary.

1. w ____ ghty
2. r ____ gn
3. financ ____ r
4. consc ____ ntious

5. rel ____ ve
6. bel ____ ve
7. surf ____ t
8. fr ____ ght

9. bes ____ ge
10. rec ____ pt
11. forf ____ t
12. v ____ n

13. unw ____ ldy
14. s ____ ge
15. th ____ f
16. rel ____ ve

17. gr ____ f
18. for ____ gn
19. h ____ fer
20. misch ____ vous

21. anx ____ ty
22. cod ____ ne
23. n ____ ce
24. sl ____ gh

Write the correct spelling of each of the words formed by joining the given prefix or suffix to the given root. Remember that in some cases you will have to add, delete, or change a letter.

Examples   run + ing   _running_

hate + ing   _hating_

lovely + ness   _loveliness_

fruit + less   _fruitless_

25. stop + ing   _____
26. equip + ing   _____

27. charge + able   _____
28. dis + appear   _____

29. close + ure   _____
30. awe + ful   _____

31. judge + ment   _____
32. luck + less   _____

33. petty + ness   _____
34. permit + ed   _____

35. continue + ance   _____
36. acquit + al   _____

37. coward + ice   _____
38. use + age   _____

39. transgress + ion   _____
40. arrange + ment   _____

41. occur + ence   _____
42. run + er   _____

43. breathe + ing   _____
44. defy + ance   _____

45. marry + age   _____
46. become + ing   _____

47. re + appear   _____
48. notice + able   _____

49. prove + ing _____   50. pre + eminent _____

51. carry + er _____   52. cruel + ty _____

53. lonely + ness _____   54. trace + able _____

55. eighty + eth _____   56. practice + able _____

57. accidental + ly _____   58. omit + ing _____

59. mat + ed _____   60. lively + ness _____

61. recur + ence _____   62. severe + ly _____

63. ninety + eth _____   64. refuse + al _____

65. angel + ic _____   66. nerve + ous _____

67. precede + ing _____   68. drag + ing _____

69. dine + ing _____   70. crab + y _____

71. dis + satisfy _____   72. holy + ness _____

73. hurry + ed _____   74. accrue + ing _____

To the right of each of the following sets of words, write the correct spelling of any misspelled word in the set. If no word in the set is misspelled, write *Correct* in the space.

Example	sophomore	aisle	roommate	sophistocated	*sophisticated*
75.	precept	enigma	sieze	science	_____
76.	conscience	dullard	saga	ricochet	_____
77.	confidence	vacume	psychology	psychiatry	_____
78.	immenent	sacrosanct	cylindrical	eminent	_____
79.	address	convoy	poligamous	cylindrical	_____
80.	lightning	mispell	prenatal	garland	_____
81.	humdrum	niece	enclosure	exagerrate	_____
82.	rhapsody	mellifluous	morgage	nicety	_____

64

All the skills you have practiced throughout this workbook are applicable to the writing tasks you will face on the job. Both academic and business writing require attention to the same elements of composition: purpose, audience, tone, style, grammar, spelling, punctuation, and organization. If anything, your business associates will be *less* tolerant of poor writing than your college teachers have been. The purpose of business correspondence is to get things done. Consequently, good business writing does not waste a reader's time. It is clear, straightforward, and, above all, efficient.

When you compare business correspondence with academic writing such as essays or term papers, you first might think of the visual differences. College papers are usually composed of uninterrupted paragraphs headed by a title. They also tend to run for a number of pages, frequently three or more. On the other hand, business correspondence uses various kinds of headings, routing instructions, and visual cues to assist the reader. With the exception of reports, most business correspondence is much shorter than college papers: letters are usually no more than a page or two, memos rarely more than three pages long.

Visual cues are important in business correspondence. Paragraphs tend to be shorter than in an essay, research paper, or novel. Lists are sometimes presented vertically, and series may include bullets (dots, asterisks, or dashes preceding listed items) or numbers that would be omitted in an essay.

The reason has to do with the way business letters and memos are used. As part of its function of getting a job done, business correspondence often serves as a reference document. Consequently, the reader must be able to find items quickly. By dividing the discussion more frequently into subtopics and by providing more visual cues, the writer aids not only the reader's understanding but also provides a fast, easy reference to specific portions of the document. (For a full discussion of business correspondence types and formats, see Section 49 of the *Prentice-Hall Handbook for Writers,* 8th edition.)

The following examples illustrate how the same topic might be treated in the opening paragraphs of a college essay and in a business memo. Notice the differences in the looks of the two examples.

Those Vital Volunteers

ESSAY
Volunteers comprise a vital part of the staff behind a city's efforts to help its disadvantaged citizens. Volunteers assist the professional personnel in many social service agencies by answering telephones, providing transportation, raising funds, and meeting clients when appropriate. Locally, volunteers serve many programs such as Legal Advocates for the Poor, Crisis Hot-Line, the Job Training Center, and the Battered Wives and Children Shelter. In recent years, the number of volunteers has decreased. Our city's Chamber of Commerce is developing a Leadership Academy to attract and train large numbers of volunteers for this important work.

To:	Barbara Swift, Mayor
From:	Stan Cox, Councilman
Date:	July 26, 1983
Subject:	Local Volunteer Leadership

MEMO   The Chamber of Commerce on July 22 approved a plan for a Leadership Academy. The purpose of the academy would be to train leaders for local volunteer work. Having attended that meeting, I recommend that the City Council endorse the Chamber's plan.

Program Priorities

The Chamber members believe our city must enlarge its dwindling corps of volunteers to assist local social service agencies. A recent Chamber survey shows that programs in great need include

- Legal Advocates for the Poor
- Crisis Hot-Line
- Job Training Center
- Battered Wives and Children Shelter

Besides using routing instructions—usual in the memo format—and short paragraphs, a list with bullets, and a heading, this memo shows two other features common to effective business correspondence: a summary beginning and streamlined sentences.

Section 46 discusses various types of beginnings for essays. Although any of these may occasionally be effective in business correspondence, most business people prefer an opening that gets right to the point—as Stan Cox does when he states his recommendation in the first paragraph. Remember, recipients of business correspondence are not reading for pleasure or for edification. They are reading because they need information to make decisions, to take action. If your letter or memo takes too long to get to the point, you will have wasted your reader's time and tried his or her patience. As a result, you are less likely to achieve the response you want from the reader.

This same principle of efficiency should be carried out in the sentence structure you use. Try to give your readers the greatest amount of necessary information in the fewest number of words. For instance, compare

The Chamber members believe our city must enlarge its dwindling corps of volunteers to assist local social service agencies.

It is believed by the members of the Chamber of Commerce that the corps of volunteers, whose numbers have decreased in recent years, needs to be enlarged by our city so that they can give assistance to social service agencies in the local area.

Obviously, the second example is much more long-winded than the first. The extra words are caused by unnecessary nominals, weak verbs, passive voice verbs, expletives, and phrases. While none of these are grammatically incorrect, they can be time wasters in business correspondence.

Nominals are nouns formed from verbs: *assistance* from *assist; opposition* from *oppose; statement* from *state.* Common suffixes added to verbs in forming nominals are *-ment, -tion, -ance,* and sometimes *-ity, -ize, -ness.*

Weak verbs such as *give, make,* or *take* often appear with nominals because, the strong verb having been changed into a noun, a new verb must be found for the sentence. The previous sample contains just such a combination of nominal and weak verb: "so that they can *give assistance.*" Notice how restoring a strong verb adds power and brevity to the sentence: "so that they can *assist.*"

Passive voice verbs tend to drain energy from sentences while adding extra words. (Passive constructions are discussed thoroughly in Sections 13 and 55.) For instance, the phrases "It *is believed* by the members" and "the corps . . . *needs to be enlarged* by our city" become more forceful when revised: "The members *believe*" and "our city *needs to enlarge* the corps. . . ."

Expletives (*it is, there were,* etc.) can also be great time wasters. The previous example shows that "It is" adds nothing important to its sentence. An expletive often occurs with a relative pronoun clause containing a sentence's real subject: "*It is* clear *that we* need volunteers." Replacing the expletive with the subject of the relative pronoun clause streamlines the sentence: "Clearly, *we* need volunteers."

Unnecessary phrases can clog writing, too. Frequently, relative pronouns can be "understood" and thus dropped from a sentence: "The Chamber of Commerce believes (*that*) our city must. . . ." Often a prepositional phrase can be rewritten as a single-word modifier: "social service agencies *in the local area*" becomes "*local* social service agencies"; "the members *of the Chamber of Commerce*" becomes "the *Chamber* members." Using the *'s* possessive form can sometimes eliminate a phrase: instead of "the decision *of the mayor*" write "the *mayor's* decision." Verbals (root verb + *ing*) can also be substituted for prepositional phrases into one short, smooth verbal phrase: *with regard to the meeting on Tuesday* becomes *regarding Tuesday's meeting.*

Nominals, passive voice verbs, expletives, relative pronoun and prepositional phrases all have their place in good writing, including good business writing. The point is, we often use more of them than we need; as a result, we use more words than we need or our readers want. Besides lengthening sentences, these constructions can add a ponderous, pompous tone to writing, creating stuffy-sounding business correspondence. Letters and memos should sound cordial and natural. You don't want a chummy, overly casual tone, but neither do you want to sound like a stuffed shirt. Avoid **business jargon**: rather than creating a business-like tone, it simply makes your writing sound stiff and old-fashioned, even cold and unfriendly. Instead of "as per your request" say "as you requested"; instead of "at the time of this writing" say "now" or "today." The following list contrasts jargon phrases to more natural, often shorter equivalents preferred in modern business correspondence.

JARGON	PREFERRED
at all times	always
due to the fact that	because
in the amount of [referring to money]	for
in the event that	if
please find enclosed	enclosed is
pursuant to	concerning

EXERCISE 64-1, SUMMARY BEGINNINGS AND ACTION ENDINGS   (49)

Much business correspondence wastes a reader's time because its subject, purpose, and main point are unclear or buried in a mass of detail. Furthermore, the ending of a business letter or memo should not leave the reader wondering what happens next. The writer should supply an "action ending" that clearly indicates the action the writer desires from the reader.

Read the following memo, paying careful attention to its organization as well as to its contents. Then write a new subject line that more accurately and specifically identifies what you believe to be the memo's true topic. Second, write a new opening paragraph that clearly expresses what you believe to be the memo's main point and purpose. Finally, write a concluding paragraph that contains an action ending.

To: Bob Jones, district supervisor

From: Melanie Harper, sales representative

Date: August 3, 1981

Subject: Sales visits

This week I called on my customers to obtain their Christmas toy orders. I was able to see buyers at all but two of the sixteen stores in my territory.

Mr. Hobson at Brown's Department Store placed orders for our full line of existing toys. He increased his order for Outdoor Andy, our male doll, noting that it sold very well during the 1980 Christmas season. Outdoor Andy seems to have done well at other stores in my territory too. I showed Mr. Hobson Sprinkle, the plastic puppy that drinks from its own dish and then wets. I explained that this new toy would be available next month in time for Christmas ordering. Mr. Hobson wasn't interested.

Only three buyers in my territory showed any interest in Sprinkle. Two said they would order a dozen in September. Can you suggest ways that I might make this toy more attractive to buyers? I think we're going to have a hard time selling it.

The promotional strategy we discussed at the district sales meeting in July focused on Sprinkle's cuteness. Most of my customers pointed out that while children may think the puppy cute, parents will object to a toy that could leave water marks on rugs and furniture. Pardon the expression, but Sprinkle is likely to be a real "dog" in terms of new sales for the company.

I plan to spend next Monday and Tuesday revisiting Toy Palace and Murphy's Play Shop to talk with the buyers I missed last week. So far, Christmas orders in my territory are about the same as or slightly lower than last year.

To: Bob Jones

From: Melanie Harper

Date: August 3, 1981

Subject: _____

Opening paragraph: _____

_____

_____

_____

_____

_____

_____

_____

_____

Concluding paragraph: _____

_____

_____

_____

_____

_____

_____

_____

_____

EXERCISE 64-2, STREAMLINING SENTENCES AND ELIMINATING JARGON (49)

The following job application letter is set out in correct business form and is well organized. However, its style is poor. The letter contains long-winded sentences and stuffy business jargon that give it an impersonal, unpleasing tone sure to create a negative impression of the job applicant. Revise the letter, eliminating nominals, weak verbs, passive voice verbs, expletives, and unnecessary phrases where doing so improves the letter's tone and readability. Substitute more cordial, natural-sounding expressions for the jargon.

329 Maple Court
Stanton, Texas
May 14, 1983

Ms. Josephine Yeager
Director, User Systems
Data Processing Services, Inc.
Industrial Park, Texas

Dear Ms. Yeager:

Pursuant to your advertisement posted in the placement office at our college, I see that you have a position open for a computer programmer. It is my hope that you will give consideration to my application for that job.

My qualifications include a bachelor's degree in computer science which will be received on June 10, 1983, from Mesa College. During the past summer I gained experience in data processing at Software Specialists, a company in the local area. This year I was also given employment on a part-time basis by Mesa College in the business office where I helped with the maintenance of the computer files of the college. I was chosen over four other students who were majoring in computer science who applied for the job.

In accordance with your request, please find enclosed a resume, which gives further details of my educational and work experience. You will see that my initiative and reliability are evidenced by the fact that most of my college education has been paid for by myself.

Due to the fact that I will be making a visit to the home of my parents soon, I would like to pay Data Processing Services a visit and discuss your job opening with you. You will get a call from me early next week to make arrangements for an interview. In the event that you have questions in the meantime, please do not hesitate to contact me.

Sincerely,

Martin Burgess

Martin Burgess

_____

_____

_____

_____

_____

_____

_____

_____

_____

_____

_____

_____

_____

_____

_____

Using your own paper, write an application letter for a job you would like. Further discussion of employment letters and resumés can be found in Section 49 of the *Prentice-Hall Handbook for Writers*, 8th edition.

65

PRENTICE-HALL DIAGNOSTIC TEST REVIEW I

The purpose of this section and the next one is to provide practice for the *Prentice-Hall Diagnostic Test for Writers.* The instructions are similar to those on the diagnostic test. This section reviews punctuation, basic grammar, and sentence recognition.

Some of the following sentences require additional punctuation. Decide if any punctuation is needed immediately *before* the italicized word, and then write the corresponding number in the blank at the right.

1. **The sentence needs a comma.**
2. **The sentence needs a semicolon.**
3. **The sentence needs a colon.**
4. **The sentence is correctly punctuated.**

Example   The course had been canceled *however,* our money was refunded.   _2_

1. If a person's job is dangerous *he* or she may find it hard to buy insurance.   _____
2. Only 3 percent of the people who apply for insurance are turned down *however,* most people think the percentage is much higher.   _____
3. Steeple jacks *test* pilots, and nuclear plant technicians are risky to insure.   _____
4. Actuaries *who* study the statistics of life, death, and injury, determine the amount of risk involved with each policy.   _____

5. The actuary figures the amount of risk *and* advises the company.   _____
6. One firm *Travelers* Insurance, insured the first astronauts to fly to the moon.   _____
7. The company's actuary gave the astronauts better odds *than* NASA did.   _____
8. Some companies insure anyone *whether* the policyholder is a trapeze artist or a police cadet.   _____
9. If a company insures only nine or ten high-risk workers *it* is likely to lose money.   _____

10. However *insuring* large numbers of such people spreads the risk.   _____
11. By insuring large numbers of people *the* company can trust "the law of large numbers" to protect it.   _____
12. If the company pays one claim *there* will still be thousands of workers paying for their policies.   _____

13. Thus *insurance* companies are built around one mathematical principle.   _____
14. Prize fighters *police,* and bomb-squad members can be insured if a company insures enough people.   _____
15. People with dangerous jobs aren't ineligible for insurance *they* simply have to look for a company large enough to insure them.   _____

Read the following sentences carefully for errors in standard English. Circle any errors, and then revise the sentences specifically to correct the errors you have circled.

Example   Was it (them) who insured the *Lusitania*?

Was it they who insured the Lusitania ?

1. Liability insurance pays whomever has been damaged in an accident.

_____

2. The most famous insurance company in the world, actually a loose association of independent businessmen, are Lloyd's of London.

_____

3. Some policies are more safer than others, of course.

_____

4. When something is insured by Lloyd's, you assume the policy is safe.

_____

5. Either the policy insuring San Francisco against earthquake damage or the policy on the *Titanic* are responsible for making Lloyd's famous.

_____

6. Having issued the policies, the claims were promptly paid by Lloyd's.

_____

7. Lloyd's insures both supertankers and jets; they have had good experience with them.

_____

8. The insuring of moon vehicles and world fairs are not a simple risk situation.

_____

9. Lloyd's members consider these policies very careful before issuing a policy.

_____

10. Each member who wants to issue a policy signs his or her name beneath the description of the policy, thus the members have come to be called "underwriters."

_____

66

PRENTICE-HALL DIAGNOSTIC TEST REVIEW II

This section reviews sentence, paragraph, and composition elements in a manner similar to the *Prentice-Hall Diagnostic Test for Writers.*

Each of the following three groups contains four sentences expressing the same general thought. Select the most precise, clear, and effective one and write its number in the blank at the right.

A. 1. Jan is overqualified for her job, and she is dissatisfied with it.
    2. Jan is a person who is overqualified for her job and a dissatisfied employee.
    3. Jan is an overqualified employee and dissatisfied.
    4. Since Jan is overqualified, she is a dissatisfied employee.   _____

B. 1. In the modern world of today we desire the world of tomorrow with impatience, but looking back from tomorrow, we may want today back again.
    2. Today we await the future impatiently, but tomorrow we may long for the past.
    3. We may be impatient for the future, but tomorrow we may long for the past.
    4. Today impatient, the past may be longed for by us tomorrow.   _____

C. 1. Some types of jobs can be boring.
    2. Somes lines of work can really be the pits.
    3. With respect to employment opportunities, some can fatigue one with tediousness.
    4. Routine, monotonous, assembly-line jobs can be very boring.   _____

Each of the following two groups contains a topic sentence for a paragraph and five supporting sentences. Read the sentences and then decide how the supporting sentences would best form a well-organized paragraph. You may decide to omit some sentences entirely. In the blank following each exercise, list the number of the supporting sentences in the order you believe they should appear in the paragraph.

A. Topic sentence: Being overqualified for a job can affect an employee's performance.
    1. This dissatisfaction may result in several kinds of behavior.
    2. Others try to change the nature of the job, actually putting in extra effort to make their job more interesting.
    3. A person who is overqualified for his or her job is often a dissatisfied employee.

4. Some employees react to job dissatisfaction by being absent from work frequently or by loafing while at work.
5. More than 35 percent of the workers in the United States believe they are overqualified for their jobs. _____

B. Topic sentence: Changing careers in middle age takes special preparation.
   1. To help people deal with these negative feelings, counselors and educators are developing courses in changing careers.
   2. Sometimes they believe themselves to be weird or different—or believe that they have failed—if they no longer like their old job.
   3. At first people considering a career change may experience overwhelming fear at the thought of leaving their old job's security.
   4. For some people, a change of career can be the best thing that ever happened.
   5. Such courses enable participants to share their fears and receive professional advice. _____

The following two groups list ideas that might be used for a 500-word essay. Read each essay assignment and choose the answer you think would be the most suitable. Write its number in the blank at the right of the exercise.

A. For an assignment requiring a 500-word essay on *computers,* which of the following topics has the best focus?
   1. The development of the computer
   2. Business uses for computers
   3. How to decide if you need a personal computer
   4. The ways in which computers affect our daily lives _____

B. For a 500-word essay on *sleep,* which of the following sentences would serve as the best central (thesis) statement?
   1. It is important to get enough sleep.
   2. Scientists have found that humans experience two types of sleep and that each type seems to serve a different purpose.
   3. Insomnia can be a real problem.
   4. Babies sleep more than adults. _____